P9-CCT-355

ROBERT LOMAS gained a first class honours degree in electronics before being awarded a PhD for his research into solid-state physics. He later worked on electronic weapons systems and emergency services command and control systems. He has established himself as one of the world's leading authorities on the history of science and lectures on Information Systems at Bradford University School of Management, one of the UK's leading business schools, where he also runs the university's highly popular website of Masonic source material (www.bradford.ac.uk/webofhiram/).

He is a frequent speaker on the Masonic lecture circuit in West Yorkshire and a regular supporter of the Orkney International Science Festival. He has written a number of bestselling books: *Turning the Hiram Key*, *The Invisible College*, *Freemasonry and the Birth of Modern Science* and *The Man Who Invented the Twentieth Century*; and co-authored *The Hiram Key*, *The Second Messiah*, *Uriel's Machine* and *The Book of Hiram*.

The Secrets of Freemasonry

Revealing the Suppressed Tradition

Selected, revised and presented by

Robert Lomas

www.robertlomas.com

www.bradford.ac.uk/webofhiram/

Magpie Books, London

Constable & Robinson Ltd
3 The Lanchesters
162 Fulham Palace Road
London W6 9ER
www.constablerobinson.com

This edition published by Magpie Books,
an imprint of Constable & Robinson Ltd 2006

Copyright © Robert Lomas 2006

The right of Robert Lomas to be identified as the author of
this work has been asserted by him in accordance with the
Copyright, Designs and Patents Act 1988.

All rights reserved. This book is sold subject to the condition that
it shall not, by way of trade or otherwise, be lent, re-sold, hired out or
otherwise circulated in any form of binding or cover other than that
in which it is published and without a similar condition including
this condition being imposed on the subsequent purchaser.

A copy of the British Library Cataloguing in
Publication Data is available from the British Library

ISBN-10: 1-84529-012-7
ISBN-13: 978-1-84529-012-2

Printed and bound in the EU

1 3 5 7 9 10 8 6 4 2

Dedication

To Bro. Michael Astell, who proposed me into Freemasonry

Acknowledgments

Firstly, I would like to thank Colin Wilson for introducing me to Duncan Proudfoot at Constable & Robinson. Colin knew I had a large amount of research material on the writers Duncan was interested in – so *The Secrets of Freemasonry* was born. Then I would like to thank Duncan for his editorial support and encouragement; he shaped the concept and encouraged me to have a go at bringing the ideas of Preston, Gould, Ward, Waite and Wilmshurst to a new audience.

I would also like to thank John Wheelwright for his excellent editing skills, cheerful comments and wry sense of humour, my agent Bill Hamilton and his team at AM Heath for sorting out the necessary details, and, finally, John Acaster for reminding me what an important influence the attitude of the United Grand Lodge of England towards free-thinkers has been over the centuries.

Contents

PART FIVE

Introduction

The Origins of the Craft

Forbidden Views

In 1871 the *Daily Telegraph* ran a leader about the origins of Freemasonry. This said:

> That Freemasonry dates from before the Flood; that it is a mere creation of yesterday; that it is only an excuse for conviviality; that it is a soul-destroying, atheistic organization; that it is a charitable association, doing good under a silly pretence of secrecy; that it is a political engine of extraordinary potency; that it has no secrets; that its disciples possess in secret the grandest knowledge vouchsafed to humanity; that they celebrate their mysterious rites under the auspices and the invocations of Mephistopheles; that their proceedings are perfectly innocent, not to say supremely stupid; that they commit all the murders which are not traced to somebody else; and that they exist only for the purpose of promoting universal brotherhood and benevolence – these are some of the allegations made by babblers outside the circle of the Free and Accepted brethren.

In 1995 I happily used this quotation to open my own first venture into understanding the origins of Freemasonry, a book called *The Hiram Key*. It went on to say:

> A great number of well-informed men have set out before us to try and find the origins of Freemasonry, and none of the obvious

possibilities have been overlooked by them, or indeed by the ranks of the romancers and charlatans who have joined in the hunt. For some the line is simple: Freemasonry is as old as its publicly recorded history (the seventeenth century) and everything claimed to predate those records is whimsical nonsense. This ultra-pragmatic attitude is clean and uncomplicated, but it is the easiest of all hypotheses to reject for many reasons, not least the fact that there is widespread evidence to show that the Order materialized slowly over more than three hundred years before the establishment of the United Grand Lodge of England.

The fact is, the organization that we now call Freemasonry was a secret society before the mid-seventeenth century, and secret societies, by definition, do not publish official histories. From the establishment of the United Grand Lodge of England in 1717 onwards the Order has been open about its existence, and only its methods of recognition have been kept from public gaze. We will not spend time on proving that Freemasonry was not a spontaneous arrival because it is a theory that has already been widely discredited.

When I first began studying the origins of Freemasonry I found it difficult to uncover real information; there were lots of opinions but few contemporary books to study. Most of the modern booklets from the United Grand Lodge of England took the view that Freemasonry started in London in 1717. Apparently it sprang, fully formed, into the minds of a small group of London 'gentlemen', who were inspired by the ideas of working builders to create a whole system of ritual and mythology that then spread throughout the world. The Masonic idea caught on quickly and took a firm hold on the imagination of a large part of humanity. Differences of race and language did not prevent its spread.

The books I consulted in my early days of studying Freemasonry all took the success of the Masonic idea for granted. They did not seem at all disturbed by the thought that the nobility of Europe had been sucked into acting out little plays that involved its members taking on the role of jobbing builders. I was fascinated. So I set out to try and discover the secret of the widespread appeal of Freemasonry, which had lasted for over three hundred years.

The ritual of Freemasonry claims that the Craft is at least three thousand years old. I soon found that not only did the opponents of the Order dismiss this possibility but the United Grand Lodge of England (UGLE) didn't accept it either. Indeed UGLE went out of its way to discourage any idea that there could be a history of Freemasonry that predated its own formation in 1717.

During the late 1980s and early 1990s the permanent officials of United Grand Lodge of England were totally hostile to any attempts to investigate their origins. They allowed their so-called 'lodges of research' to debate unendingly the limited historical evidence of who drank which toasts to whom at which lodge meeting, but anyone questioning the official viewpoint, as I did, was quickly told that they would not get any promotion within the system. Usually this was very effective at stopping ambitious insiders asking the 'wrong' questions. But, although I was by then a Masonic insider, I had no Masonic ambitions and was highly sceptical of the explanations peddled in the 'research' newsletters of lodges such as the highly opinionated Quatuor Coronati. I soon found that this lodge, which calls itself the 'premier' lodge of 'authentic' Masonic research, has a long track record of supporting the UGLE party line on the London origins of Freemasonry – which I already knew to be an untenable position.

The problem of where Freemasonry came from was obviously complex, and I considered a variety of possibilities. Was it just an organization that offered opportunities for social intercourse for individuals who chose to split off into a distinctive fraternity? This did not seem a credible motive to justify an organization that was so firmly entrenched and had drawn into its ranks all types of high-achieving people. Was it a charitable society, set up simply to further philanthropy? It certainly does that, but I soon realized that Freemasonry is not a high-grade Friendly Society, and its charitable activities are not the motive for its existence. Was it a school of morality set up with the aim of promoting peace and goodwill? Perhaps. But who needs to join a secret society, or to take obligations of secrecy to learn rudimentary ethics? Was it a device to promote the mutual interests of its members? Was it a cover for political intrigue, or a screen for propagating anti-religious ideas, or a scheme for world-domination? One question immediately provoked another.

But the view I formed of British Masonry today is that it has no such ambitions, and seems to actively discourage them. And the notorious ban on Freemasonry by the Roman Catholic Church turns out to be nothing more than a knee-jerk by Church leaders aimed at supporting the political ambitions of Jacobite pretenders to the British Crown in the eighteenth century.

I soon concluded that there is only one sensible explanation for the spread of the Masonic system, and that has to be the content and power of its ceremonial rites. This, I decided, must be part of the secret of the vitality and the development of Freemasonry. But I also found that a large majority of Freemasons only dimly recognizes the significance of this heritage. There is, though, something veiled, latent and deep in Freemasonry's rites, which speaks to all who take part in them. As we work the rituals we feel we are in the presence of a mystery that goes to the root of our being. But where did it all start?

As I began to study these questions the names of a small number of writers kept being mentioned.

'Preston wrote a book about Freemasonry in the eighteenth century,' I was told. But nobody had read it, and it was out of print.

'Gould's History of Freemasonry has everything you need to know about where we came from,' somebody else confided. 'There's a copy of it in the Lodge Library.' But when I checked it out I found it was not Gould's original work but a much later version put together by Dudley Wright.

'You should read J. S. M Ward. He had some good ideas,' another brother told me. But I struggled to locate any editions of Ward's works in print at that time.

'Waite's *Secret Tradition of Freemasonry* has all the answers,' a well-read brother told me. 'But,' he added, 'he's a very hard read.' How true this was I discovered when I managed to get hold of a first edition of this work!

Then a colleague at work introduced me to the writings of W. .L. Wilmshurst. I found his works intriguing but abstruse.

As I read more widely I realized that, from its very beginnings, the Craft has been mysterious about how it started and what it is about. But the view so rigorously enforced by United Grand Lodge of England when I started my studies was not shared by the great Masonic writers of the past – not even by Robert Freke Gould, a founder member of Quatuor Coronati. The picture I got from these early writers was far more imaginative and interesting than UGLE's party line. But the stories they told long predated the foundation of the Grand Lodge of London, on which UGLE based its claim to be the 'premier' Grand Lodge of the World.

My reason for writing this book is to revisit the ideas of five giants of the Masonic movement and to retell, in my own words, their ideas on where Freemasonry came from. They do not agree with each other, and often I do not agree with them. But their stories were all written in good faith in an attempt to understand the origin of Freemasonry. They wrote in the language of their time, which can make them hard work for some modern readers; I have therefore taken their ideas and paraphrased them into simpler words and structures, to try and bring their writings to a new generation whilst remaining true to the originals. I hope that this effort will encourage many people to consider anew both the questions they posed and the answers they gave.

I begin with William Preston.

Part One

William Preston's Story
of
The Origins of Freemasonry

Chapter 1

Early Masonry

William Preston

William Preston was a Scot. He was born in Edinburgh in 1742, and his father, who was a strong Jacobite supporter, died when he was eight. William was sent to board at the Royal High School and then trained as printer. There was an active group of Edinburgh-trained printers, most of whom were Freemasons, thriving in London at that time. Their leading members were Andrew Millar and William Strachan. At the age of eighteen Preston moved to London to work for Strachan. A few years later, in 1763, this group of Scotsmen applied to the Grand Lodge of Edinburgh for a warrant to form a lodge in London. Grand Lodge, feeling it would not be appropriate for it to form a lodge in London, referred them to the Grand Lodge of the Antients. This was a group mainly of Scots and Irish who had split from the Grand Lodge of London (which they called the Moderns). The Antients Grand Lodge issued a warrant to form Lodge No. 111, and Preston was initiated into this lodge by his Scottish brethren around the time of his twenty-first birthday. Soon afterwards he formed a new lodge, called the Caledonian Lodge on a warrant from the Moderns, and for some time had a foot in each camp.

He became interested in recording and formalizing the instructional lectures, which were a key part of Freemasonry at that time. In due course he published a whole series of lectures, rituals and other Masonic material, including his view of the origins of Freemasonry. Preston was Master of a number of lodges during his life, including one of the founder lodges of the Grand Lodge of London, now known as the Lodge of Antiquity.

At one stage he challenged the attempts of the Grand Lodge of London to control the Lodge of Antiquity and took part in a long dispute with the London Grand Lodge, which has somewhat tainted his reputation with supporters of UGLE. Typical of their attitude is a comment from a Past Master of Quatuor Coronati lodge, who said of Preston: 'It is a matter of regret that he was, on a number of occasions, guilty of mispresentation'. Perhaps he was, if you look from the rather restricted viewpoint of the United Grand Lodge of England, which became the successor to the Moderns Grand Lodge of London.

However, Preston knew the Scottish background of Freemasonry, from family connections in Edinburgh and drew freely from Scottish Masonic writings to create his famous *Illustrations of Masonry*, which ran through several editions. Preston was a Knight of Heredom, a Masonic grade awarded by the Royal Order of Scotland. He did a vast amount of work in recording and publishing the teaching lectures of the Craft, and his *Illustrations* gives an interesting insight into where he thought Freemasonry came from.

What follows is paraphrased from his 1795 edition.

The Druids

The early history of Britain is mixed with fable, but, Preston believed, there is evidence that the science of Masonry existed in the British Isles before the invasion of the Romans. The principles of Masonry were practised by the order known as the Druids, who used many rituals and practices that are known to Masons today. No written records exist from this remote period, but the Druids held their meetings in woods and groves, and kept their principles and opinions a close secret. Because of this secrecy much of their detailed knowledge died with them, but what other contemporary writers said about their ways of working survives.

They were the priests of the Britons, Gauls, and other Celtic nations and were divided into three classes. Those of the first class, poets and musicians, were called Bards. Members of the second class were known as Vates and were priests and physiologists. Adherents of the third class, known simply as Druids, studied moral philosophy as well as physiology.

Many of the Druids' doctrines were taken from the teachings of Pythagoras. They devoted their lives to study and speculation and held private sessions at which they discussed where matter came from, what laws governed its behaviour and the properties of different substances. They developed theories about the size and nature of the universe and made a general study of the hidden mysteries of nature and science. Their findings were taught to their candidates in the form of verses, to make their memorizing easier. But before new entrants were allowed to learn the ritual verses they had to take an oath never to write them down.

The Druids created many branches of useful knowledge although they hid their secrets under a veil of mystery. Their order was widely admired and respected and its members were leaders in their communities. They were entrusted with educating the young, and from their centres of learning they issued valuable instruction. They acted as judges in matters of religious and civil law, and they were tutors of philosophy, astrology, politics, ritual and ceremonial. Their bards celebrated the heroic deeds of great men in songs designed to inspire the next generation.

The Druids had a similar legend to the Greek story of the death of Dionysos. Preston reports a Druidical temple on Iona, which had a sculptured slab, dating from the time of the Druids, showing two figures greeting each other using the Masonic lion grip. The Druids used various signs in their initiation rituals, and they venerated the triangle, the swastika and a symbol showing three diverging rays of light. He is not sure if there is any direct connection between the ancient Druids and Freemasonry but says the experienced mason will see how similar the practices of the Druids are to the way our Fraternity works today.

The Roman Period

Julius Caesar and several of the Roman generals who succeeded him in the government of Britain were patrons and protectors of the Craft. The Romans encouraged the arts and sciences in Britain. As Britain became more civilized so Masonry rose in esteem. The Masonic fraternity were employed in erecting walls, forts, bridges, cities, temples, palaces, courts of justice, and other stately works. Because of the secrecy of the Craft nothing was written down about how the lodges were governed or what rituals they carried out, but they held lodges and conventions regularly. These meetings were open only to initiated fellows, who were legally restrained from mentioning the private doings of Masonry. The wars between the Romans and the native British slowed the progress of Masonry in these islands although there was a positive Roman influence on Freemasonry.

The Roman *collegium* provides a link from earlier British sources to the subsequent practice of Masonry. Most Roman trades were controlled guilds or collegia. They were powerful enough for various Roman emperors to issue edicts to try to suppress them. But these edicts were never effectively enforced against the Masons because they 'could prove their great antiquity and that they were religious in character'. Many *collegia* became charitable, religious, or funerary groups, although they kept the knowledge of their Masonic secrets. They held memorial services for members who died, marked member's tombs with the emblems of their trades, and helped support widows and children. Preston describes a Roman builder's tomb, which showed the square, the compasses, and the level used as 'emblems to mark the grave of a brother'.

The Roman colleges of architects held privileges and exemptions because of the prestige of the work they did. Their organization was similar to that of a modern Masonic Lodge, and they had constitutions and regulations to rule their actions in religious and secular matters. Roman law accepted the modern rule that 'Three make a College/Lodge'. Each meeting was presided over by a master (*magister*) and two wardens (*decuriones*). They also had a secretary, a treasurer, a chaplain (*sacerdos*), and admitted lay members who were known as patrons or speculatives. Their lodges had three grades – Apprentices, Fellows and Masters – and they had rituals of initiation that involved death and rebirth, as does the modern Third Degree. They used all the Masonic emblems: the square, the compasses, the cube, plumb-rule, circle and level. And they also used an upturned urn as an emblem of death.

A meeting hall owned by the local Masonic *collegium* was found when Pompeii was excavated in 1878. It had two columns at its entrance, and its interior was decorated with interlaced triangles, which is 'the constant badge of the masons'. There was a pedestal in the main room that held a tracing-broad in the form of a table of inlaid mosaic. In its centre was a skull with square, plumb line and other Masonic designs.

When Christianity became the official religion of Rome it attracted members of the *collegia* of Masons, but the Masons retained their links with the ancient traditions of the builders. When the Emperor Diocletian set out to destroy Christianity he dealt leniently with the *collegia* of Architects until some of them refused to make a statue of Aesculapius, but, when thus defied, he had four Master Masons and one apprentice tortured to death. Now known as the Four Crowned Martyrs, the four Masters, Claudius, Nicostratus, Symphorian and Castorius, are always shown holding the implements of their Mason's trade. [This legend would later provide the name for the Quatuor Coronati lodge.] They and the apprentice Simplicius became the patron saints of Masons throughout Europe. There is a poem about them in the oldest written record of the craft, the Regius MS, which is kept in the British Library.

A Romano-British emperor named Carausius revived the principles of Masonry. Carausius wanted to make himself and his government more acceptable to the British, so he decided to emulate the good works of the Masons, and by this means he earned the love and esteem of what Preston calls 'the most enlightened part of his subjects'. He supported learning, improved the civil arts, and employed the best workmen and artificers from throughout the country. The old Masonic constitutions say that he took on a noble called Albanus to provide his hometown of Verulamium with a wall. Not only did Albanus build a strong wall he also built a splendid palace for the emperor. He made such a good job of it all that Carausius made him steward of his household, and chief ruler of the realm.

The masons became Carausius's favourites, and he was so impressed by their teachings that he made Albanus their Grand Master. Albanus held regular lodges and conventions for the Fraternity, and the rituals of masonry thrived. Carausius was so pleased with the Masons that he granted them a charter letting them hold a general council, set up their own government, and correct errors among themselves. Albanus turned out to be a good friend to the Craft and assisted at the initiation of many candidates into the mysteries of the Order during the time he presided as Grand Master. Under this benign Masonic guidance Britain enjoyed peace and tranquillity. Preston concludes that this proves that Albanus was a celebrated architect, and an encourager of able workmen, adding that Freemasonry thrived under this eminent patron.

Verulamium was the Roman name for the city of St Alban's in Hertfordshire, and Grand Master Albanus came from one of the leading families of the city. As a young man he had travelled to

Rome, where he served the Emperor Diocletian for seven years. After leaving Rome he travelled to the town now known as Chester, where he was baptized a Christian by Bishop Amphibalus.

The venerable Bede tells how Albanus died in 303 AD. The Roman governor, told that Albanus was hiding a Christian in his house, sent a party of soldiers to apprehend him. (The Christian was Albanus's friend Amphibalus, the priest who had baptized him.) When the soldiers came Albanus dressed in the monk's habit of his guest and offered himself to the officers. He was taken before a magistrate, where he spoke in support of his friend and brother Christian. This did not please the judge, who, following the edict of Diocletian ordered Albanus to be beheaded for professing the Christian faith. Made a saint by the Christian church, he became known in England as St Alban the martyr, and eventually his home town was renamed as a memorial to him.

When the Roman Empire was destroyed by barbarian invaders the *collegia* system was destroyed except for one *collegium*, which took refuge in Comacina, a fortified island in the midst of Lake Como.

Once the Romans had left Britain, Masonry was totally neglected, because of the disruption caused by the raids of the Picts and Scots. These caused so much trouble that the southern British called in the Saxons to help repel the invaders. As the Saxons gained increased power the native Britons and their knowledge of Masonry sank into obscurity. Before long the rough, ignorant and heathen Saxons ruled southern Britain. They despised everything except war and destroyed what remained of the ancient Masonic learning. The Picts and Scots continued to raid England with unrestrained rigour, and it was not until some pious teachers from Wales and Ireland converted some of these savages to Christianity, that the attacks diminished. Only then did Masonic lodges begin to meet again.

Chapter 2

Early English Masonry

Saxon Freemasonry

Masonry continued to decline until AD 557, when Bishop Austin [here Preston probably refers to the man now better known as St Augustine, who came to southern England in AD 597] brought forty monks skilled in the science of Masonry to England. Austin, sent by Pope Gregory I to baptize Ethelbert king of Kent, went on to become the first archbishop of Canterbury, and he and his associates propagated the principles of Christianity among the British so that in little more than sixty years all the kings of southern Britain were converted. Masonry flourished under Austin's patronage, and, Preston says, he popularized the Gothic style of building introduced with his patronage of foreign Masons at this time. Austin encouraged architecture and headed the Fraternity which began the building of the old cathedral of Canterbury in AD 600, the cathedral of Rochester in 602, St Paul's, London, in 604, St Peter's, Westminster, in 605 and many others. He also supervised the building of several palaces and castles as well as fortifications on the borders of the new Christian kingdoms. Because he encouraged building work, the number of masons in England increased considerably.

In 680 Abbot Bennet of Wirral formed a lodge from a number of expert brethren who came from France. Preston says that soon afterwards Kenred, King of Mercia, appointed Bennet Inspector of the lodge, and general superintendent of masons. Then, he adds, in the year 856 Masonry received a boost from the patronage of St Swithin, who was employed by Ethelwulf, the Saxon king, to repair some pious houses [although Swithin was not a builder/stonemason but Bishop of Winchester in 852–62].

It continued to improve until the accession in 872 of King Alfred, who, Preston says, was a zealous protector of Masonry. Under his patronage it kept pace with the progress of learning. David Hume, in his *History of England* (1778), says of him:

He usually divided his time into three equal portions: One was employed in sleep, and the refection of his body by diet and exercise; another in the dispatch of business; a third, in study and devotion. And that he might more exactly measure the hours, he made use of burning tapers of equal length, which he fixed in lanthorns; an expedient suited to that rude age, when the [art of making sun-dials] and the mechanism of clocks and watches, were totally unknown. And by such a regular distribution of his time, though he often laboured under great bodily infirmities, this martial hero, who fought in person fifty-six battles by sea and land, was able, during a life of no extraordinary length, to acquire more knowledge, and even to compose more books, than most studious men, though blest with greater leisure and application, have [done] in more fortunate ages . . .

Alfred invited industrious foreigners from all quarters to repopulate his country, which was desolated by the ravages of the Danes. He encouraged inventors and improvers of ingenious art. A seventh part of his revenue was set aside to maintain workmen whom he employed in rebuilding his ruined cities, castles, palaces, and monasteries. He founded the university of Oxford.

Alfred died in 900, and his son King Edward the Elder took the throne. Preston tells us that during his reign the Masons continued to hold lodges and enjoyed the patronage of Ethred and Ethelward, the King's brother-in-law and brother. Prince Ethelward was a great scholar and a skilled architect who founded the university of Cambridge. Twenty-four years later King Edward died and was succeeded by his son, Athelstane; Prince Edward, brother of the new king, became the new patron of the Masons. Athelstane sold the Masons a Royal Charter; which gave them the right to meet every year at York and to rule themselves under a Royal Grand Master. The first Grand Lodge of England was formed at York in 926; Prince Edwin presided over the meeting, and many old Masonic writings in Greek, Latin and other languages were studied and their contents incorporated into the constitutions of the English Masonic lodges.

Preston goes on to quote from a copy of a paper which had once been part of the collection of Elias Ashmole, but which he says was destroyed towards the end of the Civil War.

Many of the ancient records of the brotherhood in England were destroyed, or lost, in the wars of the Saxons and Danes, yet king Athelstane, (the grandson of king Alfrede the Great, a mighty architect), the first anointed king of England, and who translated the Holy Bible into the Saxon tongue (A.D. 930), when he had brought the land into rest and peace, built many great works, and encouraged many masons from France, who were appointed overseers thereof, and brought with them the charges and regulations of the lodges, preserved since the Roman times; who also prevailed with the king to improve the constitution of the English lodges according to the foreign model, and to increase the wages of working masons.

That the said king's brother, prince Edwin, being taught masonry, and taking upon him the charges of a master-mason, for the love he had to the said craft, and the honourable principles whereon it is grounded, purchased a free charter of king Athelstane, for the masons having a correction among themselves (as it was anciently expressed), or a freedom and power to regulate themselves, to amend what might happen amiss, and to hold a yearly communication and general assembly.

That accordingly prince Edwin summoned all the masons in the realm to meet him in a congregation at York, who came and composed a general lodge, of which he was Grand Master; and having brought with them all the writings and records extant, some in Greek, some in Latin, some in French, and other languages, from the contents thereof that assembly did frame the constitution and charges of an English lodge, made a law to preserve and observe the same in all time coming, and ordained good pay for working masons, &c.

From this era we date the re-establishment of free-masonry in England. There is at present a Grand Lodge of masons in the city of York, who trace their existence from this period. By virtue of Edwin's charter, it is said, all the masons in the realm were convened at a general assembly in that city, where they established a general or grand Lodge for their future government. Under the patronage and jurisdiction of this Grand Lodge, it is alleged, the Fraternity considerably increased, and kings, princes, and other eminent persons, who had been initiated into masonry, paid due allegiance to that Grand Assembly. But as the events of the times were various and fluctuating, that Assembly was more or less respectable; and in proportion as masonry obtained encouragement, its influence was more or less extensive. The appellation of Ancient York Masons is well known in Ireland and Scotland; and the universal tradition is that the brethren of that appellation originated at Auldby near York. This carries with it some marks of confirmation, for Auldby was the seat of Edwin.

There is every reason to believe that York was deemed the original seat of Masonic government in this country; as no other place has pretended to claim it, and as the whole Fraternity have, at various times, universally acknowledged allegiance to the authority established there: but whether the present association in that city be entitled to that allegiance, is a subject of inquiry which it is not my province to investigate. To that assembly recourse must be had for information. Thus much, however, is certain, that if a General Assembly or Grand Lodge was held there (of which there is little doubt if we can rely on our records and constitutions, as it is said to have existed there in Queen Elizabeth's time), there is no evidence of its regular removal to any other place in the kingdom; and, upon that ground, the brethren at York may probably with justice claim to the privilege of associating in that character. A number of respectable meetings of the Fraternity appear to have been convened at sundry times in different parts of England, but we cannot find an instance on record, till a very late period, of a general meeting (so called) being held in any other place beside York.

To understand this matter more clearly, it may be necessary to advert to the original institution of that assembly, called a *General* or *Grand Lodge*. It was not then restricted, as it is now understood to be, to the Masters and Wardens of private lodges, with the Grand Master and his Wardens at their head; it consisted of as many of the Fraternity *at large* as, being within a convenient distance, could attend, once or twice in a year, under the auspices of one general head, elected and installed at one of these meetings, and who, for the time being, received homage as the sole governor of the whole body. The idea of confining the privileges of masonry, by a warrant of constitution, to certain individuals, convened on certain days at certain places, had no existence. There was but one family among masons, and every mason was a branch of that family. It is true, the privileges of the different degrees of the Order always centred in certain members of the Fraternity, who, according to their advancement in the Art, were authorized by the ancient charges to assemble in, hold, and rule lodges, at their will and discretion, in such places as best suited their convenience, and when so assembled, to receive pupils and deliver instructions in masonry; but all the tribute from these individuals, separately and collectively, rested ultimately in the General Assembly, to which all the Fraternity might repair, and to whose award all were bound to pay submission.

As the constitutions of the English Lodges are derived from this *General* Assembly at *York*; as all masons are bound to observe and preserve those in all time coming; and as there is no satisfactory proof that such assembly was every regularly removed by the resolution of its members, but that, on the contrary, the Fraternity still continue to meet in that city under this appellation, it may remain a doubt, whether, while these constitutions exist as the standard of Masonic conduct, that assembly may not justly claim the allegiance to which their original authority entitled them; and whether any other convention of masons, however great their consequence may be, can, consistent with those constitutions, withdraw their allegiance from that assembly, or set aside an authority, to which not only antiquity, but the concurrent approbation of masons for ages, under the most solemn engagements, have repeatedly given a sanction.

It is to be regretted, that the idea of superiority, and a wish to acquire absolute dominion, should occasion a contest among masons. Were the principles of the Order better understood, and more generally practised, the intention of the institution would be more fully answered. Every mason would consider his brother as his fellow, and he who, by generous and virtuous actions, could best promote the happiness of society, would always be most likely to receive homage and respect.

For many years Athelstane held his court at York. He was known as a mild king and a good Masonic brother. His brother Edwin was qualified in every respect, to preside over so celebrated a body of men as the Masons. He employed Masons to repair and build many churches and other superb edifices in the city of York, at Beverley, and other places.

Grand Master Prince Edwin died two years before the king, and Preston reports there was an unfounded rumour that Athelstane murdered him. He goes on to outline the circumstances of Edwin's death:

> The business of Edwin's death is a point the most obscure in the story of this king, and, to say the truth, not one even of our best historians hath written clearly, or with due attention, concerning it. The fact as commonly received is this: The king, suspecting his younger brother Edwin, of designing to deprive him of his crown, caused him, notwithstanding his protestations of innocency, to be put on board a leaky ship, with his armour-bearer and page. The young prince, unable to bear the severity of the weather, and want of food, desperately drowned himself. Some time after, the king's cup-bearer, who had been the chief cause of this act of cruelty, happened, as he was serving the king at table, to trip with one foot, but recovering himself with the other, 'See,' said he, pleasantly, 'how brothers afford each other help'; which striking the king with the remembrance of what himself had done in taking off Edwin, who might have helped him in his wars, he caused that business to be more thoroughly examined, and, finding his brother had been falsely accused, caused his cup-bearer to be put to a cruel death, endured himself seven years sharp penance, and built the two monasteries of Middleton and Michelness, to atone for this base and bloody fact.

Preston goes on to say that Simeon of Durham and the Saxon Chronicle say that Edwin was drowned by his brother's command, in the year 933, but that other sources place the story in either the first or the second year of Athelstane's reign and tell the story of the rotten ship and of the king punishing the cup-bearer. Preston reasons that, if Edwin was drowned in the second year of Athelstane's reign, he could not be alive in the tenth year. And he says that we should take the first date as the more probable, because there was a conspiracy against the king about that time (the plan was to dethrone him, and put out his eyes). Yet Athelstane did not put the plotters to death, so Preston thinks it unlikely that he would have ordered his brother's effective drowning upon bare suspicion? Athelstane was unanimously acknowledged as king – his brother being then too young to govern, and hence not old enough to conspire.

Preston argues that if we take the second date (933), the whole story is destroyed; the king could not do seven years penance, for he did not live so long (he died in 939). As for the tale of the cup-bearer, and his stumble at the king's table, the same story is told of Earl Godwin, who murdered the brother of Edward the Confessor. Preston claims that nothing is clearer from history than that Athelstane was remarkably kind to his brothers and sisters, for whose sakes he lived single, and therefore his brother had less temptation to conspire against him.

When Edwin died, King Athelstane personally took over the direction of the lodges and supported the art of Masonry for the rest of his life. When Athelstane died the masons dispersed, and the lodges remained in an unsettled state till the accession in 960 of Edgar, who brought the Fraternity together under the mastership of St Dunstan; they were employed to build some religious structures, but were not greatly encouraged.

When Edgar died Masonry declined for almost fifty years, but it revived in 1041 because of the interest in Masonry of King Edward the Confessor. Edward appointed Leofric, Earl of Coventry, who was an accomplished architect, as Superintendent of Masons. Under his guidance Westminster Abbey and the Abbey of Coventry were rebuilt.

Chapter 3

William the Conqueror to Bloody Mary

Freemasonry Under the Knights Templar

William the Conqueror, who took the crown of England in 1066, appointed two patrons to oversee the Craft. Preston tells us that these were Gundulf, Bishop of Rochester, and Roger de Montgomery, Earl of Shrewsbury – each of whom had expertise in both civil and military architecture. These noble patrons employed the Fraternity to begin building the Tower of London. The work was completed during the reign of William Rufus, who then employed the Masons to build the Palace and Hall of Westminster and to rebuild London Bridge.

When King Henry I came to the throne in 1100 he granted a Charter of Liberties to the Masons and encouraged the lodges to assemble. Stephen, who succeeded Henry in 1135, employed the Fraternity to build a Chapel at Westminster, which is now the Chapel of the House of Commons, and appointed Gilbert de Clare, Marquis of Pembroke, to preside over the lodges. After King Henry II came to the throne in 1154 he appointed André de Montbard, the Grand Master of the Knights Templar, to act as Superintendent of the Masons, and under a succession of Templar Superintendents the Masons were employed to build a Temple for the Order in Fleet Street. This was completed under Grand Master Gérard de Ridefort, who was also the Superintendent of Masons in 1185. A round church, it was designed to recall the circular Church of the Holy Sepulchre in Jerusalem, and the patriarch of Jerusalem consecrated it.

Masonry continued under the patronage of the Knights Templar until 1199, when King John succeeded his brother Richard I. Preston tells us that John removed Gilbert Erail, who was then the Templar Grand Superintendent of Masons, and replaced him with Peter de Colechurch, whom he designated Grand Master of Masons. Colechurch began to rebuild London Bridge with stone, and it was finished in 1209. Peter de Rupibus succeeded Colechurch as Grand Master, with Geoffrey Fitz-Peter, Chief Surveyor of the King's Works, acting as his deputy, and under these two artists Masonry flourished during the remainder of King John's reign. [Preston makes no mention of Henry III (1216–72).]

Masonry Under Three Edwards

Edward I came to the throne of England in 1272. To take charge of the Masons he appointed Walter Giffard, Archbishop of York, Gilbert de Clare, Earl of Gloucester, and Ralph, Lord of Mount Hermer. These three oversaw the completion of Westminster Abbey, which had been started in 1220.

Edward II (1307–27) appointed Walter Stapleton, Bishop of Exeter, to be Grand Master. Under his guidance the Fraternity built Exeter and Oriel Colleges at Oxford and Clare Hall at Cambridge. Masonry flourished in England under Edward III, who was a patron of science and an encourager of learning. Preston tells us that the king patronized the lodges and appointed five deputies to run the day-to-day business of the Fraternity:

John de Spoulee, rebuilder of St George's Chapel, Windsor, where the Order of the Garter was instituted in 1350
William Wykeham, later Bishop of Winchester, who in 1357 rebuilt Windsor Castle at the head of 400 free-masons
Robert Barnham, who, with 250 free-masons, finished St George's Hall in London in 1375
Henry Yevele (called the King's free-mason in the old records), who built the Charterhouse in London, King's Hall in Cambridge and Queensborough Castle, and rebuilt St Stephen's Chapel, Westminster
Simon Langham, Abbot of Westminster, who rebuilt the body of that cathedral as it now stands.

Edward III also revised and improved the constitutions and ancient charges of the Order and added several regulations to the original laws. During his reign lodges were numerous, and the regular communications of the Fraternity were held under the protection of the civil magistrates.

Preston quotes from an old record of the Society, which he says was then in his possession:

In the glorious reign of King Edward III, when lodges were more frequent, the Right Worshipful the Master and Fellows, with consent of the lords of the realm (for most great men were then masons), ordained,

That for the future, at the making or admission of a brother, the constitution and the ancient charges should be read by the Master or Warden.

That such as were to be admitted master-masons, or masters of work, should be examined whether they be able of cunning to serve their respective lords, as well the lowest as the highest, to the honour and worship of the aforesaid Art, and to the profit of their lords; for they be their lords that employ and pay them for their service and travel.

The following particulars, Preston says, were also contained in a very old manuscript, a copy of which was reputedly in the possession of the late George Payne, Esq., Grand Master in 1718:

That when the Master and Wardens meet in a lodge, if need be, the Sheriff of the county, or the Mayor of the city, or Alderman of the town, in which the congregation is held, should be made fellow and sociate to the Master, in help of him against rebels, and for upbearing the rights of the realm.

That entered prentices, at their making, were charged not to be thieves or thieves' maintainers; that they should travel honestly for their pay, and love their fellows as themselves, and be true to the king of England, and to the realm, and to the lodge.

That, at such congregations, it shall be inquired, whether any Master or Fellow has broke any of the articles agreed to; and if the offender, being duly cited to appear, prove rebel, and will not attend, then the lodge shall determine against him, that he shall forswear (or renounce) his masonry, and shall no more use this craft; the which if he presume for to do, the sheriff of the county shall prison him, and take all his goods into the king's hands, till his grace be granted him and issued. For this cause principally have these congregations been ordained, that as well the lowest as the highest should be well and truly served in this Art aforesaid, throughout all the kingdom of England. Amen, so mote it be.

In 1377 Richard II succeeded his grandfather Edward III, and he caused William Wykeham to continue as Grand Master. Grand Master Wykeham rebuilt Westminster Hall and employed the Fraternity to build New College, Oxford, and Winchester College. After Richard had been killed and succeeded by Henry IV, Thomas Fitz Allen, Earl of Surrey, replaced Wykeham as Grand Master. Henry founded Battle Abbey and Fotheringhay Abbey and built the Guildhall of London. In 1413 Henry V succeeded to the crown, and he put Henry Chichele, Archbishop of Canterbury, in charge of the Fraternity; under his guidance the lodges met frequently.

When Henry VI succeeded to the throne in 1422 he was still a minor, and during his reign an attempt was made by parliament to suppress the lodges and regular meetings of masons. Preston explains the circumstances. The Duke of Bedford, who was regent, spent much of his time in France, and so his brother Humphrey, Duke of Gloucester, ruled England and took the title Protector and Guardian of the kingdom. Humphrey had received a more learned education than was usual in his age; he founded one of the first public libraries in England and was a great patron of learned men. Preston adds that the records of Freemasonry say he was made a Freemason. But the young King Henry was educated by Henry Beaufort, Bishop of Winchester and Humphrey of Gloucester's uncle, who had political ambitions. It was the battle between the Bishop and the Protector that resulted in the hostility of Parliament to Freemasonry.

The Bishop resolved to destroy Duke Humphrey, as he felt the Duke's popularity made him dangerous. The Duke had always been a good friend to the public, and had prevented absolute power from being vested in the person of the young king, whose education and attitude of mind Beaufort controlled and attempted to subvert to his own purposes. In order to weaken his nephew, the Bishop, knowing Gloucester was supported by the Freemasons, called on Parliament to abolish the Society of Masons on the grounds that they held secret meetings.

In April 1425 Parliament met at Westminster, the servants and followers of the peers all arriving armed to the teeth with clubs and staves (this came to be called the Battle Parliament). Among the laws it passed was an act abolishing the Society of Masons by preventing its assemblies and congregations:

Masons shall not confederate in Chapters or Congregations

Whereas, by the yearly congregations and confederacies made by the masons in their general assemblies, the good course and effect of the statutes of labourers be openly violated and broken, in subversion of the law, and to the great damage of all the commons; our sovereign Lord the King, willing in this case to provide a remedy, by the advice and consent aforesaid, and at the special request of the commons, hath ordained and established that such chapters and congregations shall not be hereafter holden; and if any such be made, they that cause such chapters and congregations to be assembled and holden, if they thereof be convict, shall be judged for felons: and that the other masons, that come to such chapters or congregations, be punished by imprisonment of their bodies, and make find and ransom at the king's will.

This act never came into force, and the Fraternity was not deterred from assembling under the continuing Grand Mastership of Archbishop Chichele. As Preston explains:

The Latin Register of William Molart, prior of Canterbury, in manuscript, pap. 88, entitled *Liveratio generalis domini Gulielmi Prioris Ecclesiæ Christi Cantuariensis, erga Fastum Natalis Domini 1429*, informs us, that in the year 1429, during the minority of Henry VI, a respectable lodge was held at Canterbury under the patronage of Henry Chicheley, the Archbishop; at which were present Thomas Stapylton, the Master; John Morris, warden of the lodge of masons; with fifteen fellow-crafts, and three entered apprentices, all of whom are particularly named.

Despite the edict many lodges were formed in different parts of the kingdom, and the Fraternity prospered.

The sovereign authority vested in the Duke of Gloucester, as Protector of the Realm, meant that the execution of the laws, and all that related to the civil magistracy, centred in him. This was fortunate for the Masons at this critical juncture. The Duke, knowing the Masons to be innocent of the accusations Bishop Beaufort had laid against them, took them under his protection, and turned the charge of rebellion, sedition and treason away from them and onto the Bishop and his followers. The Duke asserted that they were the first violators of the public peace, and the most rigorous promoters of a civil discord.

Preston tells us that Beaufort, realizing that his conduct could not be justified by the laws of the land, set out to influence the young king. Beaufort persuaded the king to grant letters of pardon for all offences committed by him, contrary to the statute of provisors and other acts of præÊmunire. Then, five years later, he obtained another pardon, under the great seal, for all crimes whatever from the creation of the world to 26 July 1437. Notwithstanding the Bishop's precautions, though, in 1442 the Duke of Gloucester drew up fresh articles of impeachment against him, presented them to the king and urged the king to pass judgment on Beaufort for his crimes. The king referred the matter to his council, which was made up mainly of ecclesiastics. They favoured the Bishop and made such a slow progress in the business that the duke, weary of the delays and fraudulent evasions, dropped the prosecution.

The Bishop then accused the Duchess of Gloucester of witchcraft. It was alleged that a wax figure of the king was found in her possession, and that she and two associates, Sir Roger Bolingbroke, a priest, and Margery Jordan of Eye, melted it in a magical manner before a slow fire, with the intention of making Henry's force and vigour waste away in the same manner. This accusation, calculated to affect the weak and credulous mind of the king, gain some credence in that credulous age, and the Duchess and her confederates were tried and found guilty. The Duchess was condemned to do public penance in London for three days, and to suffer perpetual imprisonment; the others were executed.

The Duke, provoked by such insults to his Duchess, stoutly resisted these shameful proceedings, but the matter ended in his own destruction. The Bishop and his party hatched a plan to murder him. A parliament was summoned to meet at St Edmondsbury [now Bury St Edmunds] in 1447, where they expected he would be entirely at their mercy, and, having appeared on the second day of the session, the Duke was accused of treason, and thrown into prison. The next day he was found cruelly murdered. It was pretended that his death was natural. But, though his body (which was exposed to public view) bore no marks of outward injury, there was little doubt he was a sacrifice to the vengeance of his enemies. After this dreadful catastrophe, five of his servants were tried for aiding him in his treasons and condemned to be hanged, drawn and quartered. They were hanged accordingly, cut down alive, stripped naked and marked with a knife to be quartered, when the Marquis of Suffolk produced a pardon, and saved their lives. Preston describes this as 'the most barbarous kind of mercy that can possibly be imagined!' [Preston seems to miss the point that perhaps the Marquis was a supporter of Beaufort.]

Preston assures us that the Duke of Gloucester's death was universally lamented throughout the kingdom. He had long deserved, the sobriquet of 'the Good'. He was a lover of his country, friend of good men, protector of Masons, patron of the learned, and the encourager of every useful art. His persecutor, the hypocritical Bishop, scarcely survived him by two months. After a long life spent in falsehood and politics, he sank into oblivion, and ended his days in misery.

After Beaufort's death the Masons held their lodges without danger of interruption. Henry VI established various seats of erudition, which he enriched with endowments, and distinguished by peculiar immunities. He thus encouraged his subjects to rise above ignorance and barbarism, and reform their turbulent and licentious manners. In 1442 he was initiated into masonry, and, from that time, spared no pains to obtain a complete knowledge of the Art. He perused the ancient charges, revised the constitutions and, with the consent of his Council, honoured the Masons with his sanction.

Preston quotes a record from the time of Edward IV:

The company of masons, being otherwise termed free-masons, of auntient staunding and good reckoninge, by means of affable and kind meetyngs dyverse tymes, and as a lovinge brotherhode use to doe, did frequent this mutual assembly in the tyme of Henry VI in the twelfth yeare of his most gracious reign, A.D. 1434. That the charges and laws of the free-masons have been seen and perused by our late soveraign king Henry VI and by the lords of his most honourable council, who have allowed them, and declared, That they be right good and reasonable to be holden, as they have been drawn out and collected from the records of auntient tymes.

From this it appears that Freemasons were held in high esteem. Preston tells us that, encouraged by the example of the sovereign and drawn by an ambition to excel, many lords and gentlemen of the court were initiated into Masonry, and pursued the Art with diligence and assiduity.

While all this was going on in England, Masons in Scotland were encouraged and protected by King James I, who became a patron of learning and a zealous encourager of Masonry. The Scottish records say that he honoured lodges with his royal presence and settled a yearly revenue of four pounds Scots to be paid to every Master Mason in Scotland. He gave the Masons a Grand Master approved by the crown, either nobly born or an eminent clergyman, who had his deputies in cities and counties, and every new brother would pay an entrance fee to him. [This is the first mention of an initiation fee being paid to support a Grand Master and officers.] This office empowered the Grand Master to regulate the Fraternity, so that there would be no need to resort to law courts. In Scotland both mason and lord, the builder and the founder of any proposed structure, when at variance, could appeal to the king, in order to prevent lawsuits. In his absence, they appealed to his Warden.

In England Henry had presided in person over the lodges and nominated as Grand Master William Waynefleet, Bishop of Winchester, who built at his own expense Magdalen College, Oxford, and several religious houses. Eton College, near Windsor, and King's College, Cambridge, were founded in his reign, and finished under the direction of Waynefleet, and Henry also founded Christ's College and Queen's College (named for his queen, Margaret of Anjou) in Cambridge. In short, during the life of this prince, the arts flourished, and many sagacious statesmen, consummate orators, and admired writers, were supported by royal generosity.

So Masonry flourished until England's domestic peace was interrupted by the civil wars between the royal houses of York and Lancaster: the Wars of the Roses (1455–85). During this period Masonry was neglected, until revived in 1471 under the Grand Mastership of Richard Beauchamp, Bishop of Sarum, an appointee of Edward IV who was given the title of Chancellor of the Garter, for his efforts in repairing the castle and chapel of Windsor. Under Edward V and Richard III it again fell into decline until the accession of

Henry VII in 1485, when it rose in esteem once more. At this time Freemasonry came under the patronage of the Master and Fellows of the Order of Knights of St John of Malta. They held a Grand Lodge in 1500 and chose King Henry as their protector. Now under royal favour, the Fraternity revived its assemblies, and Masonry prospered.

On 24 June 1502 a Lodge of Masters was formed, at which the king presided in person as Grand Master. At this meeting King Henry appointed John Islip, Abbot of Westminster, and Sir Reginald Bray, a Knight of the Garter, as his Wardens. The Grand Officers then proceeded in ample form to the east end of Westminster Abbey, where the King laid the foundation stone of the chapel that bears his name.

Henry VII's Chapel is supported by fourteen Gothic buttresses, all beautifully ornamented, projecting from the building at different angles. It is lighted by two tiers of windows, casting a light that both pleases the eye and also affords a kind of solemn gloom. The buttresses extend to the roof, and to strengthen it, are crowned with Gothic arches. The entrance is from the east end of the abbey, by a flight of black marble steps, under a royal arch, leading to the body of the chapel. The gates are of brass. The stalls on each side are of oak, as are the seats, and the pavement is black and white marble. The ceremony of the capstone for this building was celebrated in 1507. Later in Henry VII's reign the Palace of Richmond was built under the direction of Sir Reginald Bray, and Brasenose College, Oxford, and Jesus and St John's Colleges, Cambridge, were finished.

Preston tells us that when Henry VIII succeeded his father in 1509 he appointed Cardinal Wolsey to be Grand Master. Wolsey built Hampton Court, Whitehall and Christ Church College, Oxford. In 1530 Thomas Cromwell, Earl of Essex, succeeded as Grand Master and employed the Fraternity to build St James's Palace, Christ's Hospital and Greenwich Castle. In 1534 the King and Parliament threw off allegiance to the Pope of Rome, and the King was declared supreme head of the English church. In the aftermath of the break with Rome no less than 926 religious houses were suppressed; many of them later converted into stately mansions for the nobility and gentry. Cromwell was beheaded in 1540, and John Touchet, Lord Audley, succeeded to the office of Grand Master and supervised the Fraternity in building Magdalene College, Cambridge.

Edward VI was a minor when he succeeded to the throne in 1547, and his guardian and regent, Edward Seymour, Duke of Somerset, undertook the management of the masons and built Somerset House in the Strand. Seymour was beheaded in 1552. John Poynet, the Bishop of Winchester, then became the patron of the Fraternity, and presided over the lodges till the King's death in 1553. During the nine-day reign of Lady Jane Grey and the five-year rule of Mary I the Masons remained without a patron.

Chapter 4

Elizabeth and the Stuarts

The Grand Lodge of York

When Queen Elizabeth I came to the throne Sir Thomas Sackville became Grand Master. During this period Lodges were held in different parts of England, but the Grand Lodge assembled in York, where the Fraternity were numerous and respectable.

Elizabeth, hearing that the Masons were in possession of secrets that they would not reveal, and being jealous of all secret assemblies, sent an armed force to York to break up their Annual Grand Lodge. Her design, however, was happily frustrated by the interposition of Sir Thomas Sackville. He initiated into Masonry the chief officers whom she sent to break up the meeting. They joined in communication with the Masons, and made such a favourable report to the Queen on their return, that she countermanded her orders, and never afterwards attempted to disturb the meetings of the Fraternity.

Sir Thomas Sackville remained Grand Master till 1567, when he resigned in favour of Francis Russell, Earl of Bedford and Sir Thomas Gresham, an eminent merchant. The former took on the care of the brethren in the northern part of the kingdom, and the latter was in charge of the south, where the society had considerably increased as a result of the favourable report that had been made to the Queen.

In the city of London Sir Thomas Gresham erected, at his own expense, a building for the service of commerce. He bought some houses between Cornhill and Threadneedle Street and demolished them to provide the site, and on 7 June 1566 the foundation stone of the new building was laid. The work was finished in November 1567. The building was rectangular and had Sir Thomas's emblem of a grasshopper upon a pedestal at each corner of the roof. That roof was supported by marble pillars – ten on the north and south sides, seven on east and west – forming a portico. Under the portico stood 119 shops (each seven-and-a-half feet long, and five feet broad), 25 a side on the east and west, 34 on the north, and 35 on the south, each earning Sir Thomas £41 10s. a year in rent.

When it was first built this edifice was called the Bourse. But on 23 January 1570 the Queen, attended by a great number of her nobles, came from her palace of Somerset House in the Strand, to dine with Sir Thomas at his house in Bishopsgate. After dinner Her Majesty returned through Cornhill, entered the Bourse on the south side, and viewed every part of the building. She was particularly impressed with the gallery, which extended round the whole structure and was furnished with shops filled with all sorts of the finest wares in the City. She caused the building to be proclaimed, in her presence, by a herald and trumpet, the Royal Exchange.

On this occasion Sir Thomas appeared publicly in the role of Grand Master of Masons. (The original Royal Exchange building stood till the fire of London in 1666, when it perished amidst the general havoc, but was later restored to its present magnificence.) Despite the appointment of Sir Thomas as Grand Master for the South, however, the General Assembly continued to meet in the city of York. All the records were kept at York, and appeals were made to this assembly on important occasions.

Elizabeth was now satisfied that the Masonic fraternity was made up of skilful architects, and lovers of the Arts, and that the rules of the Order forbade interference in state affairs. She became perfectly reconciled to their assemblies, and Masonry made great progress during her reign. Lodges were held throughout the kingdom, particularly in London, and its environs, where the brethren increased considerably. Under the auspices of Sir Thomas Gresham several great works were carried out and the Fraternity received every encouragement. Charles Howard, later the Earl of Nottingham, succeeded Sir Thomas as Grand Master and presided over the lodges in the south until 1588, when George Hastings, Earl of Huntingdon, replaced him.

James VI and I

When Elizabeth died the crowns of England and Scotland were united under her successor James VI of Scotland, who was proclaimed King of England, Scotland and Ireland on 25 March 1603, taking the title King James I in England. He had already been made a Mason two years earlier at Scone and had been a noted patron of the Craft in Scotland. Masonry now flourished throughout the combined kingdoms, and many lodges were convened directly under his royal patronage.

Many gentlemen were inspired by the teachings of Masonry to revive the old Roman masonry. They travelled widely and returned full of enthusiasm with fragments of old columns, curious drawings, and books of architecture. Foremost among these enthusiasts was Inigo Jones, a Londoner who had been apprenticed to a joiner and had a natural bent for design. He was renowned for his skill in landscape painting and was patronized by William Herbert, later Earl of Pembroke. Jones made the tour of Italy at Herbert's expense, and studied under the best disciples of the famous Andrea Palladio. When he returned to England, he became engrossed in the study of architecture; he came to be known as the Vitruvius of Britain and a local rival to Palladio.

King James appointed this celebrated artist his General Surveyor and later nominated him Grand Master of England and deputized him to preside over the Lodges. Under Inigo Jones the Fraternity flourished, several learned men were initiated into it, and Masonry grew in reputation. Ingenious artists were inspired to come to England, and when they did they met with great encouragement. Lodges were set up as places of instruction in the sciences and polite arts. The regular communications of the Fraternity were observed, and the annual festivals regularly celebrated.

Grand Master Inigo Jones was an accomplished architect and many magnificent structures were finished under his direction. He was instructed by King James to plan a new palace at Whitehall that would be a worthy residence for the Kings of England. Parliament, however, would not provide sufficient funds, so no more than the present Banqueting House was completed.

In 1607 the foundation stone of the Banqueting House was laid in full Masonic ceremony by King James, attended by Grand Master Jones and his wardens, William Herbert, Earl of Pembroke, and

Nicholas Stone, Esq. Many brothers, clothed in proper Masonic form, were also present, along with other eminent persons invited for the occasion. The stone-laying was conducted with great pomp and splendour, and afterwards the king laid a purse of pieces of gold upon the stone, so that the Masons might have a feast to celebrate the event.

When completed in 1622 the Banqueting House, the finest single room of its size since the days of the Roman Emperor Augustus, was intended as a place for receiving ambassadors and for other state occasions. It was three storeys high, regular and stately. Externally, the lowest level consisted of a rusticated wall with small square windows. From this plinth rose a wall punctuated with Ionic columns and pilasters with, between the columns, well-proportioned windows with alternating segmental and triangular pediments. Over this was an entablature from which rose another tier of (Corinthian) columns and pilasters, aligned above those below. From the capitals hung festoons, with masks and other ornaments suspended in the middle. This level, too, was crowned with an entablature supporting a balustrade. The relief effect created by the pilasters and engaged columns, rustication and entablatures created a happy diversity of light and shade on the outside of the building.

Inigo Jones remained Grand Master until 1618, when he retired and was succeeded by the Earl of Pembroke, under whom many eminent, wealthy and learned men were initiated, and the mysteries of the Order were held in high esteem.

Charles I

King James died in 1625, and his son Charles I succeeded, but the Earl of Pembroke continued as Grand Master until 1630, when he resigned in favour of Henry Danvers, Earl of Danby. Danby was succeeded in 1633 by Thomas Howard, Earl of Arundel and later Duke of Norfolk. In 1635 Francis Russell, Earl of Bedford, took over the government of the society, but Past Grand Master Inigo Jones having continued to patronize the lodges during his lordship's administration, was re-elected the following year and continued as Grand Master till his death in 1646.

Lodges continued to meet regularly at this time, as the diary of the antiquary Elias Ashmole shows:

I was made a free-mason at Warrington, Lancashire, with Colonel Henry Mainwaring, of Kerthingham, in Cheshire, by Mr Richard Penket the Warden, and the fellow-crafts [all of whom are specified] on 16th October 1646.

In another diary entry he says:

On March the 10th, 1682, about 5 hor. post merid. I received a summons to appear at a lodge, to be held the next day at Masons' Hall in London – March 11. Accordingly I went, and about noon were admitted into the fellowship of free-masons, Sir William Wilson knt, Capt. Richard Porthwick, Mr William Woodman, Mr William Gray, Mr Samuel Taylour, and Mr William Wise. I was the senior fellow among them, it being thirty-five years since I was admitted. There were present, beside myself, the fellows after-named; Mr Thomas Wise, master of the masons' company this present year, Mr Thomas Shorthose, and 7 more old free-masons. We all dined at the Half-moon tavern, Cheapside, at a noble dinner prepared at the charge of the new accepted masons.

Preston says that an old record of the Society describes a coat of arms much the same as that of the London Company of Freemen Masons, and it is generally believed that this company is a branch of our ancient fraternity. In former times it was a necessary qualification to be made free of that company, that a man must be first initiated in some lodge of Free and Accepted Masons. This practice is still carried out in Scotland among the operative masons.

Preston quotes this account of Masonry from an unnamed source:

He (Mr Ashmole) was elected a brother of the company of free-masons; a favour esteemed to singular by the members, that kings themselves have not disdained to enter themselves of this Society. From these are derived the adopted masons, accepted masons, or free-masons; who are known to one another all over the world, by certain signals and watch-words known to them alone. They have several lodges in different countries for their reception; and when any of them fall into decay, the brotherhood is to relieve them. The manner of their adoption or admission is very formal and solemn, and with the administration of an oath of secrecy, which has had better fate than all other oaths, and has ever been most religiously observed; nor has the world been yet able, by the inadvertency, surprise or folly of any of its members, to dive into this mystery, or make the least discover.

In some of Mr Ashmole's manuscripts there are many valuable collections relating to the history of the free-masons.

As to the ancient Society of free-masons, concerning whom you are desirous of knowing what may be known with certainty, I shall only tell you, that if our worthy brother E. Ashmole esq. had executed his intended design, our fraternity had been as much obliged to him as the brethren of the most noble Order of the Garter. I would not have you surprised at this expression or think it at all too assuming. The Sovereigns of that Order have not disdained our fellowship, and there have been times when Emperors were also free-masons. What from Mr Ashmole's collection I could gather was, that the report of our Society taking rise from a bull granted by the pope in the reign of Henry VI to some Italian architects, to travel over all Europe to erect chapels, was ill-founded. Such a bull there was, and those architects were masons. But this bull, in the opinion of the learned Mr Ashmole, was confirmative only, and did not by any means create our fraternity, or even establish them in this kingdom. But as to the time and manner of that establishment, something I shall relate from the same collections.

St Alban, the proto-martyr, established masonry here, and from his time it flourished, more or less, according as the world went, down to the days of king Athelstane, who, for the sake of his brother Edwin, granted the masons a charter. Under our Norman princes they frequently received extraordinary marks of royal favour. There is no doubt to be made that the skill of masons, which was always transcendently great, even in the most barbarous times; their wonderful kindness and attachment to each other, how different soever in condition; and their inviolable fidelity in keeping religiously their secrets; must have exposed them, in ignorant, troublesome and superstitious times, to a vast variety of adventures, according to the different state of parties and other alterations in government. By the way, it may be noted, that the masons were always loyal, which exposed them to great severities when power wore the appearance of justice, and those who committed treason punished true men as traitors. Thus, in the 3d year of Henry VI an act passed to abolish the society of masons, and to hinder, under grievous penalties, the holding chapters, lodges, or other regular assemblies; yet this act was afterwards [virtually] repealed; and even before that, king Henry and several lords of his court, became fellows of the craft.

Charles II

After the Restoration, Masonry began to revive under the patronage of Charles II, who had been received into the Order during his exile. During his reign some lodges were constituted by leave of several noble Grand Masters, and many gentlemen and famous scholars requested at that time to be admitted to the Fraternity.

On 27 December 1663 a general assembly was held, at which Henry Jermyn, Earl of St Albans, was elected Grand Master, and he then appointed Sir John Denham, Christopher Wren and John Webb as his Wardens. Preston quotes what he calls several useful regulations that were made at this assembly, for the better government of the lodges and to enable the greatest harmony to prevail among the whole Fraternity.

1. No person, of what degree soever, be made or accepted a free-mason unless in a regular lodge, whereof one to be a Master or a Warden in that limit or division where such lodge is kept, and another to be a craftsman in the trade of free-masonry.
2. No person shall be accepted a free-mason, but such as are of able body, honest parentage, good reputation, and an observer of the laws of the land.
3. No person who shall be accepted a free-mason or shall be admitted into any lodge or assembly, until he has brought a certificate of the time and place of his acceptation from the lodge that accepted him, unto the Master of lodge, shall enrole the same in a roll of parchment to be kept for that purpose, and shall give an account of all such acceptations at every general assembly.
4. Every person who is now a free-mason shall bring to the Master a note of the time of his acceptation, to the end the same may

be enrolled in such priority of place as the brother deserves; and that the whole company and fellows may the better know each other.

5. For the future the fraternity of free-masons shall be regulated and governed by one Grand Master, and as many Wardens as the said Society shall think fit to appoint at every annual general assembly.

6. No person shall be accepted, unless he be twenty-one years old, or more.

Many of the fraternity's records of this and the preceding reign were lost during the rule of Oliver Cromwell, as they were too hastily burnt by some scrupulous brothers, from a fear of making discoveries prejudicial to the interests of Masonry.

In June 1666 Thomas Savage, Earl Rivers, succeeded the Earl of St Albans as Grand Master. Now Sir Christopher Wren was appointed Deputy Grand Master and set about promoting the prosperity of the few lodges that met at this time, particularly the old lodge of St Paul's, which he patronized for upwards of eighteen years. The records of this lodge, now known as the Lodge of Antiquity, say that Bro. Wren attended the meetings regularly and that during his Mastership he presented three mahogany candlesticks to the lodge – a valuable gift still preserved and highly prized as a memento of the esteem of their donor.

Christopher Wren was born in 1632 and was the only son of the dean of Windsor. He showed an early aptitude for arts and sciences. At the age of thirteen, he invented a new astronomical instrument, which he called a Pan-organum, and wrote a treatise on the origin of rivers. He invented a new pneumatic engine, and a calculating machine for making appropriate markings on sundials. In 1646, at the age of 14, he entered Wadham College, Oxford, where he was taught and befriended by Dr John Wilkins and Dr Seth Ward, both gentlemen of great learning, and showed himself to be something of a polymath. He assisted Dr Scarborough in anatomical preparations and experiments on the muscles of the human body. Soon afterwards he wrote about the geometry and mechanisms of anatomy. He also wrote discourses on the problem of measuring longitude, on the variations of the compass needle, on how to find the velocity of a ship, about improving ship design and how to recover wrecks. Beside this he also wrote on convenient ways of using artillery aboard ship, how to build in deep water, how to build a mole into the sea and improving river navigation by linking rivers together. In short, he wrote many works of genius – so many that they appear to be the united efforts of a whole century rather than the production of one man.

The Great Fire

Preston recounts how a singular and awful event in 1666 called forth the utmost exertion of Masonic abilities. The City of London, which the preceding year had been struck by the plague, which killed more than 100,000 of its inhabitants, had scarcely recovered when a great fire reduced most of the buildings within the city walls to ashes. It started on 2 September at the house of a baker in Pudding Lane. The bakery was a wooden building coated with pitch on the outside, like the rest of the houses in that narrow lane, and the house was filled with faggots and brushwood for the ovens, which added to the spread the flames. The fire raged with such fury that it spread in four directions at once.

Jonas Moore and Ralph Gatrix, were ordered to survey the ruins afterwards, and they reported that the fire had devastated 373 acres within the walls and burnt 13,000 houses and 89 parish churches, leaving only 11 parish churches standing. Gresham's Royal Exchange, the Custom House, the Guildhall, Blackwell Hall (the centre of the cloth trade), St Paul's Cathedral, the Bridewell prison, the halls of fifty-two city livery companies, and three of the city's gates were all demolished. The cost of the damage was estimated at over a million pounds sterling.

After such a calamity, it was decided to adopt building regulations to guard against any similar catastrophe in future. All new buildings were to be built of stone and brick instead of timber. Charles II and Grand Master Earl Rivers at once instructed Deputy Grand Master Wren to draw up a plan for a new city, which, Wren decided, would have broad and regular streets. They appointed him Surveyor General and also made him Principal Architect with responsibility for rebuilding the city. He was put in charge of rebuilding the cathedral of St Paul, and all the parochial churches that had been destroyed.

Bro. Wren soon realised that this task was too big for one man, so he asked Robert Hook, Professor of Geometry at Gresham College, to assist him. Hooke set about measuring, adjusting and setting out the grounds of the private streets at once. The model and plan for the new city were laid before the king and the House of Commons, and the whole scheme shown to be practical. However, most of the citizens insisted on rebuilding their houses on the old foundations, and many were unwilling to give over their properties to public trustees unless they received more compensation. A majority were distrustful of the plan. Wren argued that removing all the churchyards, gardens, etc., to the outskirts of the city would both create more space to improve the streets and result in better churches, halls and other public buildings. But he failed to convince the owners of the burnt-out land; the citizens wanted to rebuild their old city, despite all its disadvantages. They did not understand the principles of Bro. Wren's new model city and thought it an unwelcome innovation.

Thus the opportunity of making the new city the most magnificent, and the most commodious for health and trade of any in Europe was lost, and Wren had to abridge his plans. All the same, he used all his labour, skill and ingenuity to model the city as best he could within the constraints.

On 23 October 1667 King Charles II carried out the Masonic ceremony of levelling the foundation stone of the new Royal Exchange. The building, said at the time to be the finest in Europe, was opened on the 28 September 1669 by the Lord Mayor and Aldermen. It took the form of a hollow square, and around the inside, above the arcades and between the windows, were statues of the sovereigns of England. In the centre of the square a masterly life-size white marble statue by Mr Gibbons, then Grand Warden of the society, depicted the king wearing a monk's habit. Meanwhile the Custom House for the Port of London was built in 1668 on the South side of Thames Street; it was adorned with stone columns of the Tuscan and Ionic orders. (In the same year Deputy Grand Master Wren and his Warden Mr Webb completed the Sheldonian theatre in Oxford, which was paid for by Gilbert Sheldon, then Archbishop of Canterbury.)

In 1671 Bro. Wren started work on a great monument, in the form of a great Doric column 202 feet high, to commemorate the burning and re-building of the City of London. This was finished in 1677. Around the base, were carved these words:

This pillar was set up in perpetual remembrance of the most dreadful burning of this Protestant city, begun and carried on by the treachery and malice of the Popish faction, in the beginning of September, in the year of our Lord 1666, in order to the carrying on their horrid plot for extirpating the Protestant religion, and old English liberty, and introducing popery and slavery.

Bro. Wren paid particular attention to the rebuilding of St Paul's Cathedral, even while he worked vigorously to rebuild the city. He drew several designs for it and after wide consultation drew up a final design in the best style of Greek and Roman architecture. He made a large model of it in wood, but when he showed it to the bishops they decided it was not sufficiently in the grand cathedral style, and he was ordered to amend it. He then produced the present scheme, which met with the King's approval. (The original model, which was based only on the Corinthian order, like St Peter's in Rome, was kept at the cathedral, as a curiosity.)

The foundation stone of this magnificent cathedral was laid by King Charles II in 1673. He conducted the ceremony in solemn Masonic form, supported by Grand Master Rivers, Bro. Wren, his Deputy and the architects and craftsmen. The ceremony was attended by the nobility and gentry, the Lord Mayor and Aldermen, and the bishops and clergy. Throughout the building work Deputy Grand Master Wren acted as master of the work and surveyor, and was ably assisted by his wardens, Bro. Edward Strong and Bro. Thomas Strong, his son.

Bro. Wren took great care to ensure that the new cathedral was accurately aligned due East and West, and this has meant it is set at an oblique angle to Ludgate Street. The great front gate – which has been set in line with the street, rather than the church to which it belongs – makes the statue of Queen Anne, which is exactly in the middle of the West front, seem to be thrown to one side of the straight approach from the gate to the church, and suggests the whole edifice is awry. It is the street which is misaligned, however, not the great cathedral.

When he was marking out the dimensions of the building, Wren fixed the location of the centre of the great dome, and a labourer was ordered to bring him a flat stone from among the rubbish, to leave as a marker for the Masons. The man brought a piece of a gravestone, with nothing remaining of the inscription but a single word, in large capitals, RESURGAM. This was said to have left an impression on Bro. Wren's mind that was never afterwards erased.

The Cathedral is planned in the form of a long cross with the grand dome rising on the centre of the whole building. In the great cupola, 108 feet in diameter, Wren seems to have imitated the Pantheon in Rome. Its windows shine light through the great colonnade that encircles the dome. The old church of St Paul had had a lofty spire, so Bro. Wren was obliged to give his building sufficient height that it did not suffer by comparison, and, to do this, he made the outside of the dome much higher than its inside. He achieved this by raising a brick cone over the internal cupola, which supports the stone lantern on the apex.

The noble fabric of the new St Paul's is lofty enough to be seen from the sea to the east and from Windsor to the west. It was completed within 35 years by a single architect, the great Bro. Sir Christopher Wren. It had one principal mason, Wren's Warden Bro. Edward Strong, and was completed under one Bishop of London, Dr Henry Compton. St Peter's in Rome, by contrast, took 155 years to build and was worked on by twelve successive architects.

The Masonic Fraternity were now fully employed, and together they built the following parish churches, which had been consumed by the great fire:

All Hallows, Bread Street, finished 1694; and the steeple completed 1697

All Hallows the Great, Thames Street, 1683

All Hallows, Lombard Street, 1694

St Alban, Wood Street, 1685

St Anne and Agnes, St Anne's Lane, Aldersgate Street, 1680

St Andrew's Wardrobe, Puddledock Hill, 1692

St Andrew's, Holborn, 1687

St Anthony's, Watling Street, 1682

St Augustine's, Watling Street, 1683; and the steeple finished 1695

St Bartholomew's, Royal Exchange, 1679

St Benedict, Gracechurch Street, 1685

St Benedict's, Threadneedle Street, 1673

St Bennet's, Paul's Wharf, Thames Street, 1683

St Bride's, Fleet Street, 1680; and farther adorned in 1699

Christ-church, Newgate Street, 1687

St Christopher's, Threadneedle Street (since taken down to make room for the Bank) repaired 1696

St Clement Danes, in the Strand, taken down 1680, and rebuilt by Bro. Christopher Wren, 1682

St Clement's, Eastcheap, St Clement's Lane, 1686

St Dennis Back, Lime Street, 1674

St Dunstan's in the East, Tower Street, repaired in 1698

St Edmond's the King, Lombard Street, rebuilt in 1674
St George, Botolph Lane, 1674
St James, Garlick Hill, 1683
St James, Westminster, 1675
St Lawrence Jewry, Cateaton Street, 1677
St Magnus, London Bridge, 1676; the steeple, 1705
St Margaret, Lothbury, 1690
St Margaret Pattens, Little Tower Street, 1687
St Martin's, Ludgate, 1684
St Mary Abchurch, Abchurch Lane, 1686
St Mary's-at-Hill, St Mary's Hill, 1672
St Mary's Aldermary, Bow Lane, 1672
St Mary Magdalen, Old Fish Street, 1685
St Mary Somerset, Queenhithe, Thames Street, 1683
St Mary-le-Bow, Cheapside, 1683
St Mary Woolnoth's, Lombard Street, repaired in 1677
St Mary, Aldermanbury, rebuilt 1677
St Matthew, Friday Street, 1685
St Michael, Basinghall Street, 1679
St Michael Royal, College Hill, 1694
St Michael, Queenhithe, Trinity Lane, 1677
St Michael, Wood Street, 1675
St Michael, Crooked Lane, 1688
St Michael, Cornhill, 1672
St Mildred, Bread Street, 1683
St Mildred, Poultry, 1676
St Nicholas, Cole Abbey, Old Fish Street, 1677
St Olive's, Old Jewry, 1673
St Peter's, Cornhill, 1681
St Sepulchre's, Snow Hill, 1670
St Stephen's, Coleman Street, 1676
St Stephen's, Walbrook, behind the Mansion House, 1676
St Swithin's, Cannon Street, 1673
St Vedast, Foster Lane, 1697

While these churches, and other public buildings, were going forward under the direction of Bro. Wren, King Charles commanded Sir William Bruce, The Grand Master of Scotland, to rebuild the palace of Holyrood House at Edinburgh, and it was accordingly executed in the best Augustan style.

During the prosecution of these great works the private business of the Society was not neglected. Lodges were held at different places, and many new ones constituted, to which the best architects resorted.

In 1674, Earl Rivers resigned the office of Grand Master, and was succeeded by George Villiers, Duke of Buckingham. He left the care of the brethren to his wardens and Sir Christopher Wren, who still continued to act as Deputy Grand Master. In 1679 the Duke resigned in favour of Henry Bennett, Earl of Arlington. This nobleman was too deeply engaged in state affairs to attend to the duties of Masonry, but the lodges continued to meet under his sanction, and many respectable gentlemen joined the Fraternity.

On the death of the king in 1685 his brother succeeded to the throne as James II.

James II

During his reign the Fraternity were much neglected. Unfortunately the Earl of Arlington died the year James II came to the throne, so the lodges met in communication, and elected Sir Christopher Wren Grand Master. Grand Master Wren appointed Gabriel Cibber and Edward Strong as his Grand Wardens. Both gentlemen were members of the old lodge of St Paul, where Bro. Christopher Wren was worshipful master. They had borne a principal share in the works that took place after the fire of London. Bro. Strong, in particular, had acted as Bro. Wren's Warden during the building the cathedral of St Paul.

Under the neglect of James II Masonry declined for many years, although a few lodges continued to meet occasionally in different places.

Chapter 5

Forming a Grand Lodge

William and Mary

By 1688 the Society was so reduced in the south of England that no more than seven regular lodges met in London and its suburbs. Of these only two were worthy of notice: the old lodge of St Paul's, over which Sir Christopher Wren presided during the building of that structure, and a lodge at St Thomas's, Southwark, over which Sir Robert Clayton, then Lord Mayor of London, presided during the rebuilding of that hospital.

King William was privately initiated into Masonry in 1695. He approved the choice of Sir Christopher Wren as Grand Master, and honoured the lodges with his Royal Sanction. It is said that His Majesty frequently presided at a lodge at Hampton Court, during the building of the new part of that palace. Kensington palace was also built during his reign. Sir Christopher directed the work and also oversaw the building of Chelsea Hospital, and the palace of Greenwich. Greenwich Palace has since been converted into a hospital for seamen and finished after the design of Grand Master Inigo Jones.

At a general assembly and feast of the Masons held in 1697 many noble and eminent brethren were present, among them Charles, Duke of Richmond and Lenox, at that time Master of a lodge in Chichester. The Duke was proposed and elected Grand Master for the following year, and he then appointed Sir Christopher Wren as his Deputy Grand Master, Edward Strong his Senior Grand Warden and Thomas Strong his Junior Grand Warden. The Duke of Richmond and Lenox remained in office for only one year, and then the Society once more elected Bro. Sir Christopher as Grand Master. He continued at the head of the fraternity till the death of the king in 1702.

During the following reign, Masonry made little progress. Sir Christopher's age and infirmities drew his attention from the duties of his office, the lodges decreased, and the annual festivals were neglected. The old lodge at St Paul, and a few others, continued to meet regularly, but had few members. To increase their numbers during this difficult time a proposition was made that the privileges of Masonry should no longer be restricted to operative masons, but extended to men of various professions, providing they were regularly approved and initiated into the Order. In consequence of this resolution, the Society once more rose in notice and esteem.

The Grand Lodge of London

On the accession of George I, the Masons in London and its environs, effectively deprived of Sir Christopher Wren, and with their annual meetings discontinued, decided to elect a new Grand Master and to revive the communications and annual festivals of the Society.

The only four lodges meeting in the South of England at that time convened at the Goose and Gridiron in St Paul's Churchyard, the Crown in Parker's Lane near Drury Lane, the Apple Tree Tavern in Charles Street Covent Garden, and the Rummer and Grapes Tavern in Channel Row, Westminster.

The brethren of these lodges, and a few other old brethren, met at the Apple Tree Tavern in February 1717 and voted the oldest Master Mason then present into the chair. They then constituted themselves a Grand Lodge pro tempore. At this meeting they resolved to revive the quarterly communications of the Fraternity, and to hold the next annual assembly and feast on 24 June at the Goose and Gridiron in St Paul's Churchyard, for the purpose of electing a Grand Master among themselves, till they should again have the honour of a noble brother at their head.

In the third year of the reign of King George I, 1717, an assembly and feast were held at the Goose and Gridiron to celebrate St John the Baptist's day. The oldest Master Mason who was also Master of a lodge took the chair. A list of candidates for the office of Grand Master was produced, and the then brethren elected Mr Anthony Sayer, Grand Master of Masons for the ensuing year. He was invested by the oldest Master and installed by the Master of the oldest lodge. The Grand Master appointed his Wardens, and commanded the brethren of the four lodges to meet him and his Wardens quarterly in communication. He instructed them to recommend to all the fraternity a punctual attendance at the next annual assembly and feast.

At that time it was common practice that, when a sufficient number of Masons met together within a certain district, they had the power to make Masons, and discharge every duty of Masonry, without the need of any warrant of constitution. This privilege was inherent in each individual Mason, and is a privilege still enjoyed by the two old lodges that are still extant. However, the meeting proposed:

> That the privilege of assembling as masons, which had hitherto been unlimited, should be vested in certain lodges or assemblies of masons convened in certain places; and that every lodge to be hereafter convened, except the four old lodges at this time existing, should be legally authorised to act by a warrant from the Grand Master for the time being, granted to certain individuals by petition, with the consent and approbation of the Grand Lodge in communication; and that without such warrant no lodge should be hereafter deemed regular or constitutional.

In consequence of this regulation, new lodges were convened in different parts of London, and the Masters and Wardens of these lodges were commanded to attend the meetings of the Grand Lodge, make a regular report of their proceedings, and transmit to the Grand Master, from time to time, a copy of any by-laws they might form for their own government. They were forbidden to pass any laws contrary to the general regulations by which the Fraternity was now to be governed.

As a compliment to the brethren of the four old lodges from which the new Grand Lodge was formed, it was resolved:

> That every privilege which they collectively enjoyed by virtue of their immemorial rights, they should still continue to enjoy; and that no law, rule, or regulation to be hereafter made or passed in Grand Lodge, should deprive them of such privilege, or encroach on any landmark which was at that time established as the standard of Masonic Government.

When this resolution was confirmed, the old Masons of London vested all their inherent privileges as individuals in the four old lodges, trusting that these lodges would never suffer the old charges and ancient landmarks to be infringed. The four old lodges then agreed to extend their patronage to every new lodge that should hereafter be constituted according to the new regulations of the Society. And also promised, so long as the new lodges acted in conformity to the ancient constitutions of the order, to admit their Masters and Wardens to share with them all the privileges of the Grand Lodge, excepting precedence of rank.

These matters of rank and privilege being amicably adjusted, all the brethren of the four old lodges considered their attendance on the future communications of the Society to be unnecessary, and trusted their Masters and Wardens to represent them. They were assured that no measure of importance would ever be adopted without their approbation.

But the officers of the old lodges soon realized that, with the new lodges equally represented alongside them at the communications, in process of time their votes would far outnumber those of the old ones. This would soon give the new lodges the power of majority and allow them to subvert the privileges of the original masons of England, which were centred in the four old lodges. With the agreement of their members, the old lodges formed a code of laws for the future government of the Society, and added to that code a conditional clause, which the Grand Master for the time being, his successors and the Master of every lodge to be hereafter constituted, were bound to preserve. It has been customary ever since, for the Master of the oldest lodge to attend every Grand Installation and to take precedence over all present except the Grand Master. He was to deliver the book of the original constitutions to the new installed Grand Master, on his promising obedience to the ancient charges and general regulations.

The conditional clause that the old lodges enforced runs thus:

Every annual Grand Lodge has an inherent power and authority to make new regulations, or to alter these, for the real benefit of this ancient fraternity; providing always THAT THE OLD LAND-MARKS BE CAREFULLY PRESERVED: and that such alterations and new regulations be proposed and agreed to at the third quarterly communication preceding the annual grand feast; and that they be offered also to the perusal of all the

brethren before dinner, in writing, even of the youngest apprentice; the approbation and consent of the majority of all the
brethren present, being absolutely necessary to make the same
binding and obligatory.

This remarkable clause, with 38 regulations preceding it, was printed
in the first edition of the Book of Constitutions. It was approved, and
confirmed by 150 brethren, at an annual assembly and feast held at
Stationers' Hall on St John the Baptist's day 1721, and in their
presence subscribed by the Master and Wardens of the four old lodges
on one part, and on the other part by Philip, Duke of Wharton (then
Grand Master), Theophilus Desaguliers md frs (Deputy Grand
Master), Joshua Timson and William Hawkins (Grand Wardens) and
the Masters and Wardens of sixteen lodges which had been
constituted between 1717 and 1721.

In this way the original constitutions were established as the basis
of all future Masonic jurisdiction in the south of England and the
ancient landmarks were set up as checks to innovation and secured
against the attacks of future invaders. The four old lodges continued
to act by their original authority and, far from surrendering any of
their rights, had them ratified and confirmed by the whole Fraternity
in Grand Lodge assembled. No regulations of the Society from that
time forward could be applied to those lodges, if the lodges thought
such regulations were contrary to, or subversive of, the original
constitutions by which they were governed. While their proceedings
conformed to those constitutions, no power known in Masonry could
legally deprive them of any right that they already enjoyed.

The necessity of fixing the original constitutions as the standard by
which all future laws in the Society are to be regulated, was so clearly
understood by the whole Fraternity at this time, that it was established
as an unerring rule, at every installation, public and private. It was
used in the ceremony to make the Grand Master, and also the Masters
and Wardens, of every lodge; before they could be installed they had
to promise to support these constitutions to which every Mason is
bound by the strongest ties at initiation. Without this standard being
fixed for the government of the Society, Masonry might become
exposed to perpetual variations, which would effectually destroy all
the good effects that had hitherto resulted from its universality and
extended progress.

Preston says that these particulars have been carefully extracted from old records and authentic manuscripts, and are confirmed by the old books of the lodge of Antiquity, as well as the first and second editions of the Book of Constitutions.

He adds that the following account of the above four lodges may prove useful to many readers:

1. The old lodge of St Paul, now named the lodge of Antiquity, No. 1, formerly held at the Goose and Gridiron in St Paul's Churchyard, is still extant, (in 1795,) and regularly meets at the Free-masons Tavern in Great Queen Street, Lincoln's Inn Fields, on the fourth Wednesday of every month. This lodge is in a very flourishing state, and possesses some valuable records and other ancient relics.

2. The old lodge, No. 2, formerly held at the Crown in Parker's lane in Drury Lane, has been extinct above fifty years, by the death of its members.

3. The old lodge, No. 3, formerly held at the Apple Tree Tavern in Charles Street, Covent Garden, has been dissolved many years. By the List of Lodges inserted in the Book of Constitutions printed in 1738, it appears that in February 1722–3, this lodge was removed to the Queen's Head in Knave's Acre, on account of some difference among its members, and that the members who met there came under a new constitution – though, says the Book of Constitutions, they wanted it not, and ranked as No. 10 in the List. Thus they inconsiderately renounced their former rank under an immemorial constitution.

4. The lodge, No. 4, formerly held at the Rummer and Grapes Tavern in Channel Row, Westminster, was thence removed to the Horn Tavern in New Palace Yard, where it continued to meet regularly till within these few years, when, finding themselves in a declining state, the members agreed to incorporate with a new and flourishing lodge under the constitution of the Grand Lodge, entitled the Somerset House Lodge, which immediately assumed their rank.

The above old lodges, while they exist as lodges, cannot surrender their rights. The old Masons of the metropolis have granted those rights to them in trust, and any individual member of the four old lodges might object to the surrender, in which case they can never be given up. The four old lodges preserved their original power of making, passing and raising masons, being termed Masters Lodges; other lodges, for many years afterwards, had no such power, for it had been the custom to pass and raise masons made at those lodges only at the Grand Lodge.

Under the rule of Grand Master Sayer, the Society made little progress. Several brethren joined the old lodges; but only two new lodges were constituted. Mr Sayer was succeeded as Grand Master in 1718 by George Payne, who was particularly assiduous in ensuring strict observance of the communications. He collected many valuable manuscripts on the subject of Masonry, and encouraged the brethren to bring to the Grand Lodge any old writings or records concerning the Fraternity, to show the usages of ancient times. In consequence of this general intimation, several old copies of the Gothic constitutions were produced, arranged, and digested.

On 24 June 1719 another assembly and feast was held at the Goose and Gridiron, where Dr Desaguliers was unanimously elected Grand Master. At this feast, the old, regular, and peculiar toasts or healths of the Freemasons were reintroduced, and from this time we can date the rise of Freemasonry in the South of England. The number of lodges increased considerably under this Grand Master; they were visited by many old masons who had long neglected the craft, and several noblemen were initiated.

At an assembly and feast held at the Goose and Gridiron on 24 June 1720 George Payne was re-elected Grand Master, and under his administration the lodges flourished. He decided to publish the Masonic Constitutions. Some scrupulous brethren became alarmed at this, and many of the private lodges hastily burnt valuable manuscripts concerning their lodges, regulations, charges, secrets and usages (particularly one written by Mr Nicholas Stone, the warden under Inigo Jones), to the irreparable loss of the Fraternity.

At a quarterly communication, held that year at the Goose and Gridiron on the festival of St John the Evangelist, it was agreed that in future the new Grand Master would be named and proposed to the Grand Lodge some time before the feast; if approved, and present, he should then be saluted as Grand Master elect. (An old record of the lodge of Antiquity shows that the new Grand Master was always proposed and presented for approbation in that lodge before his election in the Grand Lodge.) It was also agreed that every Grand Master, when installed, would have the power to appoint his deputy and wardens.

At a Grand Lodge held on Lady Day 1721 Bro. Payne proposed John, Duke of Montagu, as his successor, and Montagu, being present, received the compliments of the lodge. The brethren were overjoyed at the prospect of once more being patronized by the nobility. They unanimously agreed that the next assembly and feast should be held at Stationers' Hall, and that a proper number of stewards should be appointed to provide the entertainment.

Chapter 6

Rival Grand Lodges

The Grand Lodge at York

While Masonry was successfully spreading its influence over the southern part of the kingdom, it was not being neglected in the north. The General Assembly, or Grand Lodge, at York continued to meet regularly. In 1705, under the direction of Sir George Tempest, the then Grand Master, several lodges met, and many worthy brethren were initiated in York. Sir George was succeeded by the Rt Hon. Robert Benson, Lord Mayor of York, and a number of meetings of the Fraternity were held in that city. The grand feast held during Benson's mastership is said to have been very brilliant. Sir William Robinson succeeded Benson, and the Fraternity in the north increased considerably under his auspices. He was succeeded by Sir Walter Hawkesworth, who governed the Society with great credit, and when his term ended Sir George Tempest was elected Grand Master for a second time. From his election in 1714 until 1725 the Grand Lodge continued to assemble regularly at York under the direction of Charles Fairfax. During this period Sir Walter Hawkesworth, Edward Bell, Charles Bathurst, Edward Thomson mp, John Johnson md and John Marsden all in rotation regularly filled the office of Grand Master in the north of England.

This account, which is authenticated by the books of the Grand Lodge at York, shows that the revival of Masonry in the south of England did not interfere with the proceedings of the fraternity in the north. For many years there was perfect harmony between the two Grand Lodges, and private lodges flourished in both parts of the kingdom under their separate jurisdictions. The only distinction that the Grand Lodge in the north retained after the revival of Masonry in the south was in its title: The Grand Lodge of all England. The Grand Lodge in the south passed by the name of The Grand Lodge of England. The Grand Lodge at London, being encouraged by the nobility, acquired consequence and reputation. Meanwhile the Grand Lodge at York, restricted to fewer (though no less respectable) members, seemed gradually to decline.

However, the authority of the Grand Lodge at York was still unchallenged. Indeed, every Mason in the kingdom held it in the highest veneration, and considered himself bound by the charges, which originally sprang from that assembly. To be ranked as descendants of the original York masons, was the glory and boast of the brethren in almost every country where Masonry was established, for it was in the city of York that English Masonry was first established by charter. Regrettably, the history of Brethren in the north became unknown to those in the south, although, notwithstanding the pitch of eminence and splendour achieved by the Grand Lodge in London, neither the lodges of Scotland nor Ireland courted its correspondence. This was probably because it had introduced some modern innovations among the lodges in the south.

But there was another reason for the coolness between the Grand Lodge at York and the Grand Lodge at London. A few Brethren at York seceded from their ancient lodge and applied to London for a warrant of constitution. Without proper inquiry into the merits of the case, their application was honoured. Instead of being recommended to their Mother Grand Lodge to be restored to favour, these Brethren were encouraged in their revolt and, under the banner of the Grand Lodge at London, permitted to open a new lodge in the City of York itself. This illegal extension of power justly offended the Grand Lodge at York, and caused the breach.

Consolidating the Power of the Grand Lodge at London

Preston's account of how the Grand Lodge of London consolidated its social position before the formation of the United Grand Lodge of England (UGLE) is not of great intrinsic interest. But his focus on the antics of minor nobility throws considerable light on how important social rank was to become in English Freemasonry and explains how so many 'toffs' were encouraged to join the lodges attached to the Grand Lodge of London. But let Preston explain himself.

The reputation of the Society was now established and many noblemen and gentlemen wanted to be initiated into the lodges, whose number had grown considerably during the administration of Grand Master Payne. The rituals of masonry were a pleasing relaxation from the fatigue of business, and in the lodge, uninfluenced by politics or party, a happy union was effected among the most respectable characters in the kingdom.

On 24 June 1721 Grand Master Payne and his wardens, with the former grand officers, and the masters and wardens of twelve lodges, met the Grand Master elect at the Queen's Arms Tavern in St Paul's Churchyard, to which the old lodge of St Paul's (now known as the Lodge of Antiquity) had moved. The Grand Lodge was opened in ample form, and, after confirmation of the minutes of the last Grand Lodge, several gentlemen were initiated into Masonry at the request of the Duke of Montagu, among them Philip, Lord Stanhope, afterwards Earl of Chesterfield. Grand Lodge members then marched in procession from the Queen's Arms to Stationers' Hall in Ludgate Street, proudly wearing their Masonic clothing. On arrival they were joyfully greeted by 150 brethren, also properly clothed. The retiring Grand Master made the first procession round the hall, took an affectionate leave of his brethren and returned to his place in the body of the lodge. As he did, he proclaimed the Duke of Montagu his successor for the ensuing year. Grand Master Payne had compiled a set of general regulations in 1721, from the ancient records and immemorial usages of the fraternity. These were read, and met with general approval. Afterwards Dr Desaguliers delivered an elegant oration on the subject of Masonry.

Soon after his election, the new Grand Master commanded Dr Desaguliers and James Anderson, to revise the Gothic constitutions, old charges, and general regulations. This they did, and at the Grand Lodge held at the Queen's Arms, St Paul's Churchyard, on 27 December 1721 presented them for approval. A committee of fourteen learned brothers was appointed to examine the manuscript and make their report. At this meeting several entertaining lectures were delivered, and much useful information was given by some old brethren.

The committee reported back at a Grand Lodge held at the Fountain

Tavern in the Strand on 25 March 1722. They announced that they had perused the manuscript, which contained the history, charges and regulations of Masonry and, after some amendments, approved it. The Grand Lodge ordered the whole to be prepared for the press and printed as soon as possible. Some two years later it appeared in print, under the title *The Book of Constitutions of the Free Masons: Containing the History, Charges, Regulations, &c. of that Most Ancient and Right Worshipful Fraternity. For the Use of the Lodges* (London, 1723).

In 1723 the Duke of Wharton, keen to become Grand Master, persuaded the Duke of Montagu to resign in his favour. Montagu's resignation was intended to reconcile the Brethren to Wharton, who had incurred their displeasure for having convened an irregular assembly of Masons at Stationers' Hall on the festival of St John the Baptist, in order to try to get himself elected as Grand Master. Montagu, fully sensible of Wharton's impropriety, forced him to publicly acknowledge his error and promise in future to strictly conform to and obey the resolutions of the Society. After this the Brethren, approved him as Grand Master elect for the ensuing year. Wharton was regularly invested and installed by the Grand Master on 17 January 1723, when he was congratulated by some twenty-five lodges.

Masonry in the south of England made considerable progress under Wharton's enthusiastic patronage. During his presidency, he created the office of Grand Secretary, to which Bro. William Cowper was appointed, who was to execute the secretary's duties for several years. In 1723 the Duke of Wharton was succeeded by the Duke of Buccleugh, who, although proclaiming enthusiasm for Masonry, did not attend the annual festival and was installed by proxy at Merchant Taylors' Hall in the presence of 400 Masons. The following year he was replaced by the Duke of Richmond, who set up the First Committee of Charity. This scheme raised a general fund for distressed Masons; Lord Paisley, Dr Desaguliers, Colonel Houghton and a few other brethren supported the Duke's proposition, and Grand Lodge appointed a committee to consider the most effectual means of carrying it forward. The disposal of the charity was first vested in seven brethren, but this was found to be too few, and nine more were added. It was afterward resolved that twelve masters of contributing lodges, in rotation with the Grand Officers, should form the Committee, and it was determined that all Past and Present Grand Officers, with the Masters of all regular lodges that had contributed within twelve months to the charity, would be members of the Committee.

The Committee met four times a year, in response to a summons from the Grand Master or his Deputy, to consider the petitions of the brethren who applied for charity. If the petitioner was found deserving, he was immediately granted five pounds, or, if the circumstances of his case were of a peculiar nature, his petition was referred to the next Communication, where he could be granted any sum the committee specified, though not more than twenty guineas at any one time. By these means the distressed found ready relief from this general charity, which was supported solely by voluntary contributions from different lodges out of their private funds, without laying the burden on any member of the society. Preston noted that the sums annually expended to relieve distressed brethren by the Committee of Charity had for several years amounted to many thousand pounds, but there still remained a considerable sum in reserve. Any complaints were considered at the Committee of Charity, which reported to the next Grand Lodge.

Lord Paisley, later the Earl of Abercorn, who had been active in promoting this new venture, was elected Grand Master in the end of 1725 [this was the year a Grand Lodge was formed in Ireland, which Preston does not mention] and installed by proxy. Dr Desaguliers was appointed his deputy, and performed his duties conscientiously, visiting the lodges and diligently promoting Masonry. When Paisley returned to town the Earl of Inchiquin was proposed to replace him, and was elected in February 1726. Under him the Society now flourished in town and country, and the Art was propagated with considerable success.

This period was remarkable for the brethren of Wales being forced to unite under the banner of the Grand Lodge of London. This was despite the fact that in Wales there are venerable remains of ancient Masonry, and many stately ruins of castles, which demonstrate that the Fraternity met with encouragement in that part of the island in former times. To consolidate this annexation an office of Provincial Grand Master was instituted, and on 10 May 1727 the Grand Master of the Grand Lodge in London appointed Hugh Warburton, Provincial Grand Master for North Wales [thus reducing the ancient kingdom of Gwynedd to a district of London], and on 24 June 1727 Sir Edward Mansell was likewise forced onto South Wales [turning the kingdoms of the Princes of Powys into another district of London].

The Grand Lodge of London defined a Provincial Grand Master as the immediate representative of the Grand Master in the district over which he was limited to preside. He was invested with the power and honour of a Deputy Grand Master in his province and could constitute lodges therein, if the consent of the Masters and Wardens of three lodges already constituted within his district was obtained, and the Grand Lodge in London did not disapprove. He wore the clothing of a Grand Officer and ranked in all public assemblies immediately after Past Deputy Grand Masters. He had to attend in person, or by deputy, the quarterly meetings of the Masters and Wardens of the lodges in his district and, once a year, report to the Grand Lodge in London the proceedings of those meetings, along with a report on the state of the lodges under his jurisdiction.

The lodges in England now began to increase, and deputations were granted to several Brethren, to hold the office of Provincial Grand Master in different parts of England, as well as in some places abroad where lodges had been constituted by English masons. During the Earl of Inchiquin's Mastership, a warrant was issued for opening a new lodge in Gibraltar. Also during his presidency the church of the Royal Parish Church of St Martin-in-the-Fields was finished. The foundation stone for this building had been laid, in the King's name, on 29 March 1721, by Brother Gibb, the architect, in the presence of the Bro. the lord Almoner, the Surveyor General and a large company of Brethren.

King George I died in 1727 and was succeeded by his son George II. A Grand Lodge was held at the Devil Tavern, Temple Bar, a fortnight after the old king's death. Grand Master Inchiquin was present with his officers, and the Masters and Wardens of forty lodges. This meeting decided to extend the right to vote in Grand Lodge to Past Grand Wardens; previously voting had been restricted to Past Grand Masters.

Inchiquin was travelling in Ireland when his term of office expired. He wrote to William Cowper, the Deputy Grand Master, instructing him to call a Grand Lodge and nominate Lord Coleraine as the next Grand Master. A Grand Lodge was convened on 19 December 1727 and Coleraine was proposed as Grand Master elect, and unanimously approved. On 27 December he was invested at a grand feast held at Mercers' Hall. Coleraine attended two out of the four communications during his mastership. He constituted several new lodges and authorized the right to hold a lodge in St Bernard's Street in Madrid.

At the last Grand Lodge under Coleraine's auspices, Dr Desaguliers moved that the ancient office of Stewards be revived. He argued it was necessary to assist the Grand Wardens in preparing the feast. It was agreed that the appointment of Grand Stewards should be annual, and their number restricted to twelve.

Lord Kingston succeeded Coleraine on 27 December 1728. Kingston was a regular attender at the Communications, and he presented Grand Lodge with a pedestal, a rich cushion with gold knobs and fringes, a velvet bag, and a new jewel set in gold for the use of the Secretary. Under his administration the Society flourished at home and abroad. Many lodges were constituted, and the right to open a new lodge in Bengal was granted to Bro. George Pomfret, who had introduced Masonry into the English settlement in India, where it had made rapid progress. Within a few years, upwards of fifty lodges had been constituted, eleven in Bengal. The annual remittances to the charity and public funds of the Society from this and other factories of the East India Company made up a tidy sum.

Kingston was absent from the Grand Lodge held at Devil Tavern on 27 December 1729 so Deputy Grand Master Nathaniel Blackerby took the chair. Kingston wrote instructing Blackerby to propose the Duke of Norfolk as the Grand Master for the following year. This was accepted unanimously, and Norfolk was installed at Merchant Taylors' Hall on 29 January 1730. He spent most of the period of his Grand Mastership travelling around Italy and only attended one meeting, but his long-suffering Deputy Grand Master Blackerby, on whom the whole management devolved, carried on the business of the Society. During Norfolk's Grand Mastership a Provincial Grand Lodge was set up in New Jersey in America and a provincial patent was also issued for Bengal. During this period Blackerby received daily applications to establish new lodges, and many respectable characters sought to be enrolled.

Norfolk was succeeded by Lord Lovell, later the Earl of Leicester, who was installed at Mercers' Hall on 29 March 1731. Unfortunately he was so indisposed by drink during the feast that he had to withdraw from his own installation; Lord Coleraine, acted as his proxy to complete the toasts. On the following 14 May a Grand Lodge was held at the Rose Tavern in Marylebone. It was voted that in future all past Grand Masters and their deputies would be admitted as members of the quarterly Committees of Charity, and that every committee would have the power to vote five pounds for the relief of any distressed mason, but no larger sum, without the consent of the Grand Lodge in Communication.

During Lovell's presidency his status seemed to attract many of the lesser nobility. The Dukes of Norfolk and Richmond, the Earl of Inchiquin, and Lords Coleraine and Montagu became far more regular in their attendance, although the Society was struggling to finance its charity work, as the subscriptions from the lodges were small. To encourage the nobility to accept the duties and financial responsibilities of Steward, Deputy Grand Master Blackerby ordered that in future each Steward should have the privilege of nominating his successor at every annual grand feast.

Lovell made use of his family connections to encourage Francis, Duke of Lorraine, to become a Freemason. Francis, who later became Emperor of Germany, was granted the right to hold a lodge at The Hague, where he was able take the first two degrees of masonry at the hands of Phillip Stanhope, Earl of Chesterfield, the English Ambassador, but he came to England to be raised to the third degree. The ceremony was carried out at an occasional lodge convened specially for the purpose. Lovell authorized it to be held at Houghton Hall in Norfolk, the home of Prime Minister Sir Robert Walpole [who was noted for his skill in using royal patronage for political ends]. Thomas Pelham, Duke of Newcastle was also made a Master Mason at the same ceremony. [It does make one wonder if Walpole was using Freemasonry as a tool to aid his political fortunes both at home and abroad!] Under such a deluge of aristocratic and political patronage Freemasonry flourished. Around this time lodges were set up in Russia and Spain.

The next Grand Master was Lord Viscount Montagu. He was installed at Merchant Taylors' Hall on 19 April 1732. Preston picks out the Dukes of Montagu and Richmond, the Earl of Strathmore, Lords Coleraine, Teynham and Carpenter, Sir Francis Drake and Sir William Keith as worthy of mention from among the four hundred Brethren who flocked to the spectacle. At this meeting it was proposed to hold a country feast and agreed that the Brethren should dine at Hampstead on 24 June. To make the event attractive invitations were sent to all available Freemasonic nobility. On the day the Grand Master and his Officers, the Dukes of Norfolk and Richmond, Earl of Strathmore, Lords Carpenter and Teynham, and a hundred other Brethren not important enough to name, met at the Spikes at Hampstead, where an elegant dinner was provided.

After the dinner Montagu handed the Grand Mastership over to Teynham and never again bothered to attend a meeting of the Society. Montagu was fond of constituting overseas lodges, granting deputations for constituting lodges at Valenciennes in French Flanders and at the Hotel de Buffy in Paris. The Society was particularly indebted to the Deputy Grand Master Thomas Barton, who was very attentive to the duties of his office, and carefully superintended the government of the craft during this period.

The Earl of Strathmore succeeded Lord Montagu as Grand Master. He did not make the journey down from his Scottish estates to be installed, and so took office by proxy at an assembly at Mercers' Hall on 7 June 1733. On 13 December a Grand Lodge was held at the Devil Tavern, and this Strathmore managed to get to. He took as his Wardens the Earl of Crawford and Sir Robert Mansell. A number of Past Grand Officers, and the Masters and Wardens of 53 lodges came to the meeting, and they passed several regulations about the Committee of Charity – mainly concerned with keeping its outgoing under the control of the Grand Lodge in London. It was decided that any complaints, which had previously been examined by the Committee, would be referred to the next Communication of the Grand Lodge in London.

The Society at this period collected considerable donations to encourage the settlement of a new colony just established in Georgia in America. Strathmore regularly attended the meetings of Grand Lodge and gave permission for German masons to open a new lodge in Hamburg under the patronage of the Grand Lodge of England. He also authorized several other lodges, under the English banner in Holland.

The next Grand Master was the Earl of Crawford, installed at Mercers' Hall on 30 March 1734, but he showed little interest in the Society, failing to hold the regular Communications. After an eleven-month gap, however, a Grand Lodge was convened, which Crawford managed to attend and at which he apologized for his long absence. To try and make up for lost time he commanded two Communications to be held in little more than six weeks; the Dukes of Richmond and Buccleugh, the Earl of Balcarres and Lord Weymouth came to these. During his hurriedly convened meetings of Grand Lodge Crawford introduced many new regulations. In particular he ruled that if any lodge ceased to meet for twelve calendar months, it would be erased from the list, and, if reinstated, would lose its former rank. He also granted more privileges to the Stewards in an attempt to encourage more aristocrats to serve in the office; in particular it was agreed that in future all Grand Officers, the Grand Master excepted, would be elected from the Stewards. He also passed a few resolutions about illegal conventions of Masons to make sure that nobody could be initiated into Masonry too cheaply, ruling out those paying 'small and unworthy considerations'.

Crawford also encroached on the jurisdiction of the Grand Lodge in York, by constituting two lodges within its district. He also granted deputations within its jurisdiction without its consent, one for Lancashire, a second for Durham, and a third for Northumberland. The Grand Lodge of York highly resented this behaviour, and all friendly intercourse ceased, the York masons from that moment realizing that their interests were distinct from those of Masons under the Grand Lodge in London.

During Crawford's tenure Bro. James Anderson prepared a new edition of the *Book of Constitutions*, considerably enlarged and improved (it appeared in January 1738). In it he included the following comment after a list of Provincial Grand Masters appointed for different places abroad:

All these foreign lodges are under the patronage of our Grand Master of England; but the old lodge at York city, and the lodges of Scotland, Ireland, France and Italy, affecting independency, are under their own Grand Masters; though they have the same constitutions, charges, regulations, etc., for substance with their brethren in England, and are equally zealous for the Augustan style, and the secrets of the ancient and honourable fraternity.

Preston recounts how Lord Weymouth followed Crawford, and was installed at Mercers' Hall on 17 April 1735. The Dukes of Richmond and Atholl, the Earls of Crawford, Winchelsea, Balcarres, Wemyss and Loudon the Marquis of Beaumont; Lords Cathcart and Vere Bertie; Sir Cecil Wray and Sir Edward Mansell all came to watch. Weymouth constituted several lodges including the Stewards' Lodges. He granted the Duke of Richmond permission to set up a lodge at the seat of the Aubigny in France and extended the patronage of Masonry considerably in foreign countries. He issued warrants to open a new lodge at Lisbon, and another at Savannah in Georgia and issued provincial patents for South America and West Africa.

Weymouth never managed to find time to attend any of the

Communications held during his presidency, but nobody missed him as, fortunately, he had a good Deputy Grand Master in Bro. John Ward. Bro Ward 'applied the utmost anxiety to every business which concerned the interest and well-being of the Society'.

While Weymouth was Grand Master the twelve Stewards – with Sir Robert Lawley, Master of the Stewards' Lodge, at their head – appeared for the first time in their new badges at a Grand Lodge held at the Devil Tavern on 11 December 1735. As was normal for all other lodges they were not permitted to vote as individuals, but Weymouth agreed that the Stewards' Lodge should in future be represented in Grand Lodge by twelve members, each having a vote. Many lodges objected to this as an encroachment on the privilege of every lodge previously constituted. When the motion came up for debate there was such a disturbance that Deputy Grand Master Ward had to close the meeting before the sentiments of the brethren could be collected on the subject. But, even in his absence, Weymouth got his way. Each of the twelve Stewards was permitted to vote in every Communication as an individual. This row rumbled on until 1770, when, at a Grand Lodge on 7 February, held at the Crown and Anchor tavern in the Strand, the following resolution was passed:

As the right of the Members of the Steward's Lodge in general to attend the Committee of Charity appears doubtful, no mention of such right being made in the laws of the Society, the Grand Lodge are of opinion, that they have no general right to attend; but it is hereby resolved, that the Steward's Lodge be allowed the privilege of sending a number of brethren, equal to any four lodges, to every future Committee of Charity; and that, as the Master of each private lodge only has the right to attend, to make a proper distinction between the Steward's lodge and the other lodges, that the Master and three other members of that lodge be permitted to attend at every succeeding Committee on behalf of the said Lodge.

The officers of the Grand Lodge in London declared that this resolution was not intended to deprive any lodge that had been previously constituted of its regular rank and precedence. Notwithstanding this express provision, the privilege was granted to the Steward's Lodge, of taking precedence over the other lodges. Many brethren thought this measure was not compatible with the constitutions and could not be sanctioned by the rules of the Society. They argued that this privilege had been irregularly obtained, and several Lodges entered protests against it.

The Earl of Loudon succeeded Weymouth, and was installed Grand Master at Fishmongers' Hall on 15 April 1736. The Duke of Richmond, the Earls of Albemarle and Crawford, Lords Harcourt Erskine and Southwell, Mr Anstis (the Garter King of Arms), and Mr Brady (Lyon King of Arms) were on his guest list. Loudon constituted several lodges and granted three provincial deputations during his presidency: one for New England, another for South Carolina, and a third for Cape Coast Castle in Africa.

The next Grand Master was the Earl of Darnley, who was installed at Fishmongers' Hall on 28 April 1737. The Duke of Richmond, the Earls of Crawford and Wemyss and Lord Gray came to his installation, as did many other unnamed but respectable brethren. Darnley persuaded Frederick Prince of Wales to become a Freemason, and he allowed an occasional lodge to be convened at the Palace of Kew, over which Dr Desaguliers presided as Master, with Lord Baltimore and Col. Lumley as his Wardens. Together with several other brethren, they initiated the Prince of Wales. Darnley continued to authorize this occasional Kew lodge until the prince had been advanced to the second degree and eventually raised to the sublime degree of a Master Mason.

Darnley never failed to attend at Grand Lodge. Upwards of sixty lodges were represented at every Communication during his administration, and he issued more Provincial patents than any of his predecessors. Deputations were granted for Montserrat, Geneva, the Circle of Upper Saxony, the Coast of Africa, New York, and the Islands of America. At this time the authority granted by patent to a Provincial Grand Master was limited to one year from his first public appearance in that character within his province; and if, at the expiration of that period, a new election by the lodges under his jurisdiction did not take place, subject to the approbation of the Grand Master, the patent was no longer valid. Hence we find, within the course of a few years, different appointments to the same station; but the office is now permanent, and was now a sole appointment of the Grand Master.

The Marquis of Carnarvon, who later became the Duke of Chandos, was Darnley's and was invested as Grand Master at an assembly and feast at Fishmongers' Hall on 27 April 1738 attended by the Duke of Richmond, the Earls of Inchiquin, Loudon and

Kintore, Lords Coleraine and Gray, along with numerous other brethren of too low a rank to mention. Carnarvon presented a gold jewel to the Grand Lodge for the use of the Secretary: two crossed pens in a knot, the knot and points of the pens being curiously enamelled. He granted two deputations for the office of Provincial Grand Master: one for the Caribbean Islands and the other for the Yorkshire West Riding. (The latter appointment was yet another encroachment on the jurisdiction of the Grand Lodge of York, and further widened the breach between the Brethren in the north and south of England. During Carnarvon's Grand Mastership all correspondence between the Grand Lodges ceased.) Nothing else remarkable is recorded during this administration, except a proposition for establishing a plan to appropriate a portion of the charity to place out the sons of Masons' apprentices, which, after a long debate in Grand Lodge, was rejected.

Frederick the Great – then known as the Prince Royal, although he later became King of Prussia – joined Masonry on 15 August 1738. He was initiated into a lodge in Brunswick, which was warranted by the Grand Lodge of Scotland. So highly did he approve of the initiation, that, on his accession to the throne, he commanded a Grand Lodge to be formed in Berlin and obtained a patent from Edinburgh. Thus was Scottish Masonry regularly established in Prussia, and under that sanction it has flourished there ever since. Frederick's attachment to the Society soon induced him to establish several new regulations for the advantage of the Fraternity; and among others he ordained,

1. That no person should be made a mason, unless his character was unimpeachable and his manner of living and profession respectable.
2. That every member should pay 25 rix-dollars (or £4 3s. 0d.) for the first degree; 50 rix-dollars (or £8 6s. 0d.) on his being initiated into the second degree; and 100 rix-dollars (or £16 12s. 0d.) on his being made a master-mason.
3. That he should remain at least three months in each degree; and that every sum received should be divided by the Grand Treasurer into three parts: one to defray the expenses of the lodge, another to be applied to the relief of distressed brethren, and the third to be allotted to the poor in general.

About this period a number of dissatisfied brethren separated themselves from the regular lodges, and held meetings in different places for the purpose of initiating persons into Masonry, contrary to the laws of the Grand Lodge in London. These seceding brethren took advantage of the breach in the friendly intercourse between the Grand Lodges of London and York. When they were censured for their conduct they immediately assumed, without authority, the character of York masons. Taking advantage of a general murmur spread abroad on account of innovations that had been introduced, and which seemed to authorize an omission of, and a variation in the ancient ceremonies, they again rose into notice. Their actions offended many old masons, but through the mediation of Bro. John Ward the brethren were seemingly reconciled. However, this proved only a temporary suspension of hostilities, for they broke out anew, and soon gave rise to commotions, which materially interrupted the peace of the Society.

Lord Raymond succeeded Carnarvon in May 1739 but, despite an apparent flourishing of the Society, irregularities continued. Several worthy brethren, opposed to the encroachments on the established system of the institution, were highly disgusted at the proceedings of the regular lodges. Complaints were made at every committee, and the Grand Lodge Communications were fully taken up by arguments about differences and animosities. It became necessary to pass votes of censure and to enact laws to discourage irregular associations. This brought the power of the Grand Lodge into question. In opposition to the laws that had been established by that assembly, lodges were formed without any warrants, and persons initiated into Masonry for small and unworthy considerations.

To distinguish the persons initiated by these deluded brethren from regularly made Masons, the Grand Lodge in London passed imprudent measures that even the urgency of the case could not warrant. This gave rise to a new subterfuge. The brethren who had seceded from the regular lodges immediately announced their independence and took to calling themselves Ancient Masons. They insisted that they alone preserved the ancient tenets and practices of Masonry, and the new regular lodges, being composed of modern Masons, had adopted new plans, and were not acting under the old establishment. Contrary to the rule of the Grand Lodge in London, they formed a new Grand Lodge based on the ancient system, and under that banner constituted several new lodges. They justified these actions under the sanction of the Ancient York Constitution. Many gentlemen of reputation joined them, and the number of their lodges increased daily. Claiming their authority from the Constitution of the Grand Lodge of York, they formed committees, held Communications, and appointed annual feasts.

By adopting the appellation of the York banner, they gained the support of the Scottish and Irish Masons, who joined them in condemning the measures of the lodges warranted by the Grand Lodge in London, as introducing novelties into the Society and subverting the original plan of the institution. They soon acquired an establishment, and noblemen of both kingdoms honoured them with their patronage. Many respectable names and lodges were added to their list. Preston remarked that it was much to be wished that a general union among all the masons in the kingdom could be effected, 'and we are happy to hear that such a measure may soon be accomplished, by a Royal Brother at present abroad'.

During Raymond's presidency few additions were made to the list of lodges, and the nobility stopped attending the meeting of Grand Lodge. Raymond granted only one deputation for a provincial Grand Master, that of Savoy and Piedmont.

The Earl of Kintore became the next Grand Master in April 1740 and tried to discourage the alternative Grand Lodge. He appointed several new Provincial Grand Masters: one for Russia, one for Hamburg, one for the Circle of Lower Saxony, and one for the island of Barbados. Most contentiously, he authorized a replacement for Provincial Grand Master William Horton of the West Riding of York, who had died. This did nothing to improve relations with the York Masons.

The Earl of Morton was elected on 19 March 1741 and installed at Haberdashers' Hall amid a good turnout of nobility, foreign ambassadors and others. He is mainly remembered for presenting a staff of office to the Treasurer. It was of neat workmanship, blue and tipped with gold. The Grand Lodge resolved that the Treasurer should be elected annually, and, with the Secretary and Sword-bearer, be permitted to rank in future as a member of Grand Lodge. A large cornelian seal, with the arms of Masonry set in gold, was also presented to the Society by Bro. William Vaughan, the Senior Grand Warden. Bro. Vaughan was duly rewarded with the Provincial Grand Mastership of North Wales.

In April 1742 Lord Ward succeeded Morton. Ward was well

acquainted with the nature and government of the Society, having served every office from Secretary in a private lodge to that of Grand Master. He lost no time in trying to reconcile the animosities that prevailed. He recommended vigilance and care to his officers in their different departments, and by his own conduct he set an example of how the dignity of the Society should be supported. He consolidated many lodges that were in a declining state with others in better circumstances. Some that had been negligent in attending the Communications were admonished and restored to favour; any that did not comply were erased from the list

Some measure of unanimity and harmony between the lodges was seemingly restored under his administration. The Freemasons of Antigua built a large hall in that island for their meetings, and applied to the Grand Lodge for liberty to be styled the Great Lodge of St John's in Antigua, which was granted to them in April 1744. During his two-year term at the head of the Fraternity Ward constituted many lodges, and appointed several Provincial Grand Masters: one for Lancaster, one for North America, and three for the island of Jamaica.

His successor was the Earl of Strathmore, who never once attended Grand Lodge, abandoning its care and management to the other Grand Officers. He did, however, appoint a Provincial Grand Master for the island of Bermuda. Lord Cranstoun was then made Grand Master in April 1745, and presided for two years. He constituted several new lodges, and one Provincial Grand Master, for Cape Breton and Louisburg. But he also banned the traditional public processions of Masons on feast days.

Lord Byron succeeded Cranstoun, and served for five years from his installation at Drapers' Hall on 30 April 1747. He had the laws of the Committee of Charity revised, printed and distributed among lodges. His Deputy Grand Master Fotherly Baker and Secretary Revis were frequently left to get on with running the Society while Byron stayed away from London. Byron issued Provincial patents for Denmark and Norway, Pennsylvania, Minorca and New York.

On 20 March 1752 Lord Carysfort became Grand Master, and he took more interest in the fraternity than Byron, being ready to visit the lodges in person, and to promote harmony among the members. Dr Manningham, his Deputy, was also conscientious in constantly visiting the lodges and promoting union among the Brethren. This Grand Master's attachment to the Society was so obvious that the brethren, in gratitude for his services, re-elected him on 3 April 1753.

During his presidency provincial patents were issued for Gibraltar, the Bahama Islands, New York, Guernsey, Jersey, Alderney, Sark, and Man, as well as for Cornwall, Worcestershire, Gloucestershire, Shropshire, Monmouth and Hereford.

The Marquis of Carnarvon (son of the previous Grand Master Carnarvon) succeeded Carysfort in March 1754 and began his administration by ordering the Book of Constitutions to be reprinted, under the inspection of a committee of Grand Officers. Soon after his installation the Grand Lodge received a complaint against the Grand Lodge of Ancient Freemasons, saying that those Brethren were assembling without authority. The complaint said these Brethren considered themselves independent of the Society and did not accept the laws of Grand Lodge or the control of the Grand Master. Dr Manningham, the Deputy Grand Master, wanted to actively discourage their meetings, which he described as contrary to the laws of the Society and subversive of the allegiance due to the Grand Master. The Grand Lodge resolved that the meeting of any brethren under the denomination of Masons, other than as brethren of the ancient and honourable Society of Free and Accepted Masons established upon the universal system, was inconsistent with the honour and interest of the craft, and a high insult on the Grand Master and the whole body of Masons. In consequence of this resolution, fourteen brethren – members of a lodge held at the Ben Jonson's head in Pelham Street, Spitalfields, which adhered to the Grand Lodge of Ancient Freemasons – were expelled from the Grand Lodge in London, and their lodge was erased from the list.

No preceding Grand Master granted so many provincial deputations as Carnarvon. In less than two years patents were issued for South Carolina, South Wales, Antigua, and all North America where no former provincial was appointed, for Barbados and all other of His Majesty's islands to the windward of Guadeloupe, for St Eustatius, Cuba, St Martin's, and the Dutch Caribbean islands in America, for Scilly and the adjacent islands, for all His Majesty's dominions in Germany (with a power to choose their successors), and for the County Palatine of Chester, and the City and County of Chester. Most of these appointments were honorary grants in favour of individuals, and few of them offered any advantage to the Society. Carnarvon continued to preside over the fraternity till 18 May 1757, when Lord Aberdour succeeded him.

George II died at his palace at Kensington on 5 October 1760 in the

77th year of his age and the 34th of his reign. Preston says his reign was the golden era of Masonry in England: a time when the sciences were cultivated and improved, the Royal Art was diligently propagated, and true architecture clearly understood. The fraternity were honoured and esteemed, the lodges patronized by exalted characters, and charity, humanity and benevolence were the distinguishing characteristics of Masons.

Conclusions to Part One

Preston's outline of Masonic History takes a different view of the Fraternity from that currently offered by the United Grand Lodge of England. He paints a picture of an on-going battle for control of an old and well-established fraternity.

He says that Freemasonry began with the rituals of the ancient Druids of Britain and has been sustained for thousands of years by the rulers of the kingdom. Although he talks of foreign influences, he is sure Freemasonry began in Britain. It is possible that he was influenced in this idea by the popular growth of the Ancient Order of Druids, which had been formed at the Kings Arms Tavern in Poland Street in London in 1781 and had become fashionable.

The tactics of the three contenders come through clearly from Preston's descriptions. He sees the Grand Lodge of York as the true upholder of the original traditions of Freemasonry, and the Grand Lodge of London as an organization that appointed uninterested, absentee and even drunken Grand Masters in a narrow-minded attempt to gain respectability from the nobility. This strategy resulted in a split with a group Preston calls the Antients, who set up a rival Grand Lodge in London. The historical authority that, Preston implies, is attached to the Grand Lodge of York is systematically undermined by the Grand Lodge of London and its policy of pandering to any whims of the ruling nobility – as long as they condescend to take the title Grand Master.

He touches briefly on a few points that he does not develop. He mentions the role of Scotland in early Masonry but does not expand it beyond pointing out that James VI and I and Charles II were both initiated into Freemasonry. He mentions quite a long period when Freemasonry was ruled by the Knights Templar, but again does not expand on any significance of this. The third interesting point he brings out is the importance of the Grand Lodge of York and its claim to have made a better job of preserving the ancient traditions of Freemasonry than the Grand Lodge in London managed to do.

Preston's view of the origins Freemasonry and the behaviour of the Grand Lodge of London during the eighteenth century has been attacked by members of Quatuor Coronati Lodge, with one past master saying, in an introduction to a biography of Preston:

> Regrettably, the results of Preston's historical research were not based on the accuracy one might expect to find. In particular, his complete acceptance of manuscripts since shown to have been hoaxes and his promulgation of the secession theory of the Antients' Grand Lodge, since demonstrated as totally false [by another past master of Quatuor Coronati] are examples.

But Preston was too large a figure to be totally ignored by the United Grand Lodge of England and, more to the point, he left a bequest in his will to establish a fund to pay each year for 'some well-informed Mason to deliver annually a Lecture on the first, second or third degrees of Masonry according to the system practiced in the Lodge of Antiquity during my Mastership'. His idea was to preserve the spirit of free enquiry into the ancient origins of Freemasonry and its ritual that his works celebrated. After Preston's death this bequest came under the control of the Duke of Sussex, who appointed a Mason of his own choice, and naturally he chose a Prestonian lecturer who did not raise difficult questions. The lectureship was dormant for many years, but in 1924 the Prestonian Lectureship was revived under the control of the committee of UGLE for a 'suitable' Mason to deliver each year a lecture on a suitable topic, and to repeat it on at least three occasions within the year. The Prestonian Lectures continue to be delivered today. But the regular memorial lecture now given in Preston's name is closely vetted by UGLE before it is delivered. And, cynic that I am, I suspect much of Preston's material that I have just discussed would never be allowed in a modern Prestonian lecture.

For all that, though, other early Masonic writers have taken a closer look at some of the points Preston raised. I will now look at the findings of Robert Freke Gould's investigations into the role of Scotland and its line of Stuart Kings in the traditions of Freemasonry.

Part Two

Robert Freke Gould
on
Scotland's Role in
Early Freemasonry

Chapter 7

The First Scottish Statutes
of Freemasonry

Robert Freke Gould

Robert Gould was born in 1836 in England. As a young man he was
commissioned a lieutenant in the 31st Regiment of the British Army.
He was initiated into a military lodge – Royal Navy Lodge No. 429,
Ramsgate – as an eighteen-year-old officer. At the age of twenty-one
he joined the Friendship Lodge, whilst serving in Gibraltar. And he
became Master of Northern Lodge No. 570 when he was twenty-
seven, whilst serving in China.

Gould retired from military service in 1868 and at the age of thirty-
two became a barrister. He was made Senior Grand Deacon of the
United Grand Lodge of England in 1880, and in 1884 he was invited
to become a founder member of the Quatuor Coronati Lodge No.
2076, along with Sir Charles Warren, Sir Walter Bezant, George W.
Speth, W. Harry Rylands, William James Hughan, the Revd
Adolphus F. A. Woodford, John P. Rylands and Major Sisson C.
Pratt. Quatuor Coronati was the first lodge of 'research' to be allowed
within the United Grand Lodge of England.

The Quatuor Coronati lodge is noted for its long record of hostility
to any suggestion that Freemasonry might not have started in London
in 1717. (This view of the origins of Freemasonry was formulated by
the Duke of Sussex when he forced the formation of the United Grand
Lodge of England onto the reluctant Masons of England and Wales in
1813.) Quatuor Coronati produces and sells its own lodge journal, *Ars
Quatuor Coronatorum* (AQC).

The lodge's claimed object was to develop a new style of research into Freemasonry. This mainly consisted of rubbishing the work of earlier authors that did not fit the official UGLE world view – as, for example, in the blanket comments on Preston's historical work quoted on p. [9]. It proclaimed itself the 'authentic school' of Masonic thought and made sure nobody who questioned it got a hearing. In this manner it managed to reject almost all previous research as 'unreliable'.

Robert Gould had published a three-volume work, *The History of Freemasonry*, in 1883, before being asked to become a founder member (and later Master) of Quatuor Coronati, and it is from the research he published before he was absorbed into Quatuor Coronati that I have taken the ideas in the second section of this book. I have rewritten his words into simpler language but I have not changed any of his facts. If you wish to read him in the original then be sure to look for a first edition. The 1931 five-volume edition of *Gould's History of Freemasonry*, 'revised, edited and brought up-to-date' by Quatuor Coronati member Dudley Wright, is quite different, as is the 1951 version edited by Herbert Poole (who, incidentally, was also a Quatuor Coronati member). Prof. Andrew Prescott, on the website of the Centre for Research into Freemasonry at Sheffield University, finds the book's publication history

> very confusing. The first edition ... was reprinted at least nine times. In 1931 a revised version, edited and brought up to date by Dudley Wright, was published by the Caxton Publishing Company. A third edition was produced in 1951, edited by Rev. Herbert Poole, produced by the same publisher. In general, the first edition is closer to Gould's original research, which is firmly grounded on primary sources.

Gould's Scottish Research

Gould begins by saying that Masonic historians have largely relied on their imaginations to offer proofs of the antiquity of Freemasonry. This has led many readers to suppose that the Craft is a modern adaptation of defunct organizations, and that it dates from the second decade of the eighteenth century. But, he says, it is a fact that the minutes of Scottish lodges from the sixteenth century, and evidence of British Masonic life dating some two hundred years farther back, have been left unheeded among the old Scottish Lodge chests.

So much evidence has accumulated about the early history, progress and character of the craft, Gould thinks to ignore it is embarrassing. He thinks it may safely be said that the Grand Lodges of Great Britain are the direct descendants, by continuity and absorption, of an ancient tradition of Freemasonry.

The oldest lodges in Scotland possess registers of members and meetings, as well as particulars of their laws and customs, ranging back over three hundred years. Many of these lodges were among the founders of the Grand Lodge of Scotland in 1736. However, some choose not to join in the first instance but joined later. Others preferred isolation to union; indeed one had existed as an independent lodge up to the time Gould wrote his history. Gould's sketch of the main features of these ancient documents shows how they link the Lodges of modern Freemasonry with their speculative ancestors.

The Schaw Statutes of 1598 are an important Masonic document. They were sent to all the lodges in Scotland, having received the unanimous sanction of the masters convened at Edinburgh. William Schaw, the Master of Work (by royal appointment) and General Warden, signed them and enforced their observance on the Scottish craft. The following year Schaw signed another set of Statutes clarifying the relationship between the old lodges of Edinburgh and Kilwinning. The clauses of this deed are extraordinary, considering the period of their publication. They offer a better insight into the usages and customs of the Craft than any other documents that have come down to us from remote times.

The older Masonic code is dated 28 December 1598 and is written in a legible manner in the first volume of the records of the Lodge of Edinburgh. It is signed by Schaw as Master of Work. It consists of 22 unnumbered items, and master masons are obliged to faithfully keep them all. The General Warden signed the statutes, so that an authentic copy could be made and sent to all the lodges in Scotland. Unfortunately the names and numbers of these lodges are not recorded, but their scope was not restricted to the Lodge of Edinburgh, which only served as a medium for their distribution throughout Scotland.

Schaw Statutes No. 1, of 1598

In considering these rules in detail, Gould numbered the items consecutively:

1. All the good ordinances concerning the privileges of the craft, which were made by their predecessors of 'gude memorie', to be observed and kept; and especially to be true to one another, and live charitably together as becometh sworn brethren and companions of the Craft.
2. To be obedient to their Wardens, Deacons, and Masters in all things concerning the Craft.
3. To be honest, faithful and diligent in their calling, and upright with the masters or owners of the work which they undertake, whatever be the mode of payment.
4. That no one undertake work, be it great or small, unless able to complete it satisfactorily, under the penalty of forty pounds [Scots], or the fourth part of the value of the work, according to the decision of the General Warden, or the officers named in the 2d item, for the sheriffdom where the work is being wrought.
5. That no Master shall supplant another under the penalty of forty pounds.
6. That no Master take an uncompleted work unless the previous masters be duly satisfied, under the same penalty.
7. That one Warden be elected annually by every lodge, 'as thay are devidit particularlie,' to have charge thereof, and that, by the votes of the Masters of the said lodges, with the consent of the General Warden if present. Should the latter be absent, then the results of such elections must be communicated to him, that he may send his directions to the Wardens-elect.
8. That no Master shall have more than three apprentices during his lifetime, unless with the special consent of the officers previously mentioned of the sheriffdom in which the additional apprentice shall dwell.
9. Apprentices must not be bound for less than seven years, and no apprentice shall be made brother and fellow-in-craft, unless he has served an additional seven years, save by the special license of the regular officers assembled for that purpose, and then only if sufficient trial has been made of his

worthiness, qualification and skill. The penalty was forty pounds, as usual, 'besyde the penalteis to be set doun aganis his persone, accordyng to the ordr of the ludge quhair he remains.'

10. Masters must not sell their apprentices to other masters, nor dispense with their time by sale to such apprentices, under the penalty of forty pounds.

11. No Master to receive an apprentice without informing the Warden of his lodge, that his name and date of reception be duly booked.

12. No apprentice to be entered but by the same order.

13. No Master or fellow-of-craft to be received or admitted except in the presence of six Masters and two entered apprentices, the Warden of that lodge being one of the six, the date thereof being orderly booked, and 'his name and mark insert' in the said book, together with the names of the six Masters, the apprentices, and intender. Provided always that no one be admitted without 'ane assay and sufficient tryall of his skill and worthynes in his vocatioun and craft.'

14. No Master to engage in any masonic work under charge or command of any other craftsman.

15. No Master or fellow-of-craft to receive 'any cowanis' to work in his society or company, or to send any of his servants to work with them, under a penalty of twenty pounds for each offence.

16. No apprentice shall undertake work beyond the value of ten pounds from the owner thereof, under the penalty aforesaid, and, on its completion, a license must be obtained from the Masters or Warden in their own neighbourhood, if more is desired to be done.

17. Should strife arise amongst the Masters, servants or apprentices, they must inform the Wardens, Deacons or their lodges within twenty-four hours thereof, under ten pounds penalty in case of default, in order that the difficulties may be amicably settled. Should any of the parties concerned therein, refuse to accept the award made, they shall be liable to be deprived of the privileges of their lodge, and not be permitted to work during the period of their obstinacy.

18. Masters and others must be careful in taking all needful precautions as to the erection of suitable scaffolding, and

should accidents occur through their negligence, they shall
not act as masters having charge of any work, but for ever
afterwards be subject to others.

19. Masters are not to receive apprentices who 'sal happin to ryn
away' from their lawful service, under penalty of forty
pounds.

20. All members of the mason craft must attend the meetings
when lawfully warned, under 'the pane of ten punds.'

21. All Masters present at any 'assemblie or meetting' shall be
sworn by their great oath, not to hide or conceal any wrong
done to each other, or to the owners of the work, as far as
they know, under the same penalty.

22. All the said penalties shall be collected from those who break
any of the foregoing statutes, by the Wardens, Deacons and
Masters, to be distributed 'ad pios vsus according to gud
conscience,' and by their advice.

These Schaw Statutes, were signed 'William Schaw, Maistir of Wark,
Warden of the Maisonis', on 28 December 1598.

Schaw Statutes No. 2, of 1599

The Second Schaw Statutes were signed on 28 December 1599. They
drew on the code of the previous year, and were arranged specially for
the old Lodge at Kilwinning, Ayrshire. There are several points
mentioned in this document that refer specifically to Lodge
Kilwinning and its authority.

Gould numbered the thirteen items consecutively, as he had done
with the earlier regulations:

1. The Warden to act within the bounds of Kilwinning, and
other places subject to that lodge, shall be annually elected
on the 20th day of December, 'and that within the kirk at
winning', as the 'heid and second ludge of Scotland,' the
general warden to be informed accordingly.

2. The ' Lord Warden Generall,' considering that it was
expedient that all the Scottish lodges should prospectively
enjoy their ancient liberties as of yore, confirms the right of
the Lodge of Kilwinning, 'secund lodge of Scotland,' to have

its warden present at the election of wardens within the bounds of the 'nether waird of Cliddisdaill, Glasgow, Air and boundis of Carrik,' and also to convene these wardens to assemble anywhere within the district (embracing the west of Scotland, including Glasgow), when and where they are to submit to the judgments of the warden and deacon of Kilwinning.

3. The Warden General, for reasons of expediency, confirms the rank of Edinburgh as 'the first and principal lodge in Scotland,' that of Kilwinning being the second, 'as of befoir is notourlie manifest in our awld antient writtis'; and the Lodge of Stirling to be third, according to their ancient privileges.

4. The Wardens of every lodge shall be answerable to the Presbyters within their sheriffdoms, for the masons subject to their lodges, the third part of the fines paid by the disobedient being devoted to the 'godlie usis of the ludge,' where the offences were committed.

5. An annual trial of all offences shall be made, under the management of the Warden and most ancient Masters of the lodge, extending to six persons, so that due order be observed.

6. The Lord Warden General ordains that the Warden of Kilwinning, 'as secund in Scotland,' shall select six of the most perfect and worthy masons, in order to test the qualification of all the fellows within their district, 'of thair art, craft, scyance, and ancient memorie,' to the intent that the said Wardens shall be duly responsible for such persons as are under them.

7. The Warden and Deacon of Kilwinning, as the second lodge, is empowered to exclude and expel from the society all who persist in disobeying the ancient statutes, and 'all personis disobedient ather to kirk, craft, counsall', and other regulations 'to be hereafter made.'

8. The Warden General requires the Warden and Deacon (with his Quartermasters) to select a skilled notary, to be Ordinary Clerk or Scribe, by whom all deeds were to be executed.

9. The acts heretofore made by Kilwinning masons must be kept most faithfully in the future, and no apprentice or craftsman be either admitted or entered but 'within the kirk of Kilwynning, as his paroche and secund ludge;' all

banquets arising out of such entries to be held ' within the said ludge of Kilwynning.'

10. All fellow-craftsmen at their entry and prior to their admission must pay to the lodge the sum of £10, with 10s. worth of gloves, which shall include the expense of the banquet; also that none be admitted without 'ane sufficient essay' and 'pruife of memorie and art of craft,' under the supervision of the Warden, Deacon, and Quartermasters of the lodge, as they shall be answerable to the Warden.

11. Apprentices are not to be admitted unless they pay £6 towards the common banquet, or defray the expenses of a meal for all the members and apprentices of the lodge.

12. The Wardens and Deacons of the second lodge of Scotland (Kilwinning) shall annually take the oath, 'fidelitie and trewthe,' of all the Masters and fellows of craft committed to their charge; that they shall not keep company nor work with cowans, nor any of their servants or apprentices, under the penalties provided in the former acts.

13. The 'generall warden' ordains that the Lodge of Kilwinning, being the second lodge in Scotland, shall annually test every craftsman and apprentice, according to their vocations, and should they have forgotten even one point of the 'art of memorie and science' thereof, they must forfeit 20s. if fellow-crafts, and 11s. if apprentices, for their neglect. Fines to be paid into the box for the common weal, in conformity with the practice of the lodges of the realm.

The regulations are followed by a statement from the 'Generall warden of Scotland' [William Schaw] that he had subscribed to them with his hand, in token that they were to be observed, as also were the acts and statutes made previously by the officers of the lodge aforesaid, so as to preserve due regularity, conformably to equity, justice, and ancient order. The same deed empowered the officers to make acts according to the 'office and law'.

The document ends with an important certificate from William Schaw, which proves that it was intended exclusively for the Masons under the jurisdiction of the Kilwinning Lodge, for it is addressed to the Warden, Deacon, and Masters of that lodge, and testifies to the honest and careful manner in which Archibald Barclay, the Commissioner from the lodge, had discharged the duties entrusted to him. Bro. Barclay took a commission from Kilwinning Lodge to the Warden General and the Masters of the Lodge of Edinburgh; but 'by reason of the King being out of the Toun', and no Masters but those of the lodge named being convened at the time, the deputation was not successful in obtaining all that the members asked. The chief requests of the lodge were to obtain additional powers to preserve order, which the craft required for the conservation of their rights, and especially to secure from King James VI a recognition of the privileges of the lodge, including the power of imposing penalties upon the 'dissobedient personis and perturberis of all guid ordour'. These Schaw promised to obtain. The statutes were finally signed at Holyrood Palace after two long days of discussion.

The Statutes of 1599 are mainly a reproduction of the regulations that apply to a particular lodge, but they also contain an authoritative judgment about the relative precedence of the three head lodges in Scotland. Gould says it is important to notice that many of the laws in the Constitutions of modern Freemasonry are drawn from these ancient rules.

Chapter 8

The St Clairs of Roslin

The St Clairs Charters

Gould says that, even though they are not the oldest references to Freemasonry, the St Clair Charters are important. He believes there can be no doubt of their genuineness, as the signatures match with original autographs in other manuscripts of the period.

The Advocates Library in Edinburgh holds a little folio, known as the Hay manuscripts, which also contains copies of both the St Clair Charters. They are neatly copied onto scrolls of paper, one being 15 by 11 inches, and the other 26 inches long, and the same width as its companion. A few words have faded, but can easily be filled in. The larger document has lost its south-east corner. It is quite possible that the missing section contained other signatures.

Gould places the probable date of the first charter as around 1601–2, as it has been signed by William Schaw, Master of Work, who died in 1602. The names of the Deacons of the masons in Edinburgh fit this period. I have given English summaries of the charters below; the originals written in the Scots tongue, which Gould quoted in full, are reproduced in Appendix 1.

First St Clair Charter

Be it known to all men by this letter that we Deacons, Masters and Freemen of the Masons of the realm of Scotland with the express consent and agreement of William Schaw, Master of Works to our Sovereign Lord, confirm that from age to age it has been observed amongst us that the Lairds of Roslin have ever been Patrons and Protectors of us and our privileges. We acknowledge that our predecessors also obeyed and acknowledged them as Patrons and protectors but recently, through sloth and negligence, the Lairds of Roslin have been deprived of their just rights and our fine Craft has been deprived of any patron, protector and overseer. This has created much corruption and imperfection, both amongst ourselves and in our Craft, and as a result many people have formed a bad opinion of us and our Craft. Many great enterprises have failed because of bad behaviour that has not been corrected. This has come about by the deliberate exploitation of faults and by failure of honest Masons to correctly practise their Craft. When controversies break out among our brethren the lack of any Patron and Protector is a great problem. We have to appeal for judgement to the normal processes of law to remedy our grievances and to keep us in good order. We speak for all the brethren and craftsmen of the realm when, for the advancement and good government of our Craft, we consent that William Sinclair of Roslin and his heirs shall be allowed to purchase from the hand of our Sovereign Lord the freedom to rule over us and our successors for all time and to act as patrons and judges over all practitioners of our Craft within this realm. We acknowledge the said William Sinclair and his heirs as our patrons and judges under our Sovereign Lord without restrictions on his power of judgement over us and call on him to appoint and authorise judges to rule our Craft under the powers that it pleases our Sovereign Lord to grant to him and his heirs.

William Schaw, Master of Works

Second St Clair Charter

The second charter was published in 1628.

Be it known to all men by this letter that we Deacons, Master and Freemen of the Masons and Hammermen within the kingdom of Scotland have from age to age acknowledged the Lairds of Roslin as the Patrons and Protectors of us and our privileges. Likewise our predecessors have obeyed and acknowledged them as Patrons and Protectors as they held letters of authority and other documents granted to them by most noble progenitors of noble memory who were also Lairds of Roslin. These writings were destroyed by a fire within the Castle of Roslin. The destruction by fire of these letters is well known to us and our predecessor Deacons, Masters and Freemen of the Masons. Because of negligence and slothfulness, the protection of our privileges is likely to be lost and the Lairds of Roslin be deprived of their just rights and our Craft be deprived of any Patron Protector. The lack of an overseer will result in imperfection and corruptions and will cause many people to form a bad opinion of us and our Craft. Many and great enterprises will not be undertaken if this misbehaviour is not corrected. To keep good order among us in the future, and for the advancement of our Craft within his Highness's kingdom of Scotland, we in the name of all the brethren and craftsmen, and to further the polices of our predecessors made with the express consent of William Schaw, Master of Works to his Highness, and with one voice agree and that William Sinclair of Roslin, father to Sir William Sinclair, now of Roslin, for himself and his heirs should purchase and obtain at the hands of his Majesty the liberty, freedom and jurisdiction over us and our predecessor Deacons, Masters and Freemen of the said vocation, as patrons and judges over the use of the whole profession within the said kingdom. We acknowledge him and his heirs as patrons and judges of our Craft, under our Sovereign Lord, without and limits to their ability to pass judgement, under the agreement subscribed by the said Master of Works and our predecessors. In this exercising this office of jurisdiction, over us and our vocation, the said William Sinclair of Roslin continued until he went to Ireland where he presently remains. But since his departure from this realm many corruptions and imperfections have arisen both among ourselves and in our said vocation for want of a Patron and Overseer and our Craft is likely to fall into decay. And now for the safety of our Craft and having full experience of the good skill and judgement which the said Sir William Sinclair of Roslin has shown to our Craft, and to repair the ruin and manifold corruption and damage being done by unskilled workers we are all of one voice in ratifying the pervious letter of authority and freedoms granted by our brethren and his Highness's own Master of Works at the time to the said William Sinclair of Roslin, father to the said Sir William Sinclair whereby he and his heirs are acknowledged as our Patrons and Judges under our Sovereign Lord over us and all worthy practitioners of our Craft within this

his Highness's kingdom of Scotland, without any limit on their judgements in any time hereafter. And further we all in one voice confirm that the said Sir William Sinclair, now of Roslin, and his heirs are our only Patrons, Protectors and Overseers under our Sovereign Lord. This applies to us and our successor Deacons, Masters and Freemen of our vocations of Masons and Hammermen, within the worthy kingdom of Scotland and we acknowledge that the Lairds of Roslin have held this office for many ages with full power granted to them to appoint Wardens and Deputies and to call meetings at places of their choosing for the purpose of keeping good order in the Craft. We say this so that it may be known to all Masons that they may be called to account for absences and be subject to fines if they fail to carry out the responsibilities of the Craft. The Lairds of Roslin have the right to make proper use of deputies, clerks, assistants and other such officers as are needed to ensure that all transgressors are brought to order. And the same [Lairds] have the power to enforce all the privileges, liberties and immunities of the said Craft and to exercise that power as their predecessors have done and freely, quietly and in peace against any revocation, obstacle or impediment whatsoever.

Gould points out that on the basis of these documents the distinction of a hereditary Grand Mastership of the Craft has been claimed for the St Clairs of Roslin. Sir David Brewster, who edited the later editions of Laurie's *History of Freemasonry*, says:

It deserves to be remarked that in both these deeds the appointment of William Sinclair, Earl of Orkney and Caithness, to the office of Grand Master by James II of Scotland, is spoken of as a fact well known and universally admitted.

However, Gould says that the reading of the two deeds does not necessarily prove this, as he could find no direct corroboration in them. But the deeds do show that the consent of the Freemen Masons within the realm of Scotland is acknowledged and admit that William St Clair purchased the position of patron and judge from the Sovereign Lord of Scotland for himself and his heirs. Also the successors to these masons are pledged to support such an appointment. The first deed records a statement that the Lairds of Roslin had previously exercised such a privilege for many years, and the second deed, executed some thirty years later, was confirmed by the hammermen [i.e. blacksmiths] as well as the masons, and the squaremen were also party to the agreement. The squaremen included coopers, wrights (or carpenters) and slaters, who were represented on the charter by their deacons from Ayr.

The later deed contains a declaration that there was a destructive fire in Roslin Castle in which some extraordinary writings of value to the craft perished, and were thus lost to the Freemasons. Gould comments that often, when there is an absence of confirmatory evidence, it is common to refer to a fire or other visitation of Providence to turn the edge of criticism. Gould says he did not find any deeds that confer a hereditary Grand Mastership of the Craft on the Earl of Orkney in the fifteenth century.

The lodges that were parties to Charter No. 1 met at Edinburgh, St Andrews, Haddington, Atcheson-Haven and Dunfermline respectively. The second charter bears the names of the lodges of Edinburgh, Glasgow, Dundee, Stirling, Dunfermline, and St Andrews and also of the Masons and other crafts at Ayr. They united to obtain a patron for their craft. But other districts in Scotland that contained lodges at that period, such as Kilwinning and Aberdeen, were not included. It seems likely that the office of patron was sought with the object of settling whatever local disputes might occur amongst the Freemasons in the exercise of their trade. It did not usurp the rights of the king's Master of Work, who supported the petition of the lodges.

If this were the case, then it might be expected that similar powers were obtained in other counties – and that is just what Gould found. On 25 September 1590 James VI granted to Patrick Coipland of Udaucht the office of 'Wardene and Justice over the girt and craft of masonrie' within the counties of Aberdeen, Banff, and Kincardine, with the fullest liberty to act within the district named. Copland's appointment was made in response to a vote in his favour, by 'the maist pairt of the master masounes within the sheriffdomes, and because his predecessoris hes bene ancient possessouris of the said office of Wardanrie over all the boundis'.

This appointment proves beyond dispute that the kings of Scotland nominated the office-bearers of the order. But, Gould asks, what does it say about the hereditary Grand Mastership theory? If the Earl of Orkney and his heirs were empowered to act as Grand Masters of the Fraternity from the reign, and by the authority, of James II, how is it that different districts are allotted Wardens to act as judges of the Masonic Craft?

In a deed of 1590 the Master Masons within the three counties named, sought the countenance and confirmation of James VI to elect a Warden to rule over them. This suggests they did not accept that there was an existing office of Grand Master of the Freemasons. The laws promulgated on 28 December 1598 by William Schaw, Master of Work to King James VI, were in force in all other parts of Scotland. We do not even know that this Warden and Judge of 1590 was a Mason, therefore Gould will only concede that he may have been accepted as a brother, and made free of the ancient craft, out of compliment to his responsible position and to secure his co-operation and favour.

The First Grand Master Mason of Scotland

Gould then returns to the matter of the St Clairs of Roslin's claim to hereditary Grand Mastership of the Craft. At the Grand Election of the Master Mason of Scotland in 1736 fully one hundred Lodges were in being, of which no fewer than 33 were represented in the election. If there was one influence that encouraged the election of a governing Masonic body for Scotland, it is that within the short space of 13 years six prominent noblemen, all connected with Scotland, had filled the chair of the Grand Lodge of England. It seemed likely that one of these, the Earl of Crawford, might have been offered the appointment of first Grand Master of Scotland by the Grand Lodge of England, but had declined the honour.

Although the preliminaries of the Grand Election were said to have been organized by the four Lodges in and about Edinburgh, there were six Lodges in the metropolitan district at that time. The others were ignored in these proceedings. Why were they not included? Probably because they had formed themselves into separate bodies without the authority or approval of the King or his Warden General, which was an understood principle of the Craft. Despite the Lodge of Edinburgh's refusal to accord them recognition, they still remained as independent and separate units.

The main initiative to form a Scottish Grand Lodge was taken by Lodge Canongate Kilwinning. On 29 September 1735 its minutes say that the duty of framing proposals, to be laid before the several Lodges in order to implement the choosing of a Grand Master for Scotland, was passed to a committee. There is no recorded meeting of the four (subsequently) associated Lodges at which this subject was considered until 15 October 1736. Then delegates from the Lodges of

Mary's Chapel, Canongate Kilwinning, Kilwinning Scots Arms and Leith Kilwinning met and agreed to send a circular to all the Scottish Lodges inviting their attendance, either in person or by proxy, for the purpose of electing a Grand Master.

It was decided that the election should take place in Mary's Chapel on Tuesday 30 November 1736, at half-past two in the afternoon. At the appointed time representatives of 33 of the hundred or more Lodges that had been invited assembled. Present were the Master and Wardens of the following lodges:

Mary's Chapel	Falkirk
Selkirk	Cupar of Fife
Biggar	Hamilton
Kilwinning	Aberdeen
Inverness	Linlithgow
Sanquhar	Dunse
Canongate Kilwinning	Maryburgh
Lesmahagow	Dunfermline
Peebles	Kirkcaldy
Killwinning Scots Arms	Canongate and Leith
Saint Brides at Douglas	Dundee
Glasgow St Mungo's	Journeymen Masons of Edinburgh
Kilwinning Leith	Dalkeith
Lanark	Edinburgh
Greenock	Monross
Kilwinning Glasgow	Aitcheson's Haven
Strathaven	Kirkintilloch

To avoid jealousy over precedent, each Lodge was placed on the roll in the order in which it entered the hall.

No amendments were offered to the form of procedure, or the draft of the Constitutions, which had been submitted to the Lodges and, the roll having been finally adjusted, the following resignation from the office of hereditary Grand Master was tendered by the Laird of Roslin and read to the meeting:

I, William St Clair of Rossline, Esquire, taking into my considera-tion that the Massons in Scotland did, by several deeds, constitute and appoint William and Sir William St Clairs of Rossline, my ancestors and their heirs, to be their patrons, protectors, judges, or masters; and that my holding or claiming any such jurisdiction, right, or privilege, might be prejudiciall to the Craft and vocation of Massonrie, whereof I am a member and I, being desireous to advance and promote the good and utility of the said Craft of Massonrie to the utmost of my power, doe therefore hereby, for me and my heirs, renounce, quit, claim, overgive, and discharge all right, claim, or pretence that I, or my heirs, had, have, or any ways may have, pretend to, or claim, to be patron, protector, judge, or master of the Massons in Scotland, in virtue of any deed or deeds made and granted by the said Massons, or of any grant or charter made by any of the Kings of Scotland, to and in favours of the said William and Sir William St Clairs of Rossline, or any others of my predecessors, or any other manner of way whatsomever, for now and ever: And I bind and oblige me and my heirs, to warrant this present renounciation and discharge at all hands; and I consent to the registration hereof in the Books of Councill and Session, or any other judge's books competent, therein to remain for preservation; and thereto I constitute my procurators, &c. In witness whereof I have subscribed these presents (written by David Maul, Writer to the Signet), at Edinburgh, the twenty-fourth day of November one thousand seven hundred and thirty-six years, before these witnesses, George Fraser, Deputy Auditor of the Excise in Scotland, Master of the Canongate Lodge; and William Montgomerie, Merchant in Leith, Master of the Leith Lodge.

Sic Subscribitur

WM. ST CLAIR
Geo. Fraser, Canongate Kilwinning, witness
Wm. Montgomerie, Leith Kilwinning, witness

Gould says that the Brethren were so fascinated with the magnanimity, disinterestedness and zeal displayed in William St Clair's resignation, that the Deed was unanimously accepted and his abdication from an obsolete office in Masonry cleared the ground for St Clair to fill the post of first Grand Master in the Scottish Grand Lodge of Speculative Masons.

William St Clair was initiated, without ballot, according to custom in Canongate Kilwinning (No. 2) on 18 May 1736. This was just eight months after the choosing of a Grand Master had first been discussed in that Lodge. He was advanced to the Degree of Fellow Craft on 2 June following, paying into the box as usual, and raised to a Master Mason on

22 November of the same year. Nineteen days previously, on 3 November, his fellow members had decided to nominate St Clair for the chief office of the Grand Lodge they were trying to create.

Part of this story concerns Bro. John Douglas, a surgeon and a member of the Lodge of Kirkcaldy. On 4 August 1736 he was affiliated to Lodge Canongate Kilwinning and appointed Secretary for the time, with power to appoint his own Deputy, in order to make out a scheme for bringing about a Grand Master for Scotland. Two days after St Clair was made a Master Mason, Douglas signed the document that facilitated the election of a Grand Master, and three leading members of his Kirkcaldy Mother Lodge attested it.

It is Gould's opinion that Dr Douglas was introduced as part a preconceived plan whereby the election of a Grand Master would contribute to the aggrandisement of the Lodge receiving him. Douglas's subsequent advancement and frequent re-election to the chair of Substitute Grand Master suggests he held high Masonic qualifications. And the part he played in the resuscitation of the St Clair Charters and the dramatic effect that their identification had for the case of the successful aspirant to the Grand Mastership gave the formation of the Grand Lodge of Scotland a sort of legal gloss that had been wanting at the institution of the Grand Lodge of England. Whatever the motive of the originators of the scheme, Gould thinks that setting up a Grand Lodge upon the ruins of an institution that had ceased to be of practical benefit, but which had been closely allied to the Guilds of the Mason Craft, lent the new organization an air of antiquity as the lineal representative of the ancient courts of Operative Masonry.

The other Grand Officers elected on 30 November 1736 were Captain John Young, D. G. .M.; Sir William Baillie, S. G. W.; Sir Alexander Hope, J. G. W.; Dr John Moncrief, G. Treasurer; John Macdougall, G. Secretary; and Robert Alison, G. Clerk.

The first Quarterly Communication was held 12 January 1737, when the Minutes and proceedings of the Four Associated Lodges and the Minutes of the Grand Election were read and unanimously approved.

Chapter 9

The Old Lodges of Scotland

Dating the Records

Gould thought it a good idea to examine the records of all the more ancient Scottish lodges, and he dealt with the history of each separately as far as possible. There was, however, a delicate question of precedence, about which these old lodges were a little sensitive.

Gould says that some writers claim that the years when the various Scottish abbeys were built provide the best means of deciding when the lodges originated. They assume that each of them needed a lodge of Freemasons as their builders. English Freemasons say that the Masonic fraternity was organized at York in the time of Athelstan in AD 926, but Scottish Freemasons are content to trace their descent from the builders of the abbeys of Holyrood, Kelso, Melrose and Kilwinning, the Cathedral of Glasgow and other church foundations of the twelfth and thirteenth centuries. Gould did not find any evidence as to when and where the first Scottish Masonic lodge was instituted.

Holyrood and Kelso are mentioned among the earliest of the Scottish abbeys; Kilwinning is said to be older than any ecclesiastical edifice of England, and Melrose is always put forward. There is little agreement to be found under such circumstances, and Gould advances no opinion of his own as to the primogeniture of these old lodges. Several of them lament the loss of their most ancient manuscripts, whilst others lack any records whatever. Bearing in mind these difficulties, which suggest the great age of many of the lodges, he thought it safest to follow the decision of the Grand Lodge of Scotland as to their relative precedence, leaving their antiquity an open question.

Gould's discussion of the lodges followed the sequence to their positions on the roll, after which he discussed those that had ceased to exist. He also noted that the Lodge of Melrose kept aloof from the Grand Lodge of Scotland.

Mother Kilwinning Lodge, Ayrshire, No. 0

The story of the formation of the lodge and the erection of Kilwinning Abbey (1140) are weakened by the fact that the abbey was neither the first nor the second Gothic structure erected in Scotland. The lodge's verbal history says that the lodge was first presided over in year 1286 by James, Lord Steward of Scotland, a few years later by King Robert, the hero of Bannockburn, and then by the third son of Robert II (Earl of Buchan). Gould believes that these are rather improbable stories, which were propagated to secure for the lodge the coveted position of being the first on the Grand Lodge Roll, or even to give support to its separate existence as a rival Grand Lodge.

But, Gould says, whatever pre-eminence the supporters of Mother Kilwinning claimed for that ancient lodge during the early part of the eighteenth century, and however difficult it might then have been to reconcile conflicting claims, the Schaw Statutes of 1599 give precedence to the Lodge of Edinburgh, with Kilwinning having to take second place. But Gould finds it surprising that the records of neither the Edinburgh nor the Kilwinning Lodges mention these regulations, and the Scottish Craft does not appear to have had any idea of their existence until the late eighteenth century. They were not known in 1736 and during the struggles for priority and supremacy waged by the Grand Lodge and Mother Kilwinning, because their production as evidence would have settled the dispute at once. Why were they not used?

In 1861 the Earl of Eglinton and Winton presented the Grand Lodge with a copy of *Memorials of the Montgomeries, Earls of Eglinton*. Thus, through the devotion of Lord Eglinton to archaeological studies and research, the Scottish craft owes the discovery of this valuable list of Masonic laws and decisions (The Second Schaw Statutes). Gould says there is no doubt of the authenticity of the manuscript, and its preservation at the family home of the Earl of Eglinton was in all probability because of his family's former connection with the Masonic Court of Kilwinning.

Gould reports that in the 1869 edition of his history of Lodge Kilwinning D. Murray Lyon mentions the appointment of the Baron of Roslin to the Grand Mastership by James II. He also mentions theories that connect the Kilwinning Lodge with the degrees of Masonic Knights Templar, and of the Royal Order of Scotland. Gould, however, believes that, before the development of Grand Lodge masonry early in the eighteenth century, the lodge was never more nor less than a society of architects and artisans incorporated for the regulation of the business of the building trade, and the relief of indigent brethren. He says that its purely operative character merged so imperceptibly into the condition of a purely speculative one, that the precise date of such change cannot be decided upon with any certainty.

Gould feels there may be something in the suggestion that Kilwinning was originally the chief centre of Scottish Freemasonry, and the removal of the Masonic Court to Edinburgh was due to causes, which can be explained. But, he asks, if Kilwinning ever was the headquarters of Freemasonry, why did the lodge quietly accept a secondary position in 1599 and allow its authority to be restricted to Western Scotland? In 1643 it styled itself The Ancient Lodge of Scotland, but Gould thinks this only shows the vanity of its members. The Schaw Statutes effectually dispose of such pretensions, and, whilst admitting Kilwinning into the trio of head lodges, place it immediately behind its metropolitan rival.

The oldest minute-book preserved by the Kilwinning lodge is a small quarto, bound in vellum, which contains accounts of its transactions from 1642 to 1758. (This is not a continuous record, but the lapses are not evidence that the lodge suspended its meetings, for detached sheets referring to some of the missing years still exist.) It notes that the members should deplore the acquisitive propensities or careless conduct of its custodians, by which an older volume has been lost, and manuscripts of great Masonic value dispersed. It is now unlikely these will ever be restored to their rightful owners. As the record chest of the lodge has been ravaged by fire and other vicissitudes, it is no cause for wonder to learn of the shortcomings of its manuscripts. It is a matter for congratulation, under the circumstances, that so much remains of its ancient documents, and that the first minute still preserved is dated as early as 20 December 1642. The object of that meeting was to receive the submission of members to the lodge and the laws thereof. Over forty signatures follow the minute, along with the marks of the brethren, of whom a few had no mark (perhaps because they were still apprentices). Three of the members can be recognized as a deacon and two freemen of the Ayr Squaremen Incorporation, who represented trades other than the Masons. One year later 'the court of the Ludge' was held in the upper chamber of the dwelling house of Hew Smithe. 'Johne Barclay, mason-burgess of Irwine', acted as deacon, and the other brethren were referred to as masters of work. Barclay was chosen Warden, and Hew Crauford as Deacon. Several of the regulations of 1598 were recited and described as ancient statutes, and officers were appointed in charge of the districts of Carrick, Kyle, Cunningham and Renfrew. They were duly obligated to their duties, and James Ross, a notary, was appointed Clerk and also took his 'aithe' (oath). The quarterly fees were agreed for the Masters and apprentices, with the latter having to pay double if they were not prompt in settling their dues. The Quartermasters were instructed to take great pains to collect such subscriptions.

On 20 December 1643 the lodge passed a law that the Deacon Warden should pay to the box, on their first election to office, the sum of £3 each. This is a very early instance of Fees of Honour being paid to the lodge, just as are levied in modern lodges and other Masonic organizations. The Lodge of Edinburgh required no such payments, though other lodges followed the example of Kilwinning.

Gould did not find it easy to discover much that was either new or original in the practices of the lodges of today, for he said that, generally speaking, the ancient minutes offer abundant evidence that our modern Masonic usages are survivals of the time-honoured customs of former days. On 19 December 1646, the lodge assembled in the same upper room, other chief officers being recorded. Three masons were received and accepted as fellow brethren to 'ye said tred' (trade), having sworn to the 'standart of the said lodge *ad vitam*', and five apprentices were received. Hew Mure in Kilmarnock was fined ten pounds for working with cowans. Some ten years later (20 January 1656) another member was obliged to promise, on his oath, not to work with any cowans in future, under pain of being fined according to the ancient rules. Those who had been disobedient in other respects (they were not named) were required to be present at a meeting in Mauchline the following month, or be fined if they failed to attend. Gould says this meeting seems to have been a sort of Provincial Grand Lodge, as twelve delegates represented the lodges of Ayr, Maybole, Kilmaurs, Irvine, Kilmarnock, Mauchline and Renfrew. The fees charged at Kilwinning at this time were 20 shillings for apprentices and 40 shillings for fellows-of-craft, with 4s. more on selecting a mark. The fines for non-attendance were levied with military precision, and absentees were regularly named in the minutes along with those who were present.

In 1659 (20 December) the Lodge appointed representatives in the four local districts to assemble annually in Ayr on the Wednesday before Candlemas to take 'ordours with the transgressors of the actin of the court in the Mason Court buiks [books] of the Ludge of Kilwinning', so that a report could be made to the Lodge on 29 December each year.

Gould thinks these meetings were ordered because of the disaffection of the squaremen (carpenters, slaters and glaziers) of Ayr, who claimed the privileges granted to the crafts of Scotland by the charter of Queen Mary in 1564 and declined to pay dues into the Kilwinning treasury, having a box of their own. This opinion seems to be confirmed by the fact that the regular representatives of the squaremen of Ayr acted independently of the Kilwinning Lodge in joining with the lodges that signed the agreement known as the St Clair Charter No. 2 (of *c.* 1628). The motive of the deputation from the lodge for seeking the powerful authority of the king to uphold their ancient privileges is all too apparent. The monopoly the Freemasons held over the other crafts was gradually being undermined. Neither the ancient privileges nor the indignant complaints of the head lodges were able stop the growing aversion to the interference of these old associations with the development of the Masonic craft either in Kilwinning or elsewhere. The cowans in particular objected to being banished by the lodges, when they argued that they were competent to work in their trade, even though they were not Freemasons.

The introduction of a speculative element – which Gould thinks was intended to strengthen the authority of the old lodges – he says did in effect pave the way for the ultimate surrender of many rights and privileges no longer suitable to the times.

The Earl of Cassilis was elected a Deacon of the lodge in 1672, but was not entered as fellow-craft until a year later, when Cunninghame of Corsehill was his companion. Charles II created Cunninghame a Baronet of Nova Scotia in 1672. Alexander, eighth Earl of Eglinton, appeared at the annual meeting in 1674 as a 'felloe-of-craft', and was elected Chief Deacon in 1677. The office of Deputy Master (which

Gould says is an arrangement of modern times, consequent upon a Prince of the blood Royal accepting the Mastership of a lodge) had its beginning in the election of deputies for Lords Cassilis and Eglinton. They selected operative brethren to act as deputies.

Gould says at that time it was customary for the Deacons and Wardens, on their election, to subscribe to the enrichment of the Box. It may have been simply the exercise of business prudence and foresight that led the members of Kilwinning and other lodges to obtain the patronage of the aristocratic class and their money. He finds the earliest instance of such an appointment at Aberdeen Lodge, No. 34. In 1676 three candidates were proposed for the office of Deacon. The votes were signified by strokes drawn opposite each name. The result was tabulated as follows – three for Cunninghame of Corsehill, seven for Lord Eglinton, and eight for Cunninghame of Robertland, the last named being declared elected by 'a pluralitie of vottis'. We follow the same custom today, when we ballot for the Master: the brother having the greatest number of votes in his favour, of those who are eligible, is elected to the chair, even if there is not an absolute majority of those who voted.

Eglinton became Deacon again on 20 December 1678, with Lord Cochrane, eldest son of the Earl of Dundonald, becoming his Warden. At the same meeting two apprentices were entered, who paid their building money and got their marks along with Cochrane. Gould points out that Cochrane received an ordinary Mason's Mark despite clearly being a speculative or gentleman Mason.

In 1674 the payment of six pounds from fellow-crafts in Glasgow is recorded. Gould believes these brethren hailed from the mother lodge, as it was not likely the masons of the city of Glasgow recognized the right of Kilwinning to levy dues upon them. Glasgow was the first lodge to escape from the jurisdiction of Kilwinning, and Gould thinks it unlikely than an insignificant place that claimed to be the source of Scottish Freemasonry should have authority over an important city like Glasgow. It was certainly not likely that the Deacon of a lodge holding its head court in an upper chamber in a small country village should have any rule or power, Masonically or otherwise.

However, the members of Kilwinning did not want to lose their Masonic influence, and in 1677 they chartered a lodge in the city of Edinburgh. This was a direct invasion of the jurisdiction of the Edinburgh Lodge and contrary to the Schaw Statutes, No. 2. To all intents and purposes, it was a new lodge that was authorized to assemble, subject to its parent at Kilwinning. Gould says this is the first recorded instance in Great Britain of a premier lodge taking upon itself the functions of a Grand Lodge for Scotland, although he does not think it was authorized to do so.

He says it is clear that the ancient statutes were not looked upon as unalterable; frequent departures from their exact requirements were entered in the records. So long as the intention and spirit were preserved the members did not servilely obey every item. Provided any new law was passed in the regular way, the old enactments could be overruled. For example, the ninth rule of the Schaw Statutes, No. 2, which prohibited admissions taking place outside the precincts of the Kirk of Kilwinning was not always followed.

A minute of 1720 says that a plurality of members, having taken into consideration the many problems and debates occasioned by entering freemen, agreed that no freeman be entered or passed without conveying his money before he be admitted either in the lodge or elsewhere. Gould says this means it had became clear to the chief promoters of the lodge that numbers brought wealth, and rejections meant loss of funds to the box.

In 1735 two individuals claimed to belong to the court, one having been entered by a member resident in Girvan (thirty-five miles from Kilwinning), and the other under similar circumstances in Maybole. Half the fee for entry was paid at the time, and on 12 July the balance was tendered. The lodge accepted this, the members having satisfied themselves that the couple were in possession of the word. Other instances occur of private modes of admission on behalf of the mother lodge, and, so long as the fees were paid, the old regulation was ignored.

A majority of brethren at the meeting of Kilwinning Lodge held on 20 December 1725, decided to discharge two of its members from entering the 'societie of honest men' belonging to the Lodge of Kilwinning, and also to charge every freeman to give them 'no strocke of worke under the penaltie of £20 Scots, until they be convinced of their cryme'. This was a severe sentence, because it meant the Masonic criminals thus banned were unable to obtain work. Two years afterwards they again appeared before the lodge, this time to acknowledge their fault, pay their fine and be restored to membership and their means of employment. Gould thinks that in the interim they most likely asked pardon for the offence they had committed –

they certainly are minuted as regretting the consequences of their misdeeds, if not the faults themselves!

The fees for the admission of apprentices were gradually raised from 23s. 4d. in 1685-89 to 40s. 4d. in 1704-5. In 1736 Kilwinning began to charge its fees in English money. A non-working mason was charged 10s. sterling as an apprentice, and 6s. as a fellowcraft, half being placed in the box and appropriated for Liveries, etc. The fees for working masons were a crown and half-a-crown respectively, and 1s. and 6d. for liveries. It was also agreed that every gentleman Mason would pay 1s. sterling annually, and every working Mason 'or other mechannick' 6d. sterling. It was also decided that if anyone failed to pay each defaulter 'shall be distressed for the same, on a signed complaint to a justice of the peace, or other magistrate, and his warrant obtained for that effect'.

The Kilwinning version of the Old Charge included the clause to resort to the common law 'as usuallie is', in the event of the ruling of the masters and fellows not being respected, and it seems that without the occasional invocation of the strong arm of the law, the old lodges would have experienced more difficulty in collecting their arrears. Even with its aid, there were still defaulters. Unworthy members of the craft, vexed the Kilwinning brethren of those days, just as they do us today: in 1717 they passed a resolution that, 'as the lodge have been imposed upon by begging brethren, both here and at Irvine, it is resolved that no charity be given to travelling brethren without an order from the Master'.

Gould says that the records from 1720 show that so many gentlemen and tradesmen sought admission to the ranks of Kilwinning, that the lodge could no longer be thought of as operative.

The Grand Lodge of Scotland was formed in 1736; before that Head Lodges, with Kilwinning being the chief one, had exercised the Grand Lodge functions. Though they joined with the other lodges to form the Grand Lodge at Edinburgh, the Kilwinning members continued to grant warrants after 1736. The brethren were never happy at accepting the second position on the roll, and maintained their ancient right to be independent. Gould says that before 1736 Mother Kilwinning constituted at least three lodges (and probably several others): Canongate Kilwinning No. 2, Torphichen Kilwinning No. 13, and Kilmarnock Kilwinning. But, he says, there are numerous references in old papers that testify that the Kilwinningites were actively engaged in extending their influence by chartering lodges from 1670 onwards. A lodge warranted for Paisley by the authority of Mother Kilwinning took the number 77, and later charters numbered 78 and 79 were issued to Eaglesham and East Kilbride. The published lists of Kilwinning charters record only 33, so it is clear there are more than forty lodges still unaccounted for. Gould thinks these are likely to have been constituted by Mother Kilwinning before 1736, rather than later, and several were established during the latter part of the seventeenth century. This accounts for the number of old lodges that append the name Kilwinning to their own special titles, such as Hamilton Kilwinning, Dalkeith Kilwinning, Greenock Kilwinning, St John's Kilwinning and Kirkwall Kilwinning and others, whose claims to antiquity range from 1599 to 1728. The lodge issued seventy-nine warrants down to 1803, but Gould was unable to trace half that number.

Gould points out that, throughout all these vicissitudes, struggles and rivalries surrounding the formation of the Grand Lodge of Scotland, the different parties never fell out about the correct knowledge of the secrets of Freemasonry. The Grand Lodge and its subordinates accepted the *members* of Kilwinning and its offshoots as Masons, even when their lodges were not accepted. The old lodges that joined the Grand Lodge had sufficient esoteric knowledge to ensure a brotherly greeting from post-Grand-Lodge organizations. Friendly intercourse between the old and the new systems of Masonic government was uninterrupted for many years after 1736. And even when the Edinburgh Freemasons introduced changes following the visit of a Past Grand Master of the Grand Lodge of England in 1721, the fellowship between the friendly rivals remained unaltered. Gould says this proves that the old forms of reception had been retained as a common means of recognition, whatever else was added in Edinburgh from England.

The degree of Master Mason was mentioned for the first time in Kilwinning records on 24 June 1736, when a by-law was passed that 'such as are found to be qualified as apprentices and fellow-crafts shall be raised to the dignity of a Master *gratis*'. However the terms 'enter', 'receive' and 'pass', occur in the warrant to the lodge chartered by Kilwinning in 1677.

Deacon was the designation of the chief officer in Kilwinning from time immemorial, until in 1735 the presiding officer was first termed 'Master of ye Freemasons', in the following year the prefix 'Right Worshipful' was used, and soon afterwards the same officer is referred to as 'The Right Worshipful Master'. The year 1735 saw the addition of a second Warden, entitled the junior, but Wardens did not assume the chair in the absence of the Deacon; under such circumstances, the members elected the chairman.

Lodge of Edinburgh No. 1

Gould records that this ancient lodge holds records dating back to 1599 and continuing until 1736, when the Grand Lodge of Scotland was inaugurated. When this ancient lodge originated is not known, but the memorandum affixed to its title on the Poll of Lodges holding under the Grand Lodge of Scotland simply says 'before 1598'.

Its earliest minute bears the date 'Ultimo July 1599' and is a deliverance on a breach of the statute against the employment of cowans. Bro. George Patoun vexed the Deacon, Warden, and Master Masons, by employing 'ane cowane to work at ane chymnay heid'. However, when he expressed his humble penitence, the penalty was not imposed – although he, and all others, were warned of what awaited them, should they ever again violate the law, after this act of leniency. The Warden's mark is appended to the minute.

Gould says that the fact the lodge was in existence and flourishing at least a year before its earliest minute is clear from the fact that the Schaw Statutes, No. 2, rule 3, styles it the first and principal lodge *in Scotland*. The Lodge's unbroken series of minutes from 1599 continues down to 1883, extending over nearly three centuries, and Gould sees this extraordinary preservation of the records of its transactions and the continuity of its life as a lodge as the strongest link in the chain of evidence proving that several lodges, working long before the epoch of Grand Lodges, united to form such organizations. From the history of the Lodge of Edinburgh, he says, we can see that these lodges all retained their autonomy and their inherent right of assembling without warrants.

The Lodge of Edinburgh retains two items of uncertain date, but in the same handwriting as the minute of 1599. The first is a record that Wardens are to be chosen yearly upon St John the Evangelist's Day. The second says that commissioners shall be elected at the same meeting, and they are to act as conveners, by command of the General Warden (William Schaw).

Although the Schaw Statutes, No. 2, rule 13, provides for an annual test of the skill as masons of apprentices and craftsmen, neither the Kilwinning nor the Edinburgh Lodge minutes contain any account that such yearly trials of skill were carried out. It has been argued that the final examination and decision rested with the Incorporation of Mary's Chapel, so far as Edinburgh was concerned, and not with the lodge, the two being quite separate bodies. But, as the Schaw Statutes affected the lodges only, Gould does not agree with this view.

On 30 January 1683 the Edinburgh lodge objected to a son of the late Deacon Brown being passed as a fellow-craft, because he was only nineteen, and, therefore, too young to be admitted to acceptance as a Master, the minimum age being fixed at twenty-one years. Three present at the meeting are termed 'old dickins' (deacons), a description that Gould believes corresponds with a modern Past Master.

In 1714 the lodge prohibited its journeymen from acting as Deacons, Wardens, or Intendents. (The office of intendar is an ancient one, a relic of the custom of appointing operative instructors to the non-operative or speculative members.)

The Incorporation of Wrights and Masons was constituted by an act of the Magistrates and other authorities of Edinburgh in 1475, and, though originally confined to the members of those two trades, in time it received glaziers, plumbers and others, by decision of the Court of Session (1703). It was usually known as the United Incorporation of Mary's Chapel, as its meetings were held in a chapel dedicated to the Virgin Mary, which was swept away when the South Bridge was built in 1785. Since the Edinburgh Lodge met in the same building, it took the rather curious name of The Lodge of Edinburgh (Mary's Chapel).

In 1475 a petition of the Masons and Wrights was presented to the Lord Provost for the purpose of obtaining certain statutes for the regular government of the two crafts. The Provost found them to be 'gud and loveable baith to God and man', so their petition was granted. These statutes are recited in the document of 15 October 1475:

1. Two masons and two wrights were to be sworn to act faithfully as overseers of the work of the allied crafts.
2. All complaints to be referred to the deacon and the four overseers, and, in the last resort, to the Provost and Bailies (magistrates).
3. Craftsmen entering the city and desirous of obtaining work were to pass an examination before the said four men, and, if

accepted, were to give a Mark [currency unit] to the repair of the altar.

4. Masters were not to take apprentices for less than seven years; the latter to pay half a Mark at entry, and to be fined for disobedience. Apprentices duly 'passed' by the overseers were to pay half a Mark to the altar, and each man 'worthy to be a master' was to be made 'freman and fallow'.

5. Those causing discord were to be brought before the Deacon and Overmen [the four overseers], so as to secure their better behaviour, but, if still contumacious, they were threatened with the strong arm of the law,

6. The overseers were charged to take part in all general processions, 'lyk as thai haf in the towne of Bruges, or siclyk gud townes', and should one of the number die and leave 'no guds sufficient to bring him furth honestly', the wrights (or masons) shall, at their own cost, provide a befitting funeral for 'their brother of the Craft'.

7. The masons and wrights were empowered to pass other statutes, which were to have similar force to the foregoing, on being allowed by the authorities, and upon their being entered in the 'common buke of Edinburgh'.

The passing of fellow-crafts, either masons or wrights, was delegated to overseers appointed by both trades, who together formed a quartet of inspectors.

The lodge used every means in its power to prevent 'unfremen', as they were called, from engaging in work on their own account in the city of Edinburgh. In 1599 the free masters placed Alexander Scheill outside the pale; they were not allowed to employ him because he defied the lodge by working as a master without their consent. Even those who lawfully served their apprenticeships could not obtain work unless they had the consent of the lodge.

The Free Masters viewed any spirit of enterprise amongst the apprentices with great horror. They discouraged it in every possible way, even though early statutes allowed apprentices to undertake work under some circumstances. There was a case in 1607 of an apprentice who passed as a fellow-craft and received his freedom but was not allowed to take work for two and a half years from the date of being freed to do so by Mary's Chapel! Neither was such a conditional freeman allowed to work outside Edinburgh during the waiting period. He was left no choice but to keep working for his Master.

'The brethreine fremen of the masones of Edr.' in 1652, found that 'a maisone jorneyman' had wronged them in several relations, and agreed unanimously not to give the offender work within their area for seven years, and not even then until he had paid a suitable fine. They did not permit craftsmen to be imported, and set their faces against employing anyone not approved by the lodge. And in 1672 strangers hailing from a town about three miles from the city were subjected to all manner of annoyances for seven years to stop them getting work. Eventually they gave up the struggle and left in 1680.

Gould says that, beyond such exhibitions of spleen and the imposition of fines, outsiders were not otherwise interfered with – from which he infers that the lodge had no real authority over craftsmen who did not acknowledge its rights and privileges. Naturally the members were averse to seeing any of their customs neglected, especially when their funds suffered, so they were not inclined to pass apprentices to fellow-crafts unless they agreed to pay the appropriate fees.

In 1681 it was resolved that no masters should employ any apprentices who acted as journeymen, until they were passed. The Deacon, Warden and remnant Masters agreed, for the sake of their funds for the poor, that each journeyman who did not belong to the lodge should pay the sum of 12s. (Scots) per annum, for the privilege of working for a freeman. The money was to be deducted from his first month's pay by his master, and given to the Warden. If he did not pay, the journeyman was to be discharged from working in the city (which meant he could not be employed by any member of the lodge), and the Master was censured.

The Incorporation did not confine itself to following the wishes of the lodge. In 1685 it agreed to accept fees from the apprentices of journeymen (not Masters) for whom they charged wages, just as if they were regular journeymen. Although this was in direct opposition to the lodge, it was of direct benefit to their own funds.

Gould notes that, however strong their declarations of support for the Schaw Statutes, the Edinburgh Freemasons in the seventeenth century easily departed from the rules when it suited them. He cites the length of time an apprentice had to serve as a case in point. Although this was fixed by the Schaw deeds to a minimum of seven years, it was varied according to the whims of individual members of the lodge. The seven years was often reduced to a much shorter period at Edinburgh and Kilwinning. Even in those early days, the regulations of the General Warden, the highest Masonic official in Scotland, were not accepted as unalterable landmarks. As late as 1739 the Grand Lodge of Scotland agreed to bind, at its expense, the son of a poor operative mason to one of the Freemen Masons of Edinburgh, and the indentures were agreed for the period of eight years.

Just as the period of an apprenticeship varied so did the wages the masons received. In Aberdeen, a Master Mason employed on church work by the Town Council received £24 16s. 8d. Scots per quarter (a little over £2 sterling), and his journeyman 20 marks per annum (£1 6s. 8d.). In 1500 the masons engaged in building the steeple of the Old Tolbooth were paid weekly, each master 10s. Scots (10d. sterling) and each journeyman 9s. Scots (9d. sterling). In 1536 a Master Mason employed by the town of Dundee was paid every six weeks at the rate of £24 Scots, and £10 Scots per annum for his apprentice. At Lundie, in Fife, in 1661 the master had 10d. per day, and his journeyman 9d., and all their diet in the house. In 1691 the value of skilled labour had increased, for the Incorporation of Mary's Chapel ruled that no mason should work for under 18s. Scots per day in summer, and 2s. less in winter.

The hours of labour also varied. A Master Mason and his journeymen working on the college kirk of St Giles in 1491 began their work at 5 a.m. in the summer, and continued until 8 a.m. Then they were allowed half an hour's break. They started again at 8.30 a.m. until to 11 a.m., when they got a further two hours off. At 1 p.m. they started working again until 4 p.m. and then got 'a recreatioun in the commoun loge be the space of half ane hour', the remainder of the time from 4.30 p.m. to 7 p.m. was devoted to 'lawbour continually'. In winter the work started at dawn, the hours being otherwise the same, and they laboured until 'day licht begane' and darkness returned.

Although the records of Aberdeen Borough council contain the earliest use of the word 'luge' (lodge) in connection with the Scottish craft Gould notes that an earlier instance occurred at York more than a century before, in the Fabric Rolls' of York Minster. The context establishes the fact that at both periods the word 'lodge' meant a covered shed in which the Freemasons assembled to shape the stones, to which only the regular craft had access – cowans especially being excluded.

The Schaw Statutes, No. 1, said that the lodge was to make sure it recorded its decisions and actions. The members grew careless about the matter, and eventually the writing in the minutes devolved upon any member who was prepared to do it. As a result, many important matters were passed over. For example, not a single register of the annual election of Wardens was made during the seventeenth century, though their names can be traced through their signatures of those present at the meetings. From 1701 onward the annual elections were systematically recorded.

Gould tells us that the relationship of the journeymen of the Lodge of Edinburgh was fraught with difficulty. Eventually there was an open rupture with the Master Masons, and the journeymen severed their connection and created a new lodge called Journeymen Lodge, No. 8. Though they were supposed to have had a say in the affairs of No. 1 from Schaw's time, they were ignored. The Lodge of Edinburgh was virtually an extension of the Incorporation of masters, the Deacon of the masons, in his Incorporate role, was also the head of the lodge and held his appointment by virtue of the goodwill of its members, who were recognized as Master Masons by the municipal authorities.

Gould thinks that the same brother holding the offices of Deacon and Warden was a most unwise combination. From early days to the eighteenth century, the Warden acted as Treasurer, the corresponding officer in the Incorporation being the ' Box Master,' an office known in some of the seventeenth-century lodges. The unlimited powers of the Warden to dispense funds were prejudicial to the interests of the members. On St John's Day 1704 the lodge decided that no portion of the moneys in the common purse was to be disposed of without the consent of the Deacon and a quorum of the brethren.

The early minutes of the Lodges Nos. 0 and 1 make no mention of the initiation of a Clerk, but Gould sees no reason to suppose that the minute-takers were not regularly admitted. The first notice of this kind occurs in the records of No. 1, on 23 December 1706, when William Marshall, Clerk to the Incorporation, was admitted as an entered apprentice and fellow-craft and Clerk to the Brethren Masons, whom he is freely to serve for the honour conferred on him. On St John's Day 1709 Robert Alison was similarly admitted; his was the last election under the old system. Bro. Alison continued to act as Clerk to the Lodge for 43 years. In 1736 he was elected the first Clerk to the Grand Lodge of Scotland but he remained secretary of No. 1, and his son was initiated on St John's Day 1737 without cost, on account of his father's services.

It was common practice in early Scottish lodges to give glove money or make a contribution to the lodge chest. But the Incorporation of Mary's Chapel went further than this; it also kept a stock of weapons which intrants contributed to. (On 6 September 1683 the Deacons, Masters and Brethren present decided it was unprofitable, and possibly dangerous, to keep adding to their magazine the arms that each Freeman had to contribute to on admission. They decided to accept money instead, which, besides being 'usefull in the meantyme', could be used to buy implements of warfare if and when needed; so, instead of contributing to the stock of arms, Freemen paid £12 Scots to the Box Master.) Several entries of £3 10s. paid for firelocks show that the Incorporation's cash was used to provide warlike weapons, if not directly for warlike purposes. But the craftsmen of the Incorporation were not satisfied with merely having the sinews of war; they wanted arms that were useful defensively. They fortified their meeting house, and made it suitable for the safe storage of arms 'keeped and reserved' for the defence of the true Protestant religion, king and country, and for the defence of the 'ancient cittie' and their own privileges therein. They demanded of initiates that 'armes be given to the house', so that all Brethren might have the means at hand 'to adventure their lives and fortunes in defence of one and all of the objects named'. (Those craftsmen had no doubt that the Presbyterian religion was the true kind. Their meeting house was granted the right to be used as a place of Presbyterian worship in 1687.)

There are recorded instances of old Scottish lodges, allowing a widow to occupy the position of Dame, in place of a Master Mason, following her husband's death. Gould has no doubt that such occurrences were frequent, though not always cited in the records, and quotes as confirmation a minute of 17 April 1683 from the books of the Lodge of Edinburgh. The Deacon, Warden, and several Masters agreed, that a widow might, with the assistance of a competent freeman, receive the benefit of any work offered to her by the ancient customers of her deceased husband, and the freeman who thus obliged her was prohibited, under heavy pains and penalties, from taking any profit from his assistance. The widows of Freemasons occupied an anomalous position, and whilst Gould cannot help giving credit to the motives that prompted the passing of the previous resolution, it seems the members were anxious to guard against Masonic dames becoming potential rivals. The widows of Freemasons, although permitted to continue to oversee their husband's trade interests, were not permitted to join the lodge.

The early records of the lodge are mainly taken up with accounts of the admission and recording of apprentices. But, unlike today, apprentices were frequently present in the lodge during the making or passing of fellow-crafts, and they also attended as active members (apprentices are mentioned as consenting and assenting to the entries made of new receptions). Gould believes this shows that whatever Masonic secrets were known to the lodge, all its members freely participated in them, from the youngest apprentice to the oldest Master mason, until the era of separate degrees was inaugurated in the last century.

The minutes of St John's Day 1721 introduce an office which is unknown today, that of eldest entered apprentice. Alexander Smely accepted that position, and promised to be faithful therein for the ensuing year. The eldest apprentice officiated on 2 March 1732 at the passing of a fellow-craft, and it was his duty to act as president at any assemblies of apprentices. This old title later disappeared, though Gould does not say when. He does, however, give a list of the dates of the introduction of titles and their adoption into the Lodge of Edinburgh:

1598	Warden, who was president and treasurer, and clerk
1599	Deacon, who acted as president, with warden as treasurer
1710	Chairman first called 'preses'
1712	Officer, Tyler from 1763 who acted as outer guard
1731	Presiding officer designated 'Grand Master'
1735	Presiding officer designated 'Master'
1736	Depute Master first appointed
1737	Senior and Junior Wardens, treasurer, and two stewards
1739	'Old Master' ('Past Master' from 1798)
1759	Substitute Master
1771	Master of Ceremonies
1798	Chaplain
1809	Deacons
1814	Standard Bearers
1814	Inside and Outside Tylers
1836	Architect

1840 Jeweller
1848 Trustees
1865 Director of Music

The office of Clerk to the Lodge was a life appointment until 1752, when it became subject to an annual election. In 1690 William Livingstone, writer in Edinburgh, presented a petition to Parliament 'praying to be reponed in office as clerk to the Incorporation of Mary's Chapel, to which he had been appointed *ad vitam aut culpam*, and from which he had been deposed', because he refused to comply with the Test Act of 1681. His petition was granted and the Incorporation ordered to reinstate him.

Before Gould concluded these excerpts from the records of the Lodge of Edinburgh, he went on to mention the admission of speculative masons. He used the word 'speculative' to mean someone who has been admitted as a mason, without any intention of qualifying as such, save in respect of any esoteric knowledge or peculiar privileges. The earliest minute noting the presence of a speculative freeman mason in a lodge, and taking part in its deliberations, is dated 8 June 1600. When the brother in question was initiated it is impossible now to decide; suffice it to say that 'Jhone Boiswell of Aichinilek, with the other Master Masons did afxit yr markis' to witness the accuracy of the entry. The clerk styled Bro. Boiswell 'ye Laird of Aichinilek'. He was present at a special assembly at 'Halerudhous', and the 'Master of ye werk to ye Kingis Ma'stie' was present. The meeting was convened to decide how much 'Jhone Broune, Warden of ye Ludge of Edr.' was to pay for having 'contraveinit ane actt'. If it had been unusual for a non-operative or speculative brother (for they were all called brethren even then) to take part in a Masonic meeting it would never have been allowed to pass without any comment or addition of any kind in the minutes. Indeed other old lodges, such as Kilwinning and Aberdeen, permitted non-operatives to rule over them. But Gould confined himself to seventeenth-century initiations. The chief of these, accepted by the Lodge of Edinburgh, is described in the ancient records in the following manner:

The 3 day off Joulay 1634. The quhilk day the Right honirabell my Lord Alexander is admitet folowe off the craft be Hewe Forest, diken, and Alexander Nesbet, warden; and the hell rest off the mesteres off mesones off Edenbroch; and therto eurie mester heath supscriuet with ther handes or set to ther markes [Deacon and Warden's marks], Jn. Watt, Thomas Paterstone, Alexander, John Mylln.

Similar entries confirm the initiation of Anthonie Alexander, Rt Hon. Master of Work to his Majesty, and Sir Alexander Strachan of Thorntoun on the same date, and of Archibald Steuaret in July 1635. On 27 December 1636,

> Johne Myllne, dekene and warden, with the heall consent of the heall masters, frie mesones of Ednr., Dauied Dellap, prentes to Parech Breuch, is med an entert prentes.

On 25 August and 27 December 1637 David Ramsay and Alexander Alerdis were admitted to membership, the former as a fellow and brother of the craft, the latter as a 'fellow off craft in and amongst the Mrs off the loudg'.

On 16 February 1638 Herie Alexander, 'Mr off Work' to his Majesty, was received as a fellow and brother, and on 20 May 1640 James Hamiltone, Deacon, and Johne Meyenis, Warden, 'and the rest off Mrs off meson off Edenbr. conuened, admitted the Right Hon. Alexander Hamiltone, Generall of the Artelerie of thes kindom, to be felow and Mr off the forsed craft'. Further entries show the admission on 27 July 1647 of William Maxwell, 'doctor off Fisek', and on 2 March 1653 of James Neilsone, 'master sklaitter to his majestie' who had been 'entered and past in the Lodge of Linlithgow'. On 27 December 1667 Sir Patrick Flume of Polwarth was admitted as fellow of craft and Master. On 24 June 1670 the Right Hon. Mr William Morray, 'His Mai'ties Justic Deput', Mr Walter Pringle, 'Advocat', and the Rt Hon. Sir John Harper of Cambusnethen were initiated as brothers.

Gould tells us that Lord Alexander, who died in 1638, was admitted as a fellow-craft in 1634, with his brother Sir Anthony Alexander. They were the sons of the first Earl of Stirling and took an active interest in the Freemasonry; they frequently attended the meetings and signed the records, usually adding their marks (Sir Alexander Strachan also regularly signed records with his mark too). Sir Anthony Alexander, who died in 1637, was at the time of his reception Master of Work to Charles I, and presided over an important assembly of master tradesmen at Falkland on 26 October 1636. To judge from his signature, Archibald Stewart, who was initiated July 1635, was also a man of education, and – as he attended the lodge with the three brethren mentioned, and they vouched for him – it is probable that he was a personal friend of theirs.

The David Ramsay mentioned in the excerpt of 25 August 1637 was 'a gentleman of the Privy Chamber' according to Bishop Burnet and Henrie Alexander, who was passed a fellow-craft in the following year, succeeded his brother as General Warden and Master of Work to King Charles I. He became the third Earl of Stirling and was a regular attender at the Lodge of Edinburgh, and also visited Atcheson Haven Lodge on 27 March 1638.

The Right Hon. William Murray, who became a fellow-craft in 1670, was a member of the Faculty of Advocates and rose to high legal office. Walter Pringle, also an advocate, was the second son of John Pringle by his wife Lady Margaret Scott (daughter of the Earl of Buccleuch) and brother of Robert Pringle, the first baronet of Stitchel. Sir John Harper was another member of the Scottish Bar, and Sheriff Depute of the county of Lanark.

The intrants Gen. Alexander Hamilton, on 20 May, 1640, and the Rt Hon. Sir Patrick Hume, Bt., on 27 December, 1667, are specially recorded as being constituted 'felow and Mr of the forsed craft', and 'fellow of craft (and Master) of this lodg', respectively. These two brethren were speculative members, yet no objection was raised to their being raised as Masters, although Gould is confident that they did not set up as master masons on their own account!

Many of the operatives did not like the introduction of the speculative Masons, and promoters and opponents of the innovation divided into hostile camps. Eventually those supporting the Gentlemen, or Geomatic, Masons won the day, and the Domatics had to give in to the powerful influences arrayed against them. In the Lodge of Edinburgh the Domatics held the balance of power, but by 1670 the majority in the Lodge of Aberdeen were speculative members!

Gen. Hamilton was serving with the Scottish army at Newcastle on 20 May 1641, when he took part in the admission of 'Mr the Right Honerabell Mr Robert Moray [Murray], General Quarter Mr to the armie off Scotlan'. The minutes of this meeting were accepted by the authorities of the Lodge of Edinburgh as taking place beyond the boundaries of the Scottish kingdom. [General Hamilton was commanding the rebel Coventanter Army that was occupying

Newcastle in defiance of King Charles I in the early stages of the Civil War.] The minute says 'the same bing approven be the hell mester off the mesone of the Log. off Edenbroth', and the entry is ratified by the signatures and marks of four brethren, including the two Generals. The Quartermaster-General later took part in the business of the lodge held in Edinburgh 27 July 1647, on the occasion of the admission of Dr William Maxwell.

Irregular admissions were not so readily condoned in the case of ordinary operatives. It made a great difference who presided at the meetings. On 27 December 1679 John Fulton, one of the freemen, was sent to Coventry, and his servants called upon to leave his employ, because of his presuming to 'pass and enter severall gentlemen without licence or commission from this place'. Bro. Fulton chose the neighbourhood of Ayr to introduce speculative members into the Fraternity, and his conduct so greatly aroused the ire of the authorities that he humbly supplicated a return of his privileges, paid £4 as a fine, and promised to behave as a brother for the future. At this show of contrition Masters of Edinburgh relented, and he was duly 'reponed'. But he was not censured for receiving gentlemen as Masons, either in or out of the lodge: it was his failure to seek prior permission that got him into trouble.

The earliest use of the word Freemason, Gould thinks may be traced back to 1581, when the Melrose version of the Old Charges was originally written. The expression Free Mason ('Frie mason') occurs frequently, and is used synonymously with Freemen Masons, the term 'Frie-men' being cited as equivalent to Freemason. There are so many examples of the use of terms like Freemen, Freemasons, Brother Freemen, Freemen Masters, going back to the fifteenth century, that Gould says he cannot see how any other interpretation can be placed upon them.

Canongate Kilwinning Lodge, No. 2

For some lodges in the seventeenth century it was common practice to permit favoured members to enter and pass Masons at places other than their regular meeting rooms. This could cause irregularity in ceremonies and eroded the exercise of central control over admissions that is such a feature of English Grand Lodge Freemasonry. These travelling initiations were reported at the next assembly of the lodge, where they were minuted, the fees paid, and membership allowed. Such ad hoc assemblies brought together to make a Mason were not considered to be a separate regular lodge, just an irregular meeting of the main lodge. On 20 December 1677 this changed. On that date Lodge of Kilwinning, No. 0, issued the first warrant to consecrate a new lodge to several of their own members resident in the Canongate, Edinburgh. This was a direct challenge to the jurisdiction of the Lodge of Edinburgh, No. 1. This was not simply a charter to enable Kilwinning members to meet as masons in Edinburgh, it empowered them to act as an independent lodge with the same powers as Mother Kilwinning herself. It totally disregarded the proximity of what the second Schaw Statues described as the First and Head Lodge of Scotland.

Gould had already noted what he called a Masonically friendly invasion of England was consummated in 1641 in Newcastle by the Lodge of Edinburgh, No. 1. But that meeting was confined to the initiation of their own countrymen, and there the matter ended. The authority granted to the Canongate Kilwinning Lodge was a warrant for its constitution and separate existence, and it has survived to this day.

The charter of this lodge, which Gould calls the Premier Scottish Warrant of Constitution, runs as follows:

> At the ludge of Killwining the twentie day of december 1677 yeares, deacons and wardanes and the rest of the brethren, considering the love and favour showne to us be the rest of the brethren of the canuigate in Edinbroughe, ane part of our number being willing to be boked and inroled the qch day gives power and liberty to them to enter, receave, and pass any qualified persons that they think fitt, in name and behalf of the ludge of Killwinning, and to pay ther entry and booking moneys due to the sd ludge, as we do our selves, they sending on of ther number to us yearly, and we to do the lyke to them if need be. The qlk day ther names are insert into this book.

The document was signed by twelve brethren, and their marks were attached. The record of the transaction in the minutes of the Canongate Kilwinning Lodge for 1736, the year after that from which its earliest writings are believed to date, is not a correct version of the proceedings, and, Gould says, appears to have been written to sustain a claim by the members to a high position on the Scottish roll. The lodge was reorganized in 1735 by speculative Freemasons, and in that year the members first recorded their working of the third degree.

No. 2 played an important part in the inauguration of the Grand Lodge of Scotland, as it provided the First Grand Master Mason of Scotland and published William St Clair's formal resignation from a previously hereditary office, as already discussed. The newly formed Grand Lodge of Scotland acknowledged that Lodge Canongate Kilwining dates from 20 December 1677.

Scoon and Perth Lodge, No. 3

This ancient lodge is much older than No. 2, but had to be satisfied with its position as fourth on the roll, even though the Grand Lodge of Scotland agreed that it existed before 1658.

Gould tells us that the lodge holds a paper known as its Charter, which is dated 24 December 1658. This document is signed by J. Roch, Master Mason, Andro Norie, Warden, and 39 members and is quite different from any other of the seventeenth-century manuscripts. It combines features of the Old Charges with items of local interest, and also recites the Kilwinning and other legends. It speaks of the Lodge of Scoon as being second in the nation, priority being given to Kilwinning, and observes a singular reticence about Edinburgh. The Masons are frequently described as Masters, 'Friemen' and fellow-crafts, and the recital of the traditions and laws begins 'In the name of God, amen'. The conclusion is unique, and Gould gives it in full:

> And Lastlie, wee, and all of ws off ane mynd, consent, and assent, doe bind and obleidge ws, and our successoris, to mantayne and wphold the haill liberties and previledges of the said Lodge of Scoon, as ane frie Lodge, for entering and passing within ourselves, as the bodie thereof, residing within the burgh of Perth as sd is; And that soe long as the Sun ryseth in the East and setteth in the West, as we wold wish the blessing of God to attend us in all our wayes and actiones.

This reference to the movements of that glorious luminary of nature, as the ritual calls it, suggests that speculative Freemasonry was known in the city of Perth at this time. The term 'free lodge' is most expressive, pointing to the use of the word 'free' as a prefix to Mason.

Gould notes the same record as stating that, according to the 'Knowledge of our predecessoris ther cam one from the North countrie, named Johne Mylne, ane measone or man we'll experted in his calling, who entered himselff both frieman and burges of this brugh'. John Mylne went on to be Master Mason to the king and Master of the Lodge of Scoon. His son, also called John, succeeded him in both offices, and the lodge records note that:

His Majestie King James the Sixt, of blessed memorie, who by the said second Johne Mylne, was by the King's own desire entered Freeman, measone, and fellow-craft.

Gould records this additional remark about that Royal Initiation:

During all his lyfetime King James VI mantayned the same as ane member of the Lodge of Scoon, so that this Lodge is the most famous Lodge (iff weill ordered) within the kingdome.

Several generations of the Mylne family were master masons to their majesties the Kings of Scotland until 1657, when:

the last Mr Mylne being Mr off the Lodge off Scoon, deceased, left behind him ane compleit Lodge of measones, friemen, and fellow-crafts, wh such off then number as wardens and others to oversie them, and ordained that one of the said number should choyse one of themselves to succeid as master in his place.

The Master they choose was Bro. James Roch, with Andrew Norie as his Warden. Both agreed to confirm the old acts:

1. No frieman to contradict another unlawfully.
2. 'Nor goe to no other Lodge, nor mak ane Lodge among themselves, seeing this Lodge is the prime within the Shyre.'
3. If any freeman leave the lodge for another, he can only return on payment of three times the sum eligible on his joining either, and shall 'be put clean from the company of the lodge he was last in'.
4. The Master and Warden before named to see these rules carried out.
5. No master to take another's work unless so entitled.

6. Masters not to 'go between' their fellows engaged in seeking work.

7. Apprentices and journeymen belonging to this (or any other) lodge must have their free discharge from their previous masters prior to re-engagement; an exception, however, permitted in the case of twenty days' services only.

8. All fellow-crafts passed in this lodge, shall pay £16 (Scots), beside the gloves and dues, with £3 (Scots) at their ' first incoming, after they are past'.

9. If these sums are not paid at once, 'cautioners' must be obtained outside the lodge.

10. Apprentices not to take work above 40s. (Scots), and not to have apprentices under the penalty of being 'dabared from the libertie of the said Lodge'.

The Mylnes were a famous Masonic family. The third John Mylne was called to Edinburgh in 1616 to erect a statue of the king. In 1631 he was appointed Master Mason to Charles I, and in 1633 he resigned in favour of his eldest son 'Johne Mylne, younger', who was a member of the Lodge of Edinburgh. Johne Mylne the younger became Deacon and Warden of the Lodge of Edinburgh in 1636. He served as Deacon for many years, being re-elected ten times during twenty-seven years. This John Mylne was at the Masonic Meeting at Newcastle in 1641 that initiated Sir Robert Moray [who would go on to be a founder member of the Royal Society]. John's brother Alexander was passed on 2 June 1635 at a meeting attended by Lord Alexander, Sir Anthony Alexander and Sir Alexander Strachan, in addition to his brother. Alexander Mylne's son Robert was apprenticed to his uncle John in Lodge No. 1 on 27 December 1653 and was elected Warden in 1663. In 1681 he became Deacon and continued to take a leading part in Masonic business until 1707.

Robert Mylne succeeded his uncle as Master Mason to Charles I, for the records of the Perth authorities describe him as the King's Master Mason when he signed an agreement with the burgh of Perth to rebuild the cross that had been removed from High Street, whilst Oliver Cromwell occupied the city. William Mylne, eldest son of Robert, was received into the Lodge of Edinburgh on 27 December 1681 and was Warden several times from 1695; he died in 1728. William's eldest son, Thomas Mylne, was entered and admitted as apprentice in the Lodge of Edinburgh on 27 December 1721. He went on to be chosen Eldest Prentice on 27 December 1722 and was admitted and received a fellow-craft on 27 December 1729. He became Master of the Lodge on 27 December 1735.

Robert and William Mylne (sons of Thomas) were also members of the lodge of Edinburgh. When Robert died, in 1811, he was buried in St Paul's Cathedral, having been surveyor of that building for fifty years. With the deaths of these two brothers the Mylne family's connection with the Lodge of Edinburgh, which had lasted five successive generations, came to an end.

Gould tells us that the ancient lodge at Perth joined the Grand Lodge of Scotland in 1742, not having taken any part in its creation.

Lodge of Glasgow St John, No. 3 bis

This is undoubtedly an old lodge, Gould says, as its name appears in the second of the St Clair Charters, which dates to 1628. A history of the lodge is attached to its by-laws (1858), and Gould adds that, if we concede its authenticity, he fails to see that the pedigree of the lodge could be any higher.

Money was needed to restore Glasgow's cathedral, and for this purpose the patronage of the king was sought. The charter states that

> The fraternity appointed by the Right Rev. Jocylin, Bishop of said Cathedral, with advice of the Abbots, Priors, and other clergy of his diocese, we devoutly receive and confirm by the support of our Royal protection, aye and until the finishing of the Cathedral itself; and all the collectors of the same fraternity, and those who request aid for its building, we have taken into our favour.

Gould does not accept that the word fraternity in this context means the lodge and sees the inference that the charter referred to a Masonic lodge as unwarranted by the context. He believes the intention was to describe a religious fraternity that had been formed to promote the renovation of the cathedral.

The first notice in the minutes of the Glasgow Incorporation of Masons bears the date 22 September 1620, and says:

> Entry of Apprentices to the Lodge of Glasgow, the last day of december 1613 years, compeared John Stewart, Deacon of

Masons, and signified to David Slater, Warden of the Lodge of Glasgow, and to the remenant brethren of that Lodge; that he was to enter John Stewart, his apprentice, in the said Lodge. Lykas upon the morn, being the first day of January 1614 years, the said warden and brethren of the said Lodge entered the said John Stewart, younger, apprentice to the said John Stewart, elder, conform to the acts and liberty of the Lodge.

In 1601 the Deacons' courts were made up of a Deacon, six Quartermasters, two Keepers of the Keys, an Officer, and Clerk. On 1 May 1622 James Ritchie of the Ludge of Glasgow was accused of hiring a cowan, although the records of the Incorporation say that the cowan in question was entered with a ludge, and had a discharge of a master in Paisley.

Although Gould can discover no old minutes of the lodge, he remarks that the above record proves its existence early in the seventeenth century. The Incorporation has existed from 1600 to the present time, and he has no doubt that the lodge also continued from at least 1613 to the start of its existing minutes, in 1628. It was represented on the occasion of the second St Clair Charter, as the signatures of 'The Ludge of Glasgow, John Boyd, deakin; Rob. Boyd, ane of the mestres' showed the assent of the lodge to the charter. The lodge was not put on the roll of the Grand Lodge of Scotland until 1850 when it was given the number 3 bis. It was not the fault of the members, Gould says, that they did not get a higher position. By then all the old lodges had joined the Grand Lodge, except the old Lodge of Melrose, which preferred isolation and independence.

The Lodge of Glasgow, unlike other pre-eighteenth-century lodges, was exclusively operative. Gould is satisfied it gave the Mason Word to entered apprentices, but it recognized no one as a member until they joined the Incorporation, which was composed of Mason Burgesses. The consecration of St Mungo's Lodge in 1729 was the result of a split brought about after an unsuccessful attempt to introduce non-operatives into the lodge. St John's Lodge, Glasgow did not admit non-operatives until 1842.

Canongate and Leith, Leith and Canongate Lodge, No. 5

This lodge dates from 1688 and arose from a schism with the Lodge of Edinburgh. The group who left were Masons in Leith and the Canongate, but, because they could not agree on the order of precedence of these locations, they named the lodge with each of them first and each last. They were accused of disobeying the Masonic laws by entering and passing Masons within the area controlled by the Lodge of Edinburgh and so forming a lodge amongst themselves without the authority of any royal or general warden.

The minutes of the Lodge of Edinburgh then contain a long list of pains and penalties that were to be used to stamp out the rebellion. They were not successful, however, as only one of the defaulters, James Thomson, returned to the fold. (He was pardoned when he paid a fine of £10 Scots.) The earliest minutes the lodge now possesses begin in 1830, but its charter of confirmation is dated 8 February 1738. The Grand Lodge of Scotland acknowledges this earlier date and also accepts that No. 5 is descended from the Mason lodge of Mary's Chapel in Edinburgh and the daughter lodge existed from 29 May 1688. The lodge was mainly a speculative one, for Gould records that, of the 52 names enrolled on 30 November 1736, only 18 were operative Masons!

Lodge of Old Kilwinning St John, Inverness, No. 6

The Grand Lodge of Scotland granted a charter of confirmation for this lodge on 30 November 1737. It admits the lodge had existed since 1678. Gould could find no record of its antiquity in the registers of Mother Kilwinning, though he quotes Laurie as saying, 'it goes the farthest back of all the Kilwinning lodges, none of the others going beyond 1724'. Gould believes this opinion is open to question.

Hamilton Kilwinning Lodge, No. 7

This lodge is admitted by the Grand Lodge of Scotland to date from the year 1695. Gould could find little of its history.

Lodge of Journeymen, Edinburgh, No. 8

This lodge is said to have been formed in 1709. Gould says that the Journeymen of Edinburgh have good reason to be proud of their position, considering the strong influence originally brought to bear against their lodge at its beginning.

The journeymen Masons were kept in a subordinate position. This was caused by the introduction of non-operative Masons into the Lodge of Edinburgh and by the domineering spirit of the Masters in both the Incorporation of Mary's Chapel and the lodge. The journeymen did not submit to this easily; as they increased in knowledge and the Master's monopolies were gradually abolished, they rebelled. In 1705 they were forbidden to work without a Master to employ them and take his share of the profit, if not the work. Gould thinks that the suppression of the journeymen in the lodge arose from their condition in life, rather than from their belonging to a lower grade in speculative Masonry. The masters were simply masters in trade, and not masters in the sense in which we now regard Master Masons in Masonic lodges, and were jealous of their trade monopolies.

The old records of No. 8 start in 1740, anything earlier being lost, but there is evidence that its origin and separation from No. 1 was in 1707, not 1709. In 1708 the journeymen of the No. 1 passed a resolution to raise money for the poor members. It was signed by 44 brethren. On 27 December 1708 the Journeymen presented a petition to the Lodge of Edinburgh asking for closer inspection of the accounts, and in response six discreet fellows were nominated as a committee of inspection. The smouldering embers of discontent were fanned into renewed life by the imposition of an annual subscription of 20s. Scots, to be paid by journeymen for the privilege of being employed by Masters of the Incorporation.

The decisions of the Lodge of Edinburgh in August 1712 completed the rupture. The Masters rescinded the resolution appointing the committee of inspection. When this resolution was passed all the journeymen but two left the lodge. They were led by James Watson, Deacon of the Incorporation, and Master of No. 1. Then war to the knife was declared. Those left behind in the lodge agreed that not one the journeymen should be taken back unless they gave full satisfaction for their contemptuous conduct, and the Masters forbade the apprentices to assist the journeymen and would not allow journeymen to enter their own apprentices, under the threat of being disowned by the parent lodge.

Gould says the desertion from No. 1 of the Deacon and Master (James Watson) was a severe blow to its prestige, but it meant the journeymen had a competent master to preside over them. On 9 February 1713 the parent lodge met and elected David Thomson to be Master of No. 1. He was succeeded by William Smellie, a determined antagonist of the breakaway journeymen, who put stringent measures in place against them. Meanwhile the journeymen were active and lost no opportunity to enter and pass Masons within jurisdiction of No. 1 to the detriment of the original lodge. The journeymen would not dissolve their society, despite the severity of the measures taken against them; even the united influence of the old Lodge and Incorporation could not suppress them. The opposition they met, and the indomitable courage they showed are unparalleled in the early history of the Scottish craft, Gould tells us, adding that the story shows how the powerful influence that the Lodge and Incorporation had wielded in the sixteenth and seventeenth centuries was on the wane.

The Lodge of Edinburgh assumed that the journeymen would be overawed and succumb of the law. The Incorporation and lodge jointly agreed to obtain a warrant for the capture and detention of two of the malcontents, William Brodie and Robert Winram, and these two journeymen were confined in the city guardhouse, and the books of their society seized. How long the detention lasted Gould could not discover, but the journeymen countered by bringing an action against the Deacon of the Wrights, the Deacon of the Masons (representing the Incorporation) and the Master of the Lodge for unlawful imprisonment of two of their number and the seizure of their records. The damages claimed were considerable. While the case was before the Lords of Council and Session, the dispute was referred to the arbitration of Robert Inglis (late Deacon of the Goldsmiths) on behalf of the plaintiffs, and Alexander Nisbet (late Deacon of the Surgeons) on the part of the defendants. They were unable to reach an amicable settlement, so the final decision was left to John Dunbar, Deacon of the Glovers, who was given full powers to obtain all necessary testimony. This was arranged on 29 November 1714. A 'Decreet Arbitral' was accepted and subscribed to on 8 January 1715 – a document that is without parallel Masonically. As Gould remarks, it proves that the craft had no insuperable objection to its disputes being settled under the sanction of the law.

The arbitrators awarded £100, to be paid to Brodie and Winram by the two Deacons, because they had used undue severity, and ordered that the books must be returned to their lawful owners on a receipt being given by the plaintiffs. They next decided that the Deacons and the whole body of Freemen Masters of the Incorporation of Masons were absolved from accounting to the journeymen for the money received for giving the mason word, as it is called, either to Freemen or journeymen, prior to the date of the Decreet Arbitral. To put an end to the disputes arising between the Freemen and journeymen about the giving of the mason word, the two Deacons were ordered to procure from their Incorporation an act or allowance permitting the journeymen to meet 'together by themselves as a society for giving the word'.

Two provisions were added to this judgment. The first was that the journeymen's meetings, actings and writings be only concerning their collecting the moneys for giving the mason word. The second was that the moneys thus obtained be used only for charitable purposes connected with themselves, that a register be kept of the moneys so received and disbursed, and that a chest be provided with two different locks, one key being kept by a Freeman mason elected annually by the Incorporation, and the other by one of the journeymen to be elected by themselves. The said Freeman was to attend the meetings, see all was done in order, and report, if need be, to his Incorporation. The journeymen were also ordered to produce their books and accounts to the Deacon of the Masons and the Incorporation each half-year. It was allowed that five journeymen could form a quorum to meet. Both parties were warned that if they broke the agreement they would be fined £100 Scots, but the Lodge of Edinburgh persistently ignored the award. The journeymen had to take further steps to enforce their claims, as well as to force return of their books.

Gould explains that this charge was discovered in the mid-nineteenth century by Mr David Laing of the Signet Library and deposited in the charter-box of the Lodge No. 8. Gould admits he cannot report the final result of the law case, as the records of the parent lodge, although containing a minute of its decision to contest the claim, are silent about the ultimate result. What they do say, however, is that the obnoxious resolutions were rescinded, and the journeymen readmitted upon certain conditions mentioned in 'a paper apart signed and approven of both masters and jurnaymen', suggesting that they concocted another agreement. In 1719 Deacon Watson was re-elected to his former position in the old Lodge and the

Incorporation. Further difficulties cropped up about the independence of the Journeymen Lodge, but eventually lodges and incorporations parted company, free trade in mason-making became popular, and the long-standing bone of contention between the Lodge of Edinburgh and its youngest daughter being thus removed, the Journeymen Lodge was left in full and undisturbed possession of its privileges.

Lodge of Dunblane, No. 9

The surviving minutes of the Lodge of Dunblane begin in January 1696, and differ from the generality of old Masonic records in that they do not contain any Mason's marks. In that year John Cameron of Lochiel was a member of the lodge. Cameron had served with the Earl of Mar in the Rebellion of 1715, and his eldest son Donald became one of the most influential chiefs to join Prince Charles Edward Stuart, and the first to take possession of Edinburgh with the Highlanders in 1745. John Cameron was married to Isabel Campbell, whose brother Sir Duncan Campbell, was initiated into Freemasonry by Dr Desaguliers at Edinburgh in 1721.

Gould records that the majority of the brethren of the Lodge of Dunblane were both speculative Masons and noted Jacobites. Notable supporters of the Stuart side in the risings of 1715 and 1745 were Lord Strathallan (Master in 1696) and Lord John Drummond, brother of the Duke of Perth (initiated 13 March 1740 and Master 1743–5). Records dated 28 January 1696, the list of members present and show the operative masons to be in the minority. Gould has no doubt that this meeting was not the first of its kind and he cannot understand why the lodge should only be accorded precedence from the year 1709 on the official roll.

The business transacted that day in 1696 was in a Masonic court, as it was termed. The meeting was called The Lodge of Meassones in Dunblane; Lord Strathallan (the second viscount) was referred to as the 'Master Meassone', Alexander Drummond of Balhadie, Warden and 'eldest fellow of craft', was appointed, along with a Deputy Master, a Clerk, a Treasurer, an Officer, and a 'Pror. Fiscall'. These made up the court. Each workman on his entry was required to pay £6, and half that sum on his passing, as well as his ordinary dues. It was agreed that no one present, or any one who joined subsequently, should divulge any of the acts passed by the court to any person whatsoever who was not a member of the lodge 'under the breach of breaking of their oath'. Many of the laws passed at this meeting, and others in 1696, relate to the operative character of the craft.

The Lodge of Dunblane allowed its members to initiate suitable persons at a distance from the town, provided that they could get together 'such members of this lodge as can be conveniently got', or, in case of necessity, borrow from another lodge 'as many as shall make a quorum'. Gentlemen entered in this fashion were later passed in the lodge. [This is similar to the way Sir Robert Moray was initiated in Newcastle by members of the Lodge of Edinburgh in 1641.] In September 1716 the court prohibited both entry and passing at the same time, but made an exception in favour of gentlemen who lived far away and could not easily attend twice.

On 8 January 1724 three speculative intrants were presented with aprons and gloves and in turn presented the lodge with a copy of the *Constitutions of the Freemasons* (1723). Gould records an interesting minute of 1720 referring to ritual proceedings:

Dunblane, the twenty-seventh day of December 1720 years. Sederunt: [i.e. There sat in session] Robert Duthy, deacon; Wm. Wright, warden; Wm. Muschet, eldest fellow of craft. Compeared John Gillespie, writer in Dunblane, who was entered on the 24 instant, and after examination was duely passt from the Square to the Compass, and from an Entered Prentice to a Fellow of Craft of this Lodge, who present as said, is bound, obliged, and enacted himself to stand by, obey, and obtemper, and subject himself unto the heall acts and ordinances of this Lodge and Company.

On 28 November 1721 another apprentice was passed after due examination, and on 6 September 1723 others gave 'satisfieing answers of their knowledge' before being promoted. A remarkable entry occurs, dated 27 December 1729. Two apprentices (one a merchant in Dunblane), who were already members of the Lodge of Kilwinning, applied to be entered as apprentices in the Dunblane lodge. They were then passed as fellow-crafts. Bro. James Muschet was instructed

to examine them as to their qualifications and knowledge, and having reported to the lodge that they had a competent knowledge of the secrets of the mason word their petitions were duly attended to.

These minutes speak of the 'secrets of the mason word', whereas the Decreet Arbitral affecting the Lodge of Edinburgh mentions only the 'mason word'. Gould says that the records of Dunblane, and also those of Haughfoot are more explicit than those of Edinburgh and of the Edinburgh Journeymen, in that they testify that the esoteric consisted of secrets. He notes that the Lodge of Dunblane did not join the Grand Lodge of Scotland until 1761; therefore its proceedings are more valuable, because they are uninfluenced by more modern organizations.

The minutes of Dunblane contain numerous references to the appointment of instructors, for the intrants. These are referred to as intenders. (The books of the Lodge of Edinburgh in 1714 also describe such an officer.) In 1725 the lodge at Dunblane said that the duties of an intender consisted of perfecting apprentices, so that they might be 'fitt for their future tryalls'. The Lodge of Peebles also appointed intenders and continued to do so for over a century and a half. The Lodge of Aberdeen used a similar officer as early as 1670.

Peebles Kilwinning Lodge, No. 24

Peebles was at work in 1716, but is only recognized by the Grand Lodge of Scotland from 1736. Gould found this lodge interesting because he discovered that from 1716 to the end of the nineteenth century, the lodge observed the custom of holding an annual trial of the apprentices and fellow-crafts. In 1726 an inventory of its property was made in the minute-book, consisting of 'Ane Bible, the Constitutions of the haill Lodges in London, the Square, and a piece of small tow.' Next year the entry reads 'Square, tow, and compass'.

Some of the marks registered by its members are complex. A captain of the King's Foot Guards held a mark described as 'a V-shaped shield, bearing on each half a small cross, the whole being surmounted by a cross of a larger size'. Amongst other marks are a slater's hammer and a leather cutter's knife, whilst the mark taken by a wigmaker in 1745 was a 'human head with a wig and an ample beard'.

The lodge opening ceremony began with a prayer, and the brethren were sworn to 'refrain from undue partiality in the consideration of the business'. This was called Fencing the Lodge' and continued to be observed in Peebles for many years. The lodge was largely speculative from its origin in 1716, and it continued to practise ancient customs long after they had disappeared from other lodges. For example, they appointed intenders to instruct new apprentices and also tested the apprentices and fellows each year.

The first record of the lodge is dated 18 October 1716. It reports that the lodge was self-constituted by 'a sufficient number of Brethren in this Burgh', because they felt they were suffering 'by the want of a Lodge'. The minute is signed by twelve members, who were already Masons, as they attached their marks. During that first meeting a Deacon, Warden, and other officers were elected. The lodge annually celebrated the Festival of St John the Evangelist, and on this day the officers were elected and the annual subscriptions had to be paid.

A local merchant John Wood was 'gravely and decently entered a member of the said ludge' on St John's Day 1717, and the lodge did not fix a fee for initiation but left to him the matter of how much he chose to make as a gift saying, 'any complement to be given being referr'd to himself'.

On 19 December 1718 John Douglass, brother to the Earl of March, and a Captain Weir, were admitted members. Each chose a mark and two Intenders. They paid a guinea and half a guinea, respectively, to the Box. After that the 'honourable society having received ane handsome treat,' gave them a handsome feast, 'being that which was due to their carecter'.

On 13 January 1725 Bro. David White was charged that he threatened to enter some persons in a certain parish, and to set up a lodge there. He was found guilty, and 'ordained to beg God and the honourable company pardon, and promise not to doe the like in time coming, which he accordingly did'. On 27 December 1726 the members, finding that the annual subscription of one shilling each (payable by the brethren who were not workmen) was considered excessive, agreed 'to restrict in all time coming the sd shilling to eightpence'.

In 1716 the delta was not a prohibited mark, as in these modern times. A collection of old marks is scattered over so many volumes of ancient records with many being really good geometrical figures which would provide an excellent assortment for the registrars of mark lodges. Gould remarks that they prove the absurdity of limiting the choice of marks to any set number of lines or points.

Lodge of Aberdeen, No. 34

Gould says the ancient Lodge of Aberdeen really deserves a volume to itself, but a sketch of its history is all he can offer. The original formation of the lodge lies so far back in antiquity that it wholly eludes his research. The records of the burgh of Aberdeen offer rare glimpses of the social hierarchy, as seen through the prism of legal pleadings, and Gould remarks that their historical importance has long been acknowledged by those who have had access to them. They comprehend the proceedings of the Council, and of the Baillie and the Guild Courts, from 1398 to 1745. The records extend to 61 folio volumes, each averaging about 600 pages, and, with the exception of the years 1414–33, there are no gaps.

The first volume (1399) contains an account of an early contract between the 'comownys of Ab'den' on the one part, and two 'masonys' on the other part, which was agreed to on the Feast of St Michael the Archangel. The work contracted for was 'xii durris and xii wyndowys, in fre tailly', and the work was to be delivered in good order at any quay in Aberdeen.

On 27 June 1483, it is noted that the 'master of the kirk wark', decreed that the 'masownys of the luge', consisting of six members whose names are duly recorded, were to pay 20s. and 40s. to the Parish Church, 'Saint Nicholace Wark', for their first and second offences respectively. If either of them raised any controversy, for there had been previous disputes, it was also provided that 'gif thai fautit the thrid tym', they were 'to be excludit out of the luge as a common forfactour'. It was common practice to give two warnings, and to inflict increasing fines, before the exclusion that followed the third offence. A by-law is certified to have been agreed by the lodge members concerned and approved by the aldermen and Council, the masons being obligated to obedience 'be the faith of thare bodiis'. Two Masons, who were singled out as offenders, were cautioned that, should either of them break the rule they had agreed to, 'he that beis fundyn in the faute thairof salbe expellit the luge fra that tyme furtht'.

On 15 November 1493 three Masons were hired by the Aldermen and Council to spend a year:

> in thar service, live in the luge and travel to Cowe, thar to hewe and wirk one thar aone expensis, for the stuf and bigyne of thar kirk werke, and thai bane sworne the gret bodely aithe to do thax

saide seruice and werk for this yer, for the quhilkis thai sal pay to ilk ane of the said masonis xx merkis vsuale money of Scotland alarnelie, but al accidents of trede.

One of these masons, named Mathou Wricht, is also mentioned in the decree of 1483, and again in 22 November 1498 as agreeing 'be his hand ophaldin, to make gude sernice in the luge' and on the same day that 'Nichol Masone and Dauid Wricht oblist thame be the fathis of thar bodiis, the gret aithe sworne, to remane at Sanct Nicholes werk in the luge . . . to be leile trew in all pontis'.

These are only a few of the early uses of the word Lodge, then spelt *Luge*, and the context in each case, by mentioning the penalty of exclusion, shows that it meant something more than a mere covered building. Certainly, though, in fifteenth-century Aberdeen there was a private building strictly devoted to the purposes of Masonry. To work within the company of this lodge was the privilege of Freemasons. Cowans and disobedient members were excluded. Interestingly, as it was a covered building, it was tyled or healed – thus showing an early use of the words 'Tyler' and 'heal' (or 'hele') in Freemasonry.

It was ordered on 1 February 1484 that Craftsmen should bear their tokens on their breasts on Candlemas Day, and on 23 January 1496 it was agreed that every craft should have its standard. These were carried in processions. On 22 May 1531 the Provost and Council agreed that in

> honour of God and the blessit Virgin Marye, the craftismen, in thair best array, keep and decoir the processioun on Corpus Cristi dais, and Candilmes day, every craft with thair awin baner, with the armes of thair craft thairin ... last of all, nearest the Sacrament, passis all hammermen, that is to say, smythis, wrichtis, masonis, cuparis, sclateris, goldsmythis and armouraris.

According to a rule of 4 October 1555, a visitor was chosen every year by each of the crafts to be sworn before the 'Provost and Baillies in judgment'. His duty was to see that all the statutes and ordinances were faithfully kept, and that

> thair be na craftisman maid fre man to use his craft except he haf seruit as prentise under ane maister Mire yeiris, and be found sufficiee and qualifeit in his craft to be ane maister.

Gould quotes this regulation to emphasize the fact that the prefix 'free' was applied to those Scottish craftsmen who were free to exercise their trades, by virtue of due service and qualification, hence Free Mason, as well as Free Gardener, Free Carpenter and the like.

The first cathedral church of Aberdeen stood for only about 200 years. It was demolished by Bishop Alexander, who thought it too small for a cathedral and founded the present edifice in 1357. Gould says that whatever truth there may be in the early tradition of the craft, it is evident that Freemasons erected the present building. He explains that Mason's marks can be found from the foundation upwards. These marks were common among the fraternity. Masons' marks have also been found on Greyfriars Church, founded in 1471, and in King's College and Chapel, founded in 1494, as well as on the Bridge of Dee, which was started in 1505 and finished in 1527.

Gould alludes to a tradition that Matthew Kininmonth, Bishop of Aberdeen, employed a mason named Scott, with several assistants from Kelso, in 1165 to build St Machar's Cathedral. Scott and his associates are said to have founded the Aberdeen Lodge. Even without recourse to the traditions of the craft, the fact that the Lodge of Aberdeen existed at a very early date can be verified. And fifteenth-century references to the lodge in that city abundantly prove that the Masons assembled in a lodge, and not always for strictly operative purposes – although Gould says that the original object of building a lodge was to secure privacy for those who were fashioning the stones for the kirk.

It is impossible to prove that the ancient Lodge of Aberdeen is the one described in the Burgh Records of 1483, but Gould sees no reason to doubt that they were one and the same. In early days there was never more than a single lodge in each town or city, and this would have a monopoly on the rights and privileges of the trade. It was later secessions, such as that of the Edinburgh Journeymen in the seventeenth century, that gradually led to the formation of more than one lodge in a city.

On 6 May 1541 the Masons and Wrights were granted their seal, under the common seal of the burgh. Known as a 'Seal of Cause', it included the coopers, carvers and painters, and it allowed them to meet and govern their own trade. From this confirmation of their right to meet and control their Craft the brethren in Aberdeen date the institution of their lodge, and the Grand Lodge of Scotland, on granting a warrant to it on 30 November 1743, acknowledged that year as the time of its formation. It was likewise recited on the charter 'that their records had by accident been burned, but that since December 26, 1670, they have kept a regular lodge, and authentic records of their proceedings'. Gould says the members could as well claim from 1483 as from 1541, although their lodge is now only officially acknowledged as before 1670, for he says it is an undoubted fact it must have been at work long before the declaration of its records, which commence in 1670.

Gould complains that the lodges in both England and Scotland have been numbered capriciously, but he says that the assignment of the thirty-fourth place on the Masonic roll of Scotland to the 'Luge of Aberdeen' must strike everyone as a patent absurdity. He has no doubt of its relative antiquity, and inferentially concludes that it dates from a far more remote period than is attested by existing documents. Yet, even restricting its claims to the limits imposed by the rules of 1737, there are only two or three lodges in all Scotland that are entitled to take precedence above it. But, he points out, several bodies chartered late in the seventeenth century are listed above it on the register of the Grand Lodge.

The Lodge of Aberdeen made a dignified protest against its comparative effacement, but it failed to avert the calamity. Gould points out that, had its members not been more concerned to preserve and extend brotherly love and concord, rather than haggle for precedence, there might have been a rival Grand Lodge formed in the North of Scotland, as well as Mother Kilwinning in the South.

Before looking at the actual records of the lodge, Gould notes that a grant was made in favour of Patrick Coipland of Udaucht as warden 'over all the boundis of Aberdene, Banff, and Kincarne', by no less a Masonic authority than King James VI. The original deed is contained in the Privy Seal Book of Scotland. The terms of the grant are:

   (a) that the Laird of Udaucht possessed the needful qualifications to act as a warden over the 'airt and craft of masonrie';
   (b) that his predecessors had of old been wardens in like manner;
   (c) the said Patrick Coipland having been 'electit ane chosin to the said office be common consent of the maist pairt of the Master Masounes within the three Sherriffdomes';
   (d) the king graciously ratifies their choice, constitutes Coipland 'Wardane and Justice ovir them for all the dayes of his lyif;' and

(e) empowers him to act like any other warden elsewhere, receiving all fees, etc., holding courts, appointing clerks and other needful officers, etc.

The grant is dated 25 September 1590, and is a remarkable instrument. It has been suggested that it proves beyond dispute that the kings nominated the office-bearers of the Order, but Gould thinks it does no such thing. He says that, as with the St Clairs, the appointment was a civil one. If the St Clair family had held the office of Grand Master for all Scotland, clearly Coipland's appointment would never have been made by the King, neither would the Masons of Edinburgh, Perth and other cities have allowed it to pass without protest.

But Gould points out that it does show that Coipland's succeeded to a semi-hereditary office of warden for the counties named, subject to the consent of the Master Masons and ratification by the king. The grant of 1590 contains no mention of Lodges, though. Gould believes it was to settle the various trade disputes connected with the Masons – to settle matters affecting their interests, in or out of lodges, and to see that they obeyed the general statutes – that the Laird of Udaucht was appointed. This seems clear from the fact he was empowered to act in a magisterial capacity. It also seems probable that the old Aberdeen Lodge was a party to his election, and acknowledged him as its warden by royal authority. This appointment, however, was purely local. It was confined to the districts named, with other wardens acting in a similar capacity for the other counties. Ruling over all these district wardens was the General Warden, William Schaw.

In subsequent years the operatives who this high official was to regulate and control considered it only right that they should have a say in his appointment. The Acts of the Scottish Parliament, under the year 1641, contain this statement:

the humble remonstrance of all the Artificers of the Kingdome, who in one voyce doe supplicate his Majestie and the Estates of Parliament, least men incapable of the charge of Mr of Work may attaine to that: therefore it may be enacted that none shall ever bruik or be admitted to that place of Mr of Work, but such as shalbe recommended to his Majestie as sufficiently qualified, by the whole Wardens and Deacons of the Masons, Wrights, and others chosen by them, assembled for that purpose by the Parliament and Priuie Councell when the place of Mr of Work shall happen to be vacant.

This petition appears to have been dictated by the fear that an unfit person would be put in charge of the king's works. The petitioners lay great stress on the importance of the 'Wisdome, Authoritie, and Qualities' of this high officer, being such 'as may make him deserue to be Generall Wardene of the whole artificers of buildings, as worthy men haue euer formerly bene'.

The actual records of the lodge date from 1670, and Gould records that the book in which they are entered measures about 12 inches by 8, each leaf having a double border of ruled lines at the top and sides, the writing being on one side of the page only, and the volume originally consisted of about one hundred and sixty pages. According to a minute of 2 February 1748 the Box-Master, Bro. Peter Reid, was ordered to have the precious tome rebound, as it was being damaged by the iron clasps that held its leaves. Whatever special talents Reid may have possessed, Gould tells us, book-binding was not among them. Instead of having more pages inserted, as he was told to, Reid removed all save about thirty, and arranged those in an odd order. But the Lawes and Statutes of 1670 remain intact, if not undisturbed. Also the Measson Charter, the general laws, the roll of members and apprentices, and the register of their successors have been preserved. Many of these documents have unique features, whilst some are unsurpassed in interest and value.

The first volume of records that has been preserved has long been known as the Mark Book: it is a register of the names and marks of each member and apprentice. The old seal of the lodge is lost, and the present one dates from 1762. The 1762 seal serves as a frontispiece to the lodge by-laws of 1853. It is divided into four quarters: in the first are three castles; in the second, the square and compasses with the letter G in the centre; in the third are four working tools, the level, plumb-rule, trowel and gavel; and in the fourth, the sun, moon and ladder of six staves. The whole is surmounted by the motto Gould records as *Commissum tege et vino tortes et ird*.

Gould says it is known that an edition of the rules was printed in either 1680 or 1682, but no copy can now be found. It is very possible that a history of the lodge was bound up with these regulations, which, if discovered, would be of great value to the student of

Masonic history. The search for this missing record has proved abortive, but he hoped that the living representatives of former members might be encouraged to carefully examine all books, papers and bundles of documents among which such a copy of by-laws might possibly have been preserved. [A sentiment I entirely endorse. RL]

The *Lawes and Statutes* ordained *by the honourable Lodge of Aberdein, December 27, 1670*, consist of eight rules. Gould said that careful scrutiny reveals they are original and independent regulations, agreed by the members, and compiled to meet the wants of the lodge without respecting either the ancient ordinances or the *Measson Charter*. They differ materially from all other laws of the period and offer a vivid picture of the customs of the fraternity at the time. Gould reproduced them thus:

The Laws and Statutes of the Lodge of Aberdeen, AD 1670

First Statute – Article for the Maister: The master masons and 'Entered Prentises' who are subscribers to the book, vow and agree to own the lodge on all occasions unless prevented by sickness or absence, as they did at their entry, and on receiving the 'Mason Word'.

Second Statute – Maister Continued: The master to act as judge in all disputes, to inflict fines, pardon faults, 'always taking the voice of the honourable company', and he may instruct his officer to impound the working tools of malcontents, who, if they are further rebellious, shall be expelled from the lodge.

Third Statute –Wardens: By the oath at entry, the warden is acknowledged 'as the next in power to the Maister', and in the absence of the latter he is to possess similar authority and to continue in office according to the will of the company. The master is to be annually elected on each St John's Day, also the box-master and clerk, no salary being allowed the latter, it being 'only a piece of preferment'. The officer to be continued till another be entered in the lodge. No lodge was to be held within an inhabited dwelling-house, save in ill weather, then only in such a building where 'no person shall heir or see us'. Otherwise the meetings were to take place 'in the open fields'.

Fourth Statute – Box for our Poor, Etc: Of this lengthy regulation Gould presents no abstract, only overall comments. From its tenor he is inclined to believe that in 1670 there was a reorganisation of the lodge; owing to the unsettled condition of the country the meetings for many years previously had been held infrequently. The Masons of Aberdeen had a tent that was erected, for the purpose of carrying out an initiation, in the hollow at Cunnigar Hill, at Carden Howe, or at the Stonnies in the hollow at the Bay of Nigg. These sites offered private facilities for such assemblies. The members describe themselves as the authors of the 'Measson Box', a charitable scheme that they thought up themselves. They pledged their own support and also that of their successors. Several of the clauses are still worthy, though we may fail to appreciate the rule which permitted money to be taken from the treasury 'to give a treat to any nobleman or gentleman that is a measson', considering that the funds were to be devoted to the sacred purposes of charity.

Fifth Statute – Entered Prenteses: Each apprentice was required to pay four rix dollars at his admission, and to present every member of the lodge with a linen apron and a pair of gloves. If he was too poor to clothe the lodge, as this custom was called, a payment of money was substituted for the one in kind. Instead he would pay two additional dollars and pay for a feast with wine. But he had to pay, one mark piece for his mason mark, and another to the convener (officer) of the lodge. When he was made a fellow craft he was expected to pay for another dinner and pint of wine. If a Mason from another lodge elsewhere, known as a stranger, wanted to be entered as a master mason at Aberdeen, he had to pay two dollars and the invariable pint of wine, or more if he was a gentlemen mason. Apprentices were to pay fifty marks at their entry along with the customary dues, but if they were unable to provide the money, instead they could serve their masters for three years without pay before receiving their fellowship. The funds the lodge received were to be divided equally between the box and the entertainment of the Brethren. The eldest sons of the 'authoires of the Book' and all their successors were to receive the benefit of the 'Mason Word' free of all dues, except those for the box, the mark, the dinner and that indispensable pint of wine! Anyone who married the eldest daughter of a brother was granted similar privileges. The statutes call for apprentices to be entered in the 'antient outfield luge, in the mearns in the Parish of Negg, at the stonnies at the poynt of the Ness'.

Sixth Statute – For the Box Maister: This official did not keep the sums he received. They were placed in the box, which required the consent of three masters of the keys, each with his own different key, to be opened.

Seventh Statute – St John's Day: All apprentices and fellow-crafts had to pay twelve shillings Scots to the master mason or his warden at each St John's Day. If they did not, their tools were seized and kept in pledge until they paid up. St John's Day was to be a day of rejoicing and feasting, and the fees went to pay for the celebrations, as decided by the votes of those Brethren present. Any absentees were fined, and the fines further contributed to the festivities. The rules were to be read at the entry of each apprentice, 'that none declare ignorance'.

Seventh Statute – Second Part – Intenders: Apprentices could only be instructed by their 'Intenders' until that teacher was ready to give them over as being instructed. This was tested by an inter-rogation at a full meeting of the lodge. The Apprentice was fined for forgetfulness as 'the company thinks fit', unless they could prove that they were 'never taught such a thing', in which case the penalty had to be paid by their intender. All were to love one another as brothers born, and each man was to have a good report behind his neighbour's back 'as his oath tyes him'. The Lord's Day was to be kept holy, and Sabbath breakers, habitual swearers, unclean persons and drunkards were to be severely punished.

Eighth Statute – The Book: A book of laws was to be kept in the box, securely locked, unless required to be carried to any place where an apprentice was to be initiated. Only the clerk was allowed access to the volume for the purpose of making entries in it. The three key masters had to be present when this was done. Future members were bound by an oath, taken at their entry, not to blot out the names of any of the then subscribers, nor let them decay, but to uphold them for all time as their patrons. The regula-tion ends with the statement that there was never a poor-box amongst the Masons of Aberdeen, within the memory of man, until established by the authors of the book.

The document ends with a general clause that tells of the brotherly feeling that prevailed at the time. The subscribers invoke the blessing of God on all their endeavours and on those of their successors. The example set by the Masons of 1670 has been continued by the brethren of later years, who cherish an affectionate remembrance of their worthy predecessors, of 1670.

Gould states that these bygone ordinances record that Speculative Masonry existed in the seventeenth century. The list of members of the Lodge of Aberdeen affords conclusive evidence not just of speculative practices but also of a speculative ascendancy in the year 1670. The Lodge of Aberdeen provided for gentlemen-masons to pay higher fees at entry, but their presence was heartily welcomed at the festivals of the lodge. The power of the Master then was absolute, and the duties of the Warden corresponded closely with those of the modern office. The officers received a gratuity in those days from initiates, much as many Tylers do now. Privacy was guarded as closely then as it is under the modern system. The charitable nature of the fraternity shows in the rules for the Poor-Box, an article of furniture that still figures in our own ceremonies, while the regulations for the annual festivals remain alike in character.

The role of the Intenders is now taken on by the proposers of candidates, who see that the latter are qualified to pass their questions before promotion. And the careful preservation of the minute-books is something modern lodges have not lost sight of.

The Measson Charter immediately follows the Lawes and Statutes of 1670. Gould notes that this version of the Old Charges is chiefly noticeable from the absence of the terminal clauses common to the generality of these documents. The Mason Charter, as well as the regulations contained in the mark book, was read at the Initiation of each apprentice. The ceremonial of reception in those days must have been a protracted affair, and of little practical benefit to the parties chiefly concerned, who could have carried away but a faint recollection of the curious traditions and quaint customs which were rehearsed to them. The Scottish craft was both independent and original, especially in the scope and intent of its laws and customs.

The general laws of the crafts in Aberdeen are similar to those of the Lodge of Aitcheson Haven of 1636. Gould says that they confirm his view that the prefix 'free' constituted their rights to certain privileges, with unprivileged companies being denied these liberties. He confirms that these Aberdeen records show a speculative ascendancy as early as 1670. (Gould adds that he uses the word speculative to mean a non-operative Mason, and, when applied to tools, to refer to moral symbolism drawn from operative implements of labour.)

Gould regrets that it was not possible to present in facsimile the remarkable list of members of the Lodge in 1670. James Anderson, the clerk was a glazier by trade and styles himself 'Measson and Wreatter of this Book'. The initial letters of the Christian and surnames are elaborately sketched, and he took great care to make the calligraphy worthy. He succeeded because the list is easily read even after a lapse of more than two centuries. The names are legibly written, and after each is the Masonic Mark. This list was intended to exist as an enduring monument of the 'authoires of the Book'. They were as follows:

The Names of Us All Who are the Authoires of and Subcryuers of this Book in Order as Followeth 1670

1. HARRIE ELPHINGSTON: *Tutor of Airth Collector of the Kinges Customes of Aberdein, Measson and Master of our Honourable Lodge of Aberdein*
2. ALEXANDER CHARLLS: *Wrighte and Measson and Master of our Lodge. PA*
3. WILLIAM KEMPTE: *Measson*
4. JAMES CROMBIE: *Measson*
5. WILLIAM MACKLEUD: *Measson and Warden of our Lodge*
6. PATRICK STEUISON: *Measson*
7. JOHN ROLAND: *Measson and Warden of our Lodge. And ye first Warden of our Lodge*
8. DAVID MURRAY: *Measson. (Key Master, 1686–7, Master 1693)*
9. JOHN CADDELL: *Measson*
10. WILLIAM GEORG: *Smith and Measson and Maister of our Lodge*
11. AMES ANDERSON: *Glassier and Measson and Wreatter of this Book, 1670 (And Master of our Lodge in ye year of God 1688 and 1694)*
12. JOHN MONTGOMRIE: *Measson and Warden of our Lodge*
13. THE EARLE OF FINDLATOR: *Measson*
14. THE LORD PITSLIGO: *Measson*
15. GEORGE CATTANEUCH: *Piriwige Macker and Measson*
16. JOHN BARNETT: *Measson*
17. Mr WILLIAM FRASSER: *Minister of Slaines and Measson*
18. Mr GEORG ALEXANDER: *Aduocat in Edinburghe and Measson*
19. ALLEXANDER PATTERSON: *Armourer and Measson. [And mr of our Lodge in the year of God 1690 + 1692 + 1698]*
20. ALEXANDER CHARLES, *Yongere: Glassier and Measson*

21. JAMES KING: *Wrighte and Meason and Theassurer of our Lodge*
22. Maister GEORG LIDDELL: *Professor of Mathematickes*
23. Mr ALEXR TRUING: *Measson*
24. WALTER SIMPSON: *Pirwige Macker and Meason*
25. WILLIAM RICKARD: *Merchand & Measson and Treassurer of our Lodge*
26. THOMAS WALKER: *Wright and Measson*
27. JOHN SKEEN: *Merchand and Measson*
28. JOHN CRAURIE: *Merchand and Measson*
29. WILLIAM YOUNGSON: *Chyrurgeon and Measson*
30. JOHN THOMSON: *Chyrurgeon and Measson*
31. EARLE OF DUNFERMLINE: *Measson. [1679]*
32. EARLE OF ERROLLE: *Measson*
33. JOHN GRAY *Younger: of Chrichic and Measson*
34. Mr GEORG SEATTON: *Minister of Fyvie and Measson*
35. GEORG BAIT: *of Mideple, Measson [1679]*
36. JOHN FORBES: *Merchand and Measson*
37. GEORG GRAY: *Wrighte and Measson*
38. JOHN DUGGADE: *Slelaiter and Measson [1677]*
39. ROBERT GORDON: *Carde Macker and Measson*
40. PATRICK NORRIE: *Merchand and Measson*
41. JAMES LUMESDEN: *Merchand and Measson*
42. JOHN COWIE: *Merchand and Theassurer of our Lodge*
43. ALLEANDER MOORE: *Hook Macker and Measson*
44. DAVID ACHTERLOUNIE: *Merchand and Measson*
45. Mr GEORG TRUING: *Measson and Preacher*
46. PATRICK MATHEWSON: *Sklaiter and Measson*
47. JOHN BURNET: *Measson*
48. WILLIAM DONALDSON: *Merchand and Measson*
49. ALEXANDER FORBES: *Sklaiter and Measson*

'So endes ye names of us all who are the Authoires off this Book and ye meassonis box in order, according till our ages, as wee wer made fellow craft (from qth wee reckon our age); so wee intreat all our good successores in ye measson craft to follow our Rule as yor patternes and not to stryve for place, for heir ye may sie above wr' and amongst ye rest our names, persones of a meane degree insrt be for great persones of qualitie. Memento yer is no entered prentises insrt amongst us who are ye Authoires of yis book. And therefor wee ordaine all our successoires in ye measson craft not

to Insrt any entered prenteise until lie be past as fellow craft, and lykwayes wee ordaine all our successores, both entered prenteises and fellow crafts, to pay in to ye box ane rex dollar at yer receaving, or ane sufficient taut' for it till a day by and attour yr composit'. Wee ordaine lykwayes yet ye measson charter be read at ye entering of everie entered prenteise, and ye wholl Lawes of yis book, yee shall fynd ye charter in ye hinder end of yis book. Fare weell.'

The Names of the Entered Prenteises of the Honourable Lodge of the Meassone Craft of Aberdene in Order as followes (Mark of James Anderson)

1. GEORGE THOM
2. WILLIAM FORSYTH
3. WILLIAM SANGSTER
4. WILLIAM MITCHELL
5. KENETH FRASSER
6. WILLIAM MONTGOMRIE
7. TAMES BAUERLEY
8. WILLIAM CHALLINER
9. IOHN ROSS
10. PATRICK SANGSTER
11. WILLIAM ROUST

Then a list is inserted, entitled, *Heir Begines the names of our Successores of the Measson Craft in order as Followes as Maister Meassones,* which, according to the instructions of the 1670 rules, was not to contain the names of any apprentices. The foregoing eleven 'Prenteises' and the forty-nine 'Authoires and Subscryuers of this Book' composed the lodge in that year. In subsequent years apprentices who became Fellow-Crafts or Master Masons, signifying passed apprentices who were out of their time, received the dignity of having their names added to the roll of Successors, and, judging from the similarity of names and marks, Sangster (3), Frasser (5), Bauerley (7) and Roust (11), were duly passed, and honoured accordingly.

Gould comments that the mark of William Kempte, No. 3 of the 'Authoires', is the same as follows another of that name, who is the thirty-third of the 'Successors'. Alexander Kempte, No. 13, and AM— Kempt, Elder, No. 29 of the *Successors*, have each the same mark, but Alex Kempt Yor, No. 32, chose quite a different one. The marks are composed sometimes of an even or odd number of points, several being made up of the initials of the Christian and surnames, as monograms. Some represent an equilateral triangle, one or two being used to furnish a single mark, but in the forty-seven marks attached to as many names in the first roll, no two are exactly alike. The apprentices had similar marks to the Master Masons, and on being promoted to a higher grade they kept their mark. It was generally believed that marks were conferred on Fellow-Crafts only, a fallacy that, Gould says, the Aberdeen records dispel.

Amongst the 'Successors' the speculative element is still strong. The fourth entry is Alexander Whyt, *merchand*, the fifth Thomas Lushington, *merchand in London*, the seventh Patrick Whyt, *hookmaker and measson*, and the eighth George Gordon, *taylior and measson*, the mark of the last being a pair of scissors. The clerk never distinguishes present from past rank, simply recording a member's office (whenever held) against his name; each list therefore reads as if there were several wardens and masters at the same time. Owing to the predominance of the speculative element the same care was not always observed in registering these members' marks, as they did not have the same need for them as the operatives.

The later registers are not so complete as those of 1670, and it is possible that the operatives kept a separate mark book for themselves from soon after the reconstitution of the lodge. In 1781 the bulk of the operatives left the old lodge, taking their mark book with them, and established the Operative Lodge, No. 150, on the roll of the Grand Lodge of Scotland. Since then the senior Lodge of Aberdeen has ceased to register the marks of its members, a circumstance to be regretted, as such an ancient custom was well worthy of preservation.

Gould enthuses over the remarkable list of members the register of 1670 discloses, and he goes on to point out that it was compiled nearly fifty years before the assembly of the four London lodges in 1717. Since it has become the fashion to trace the origin of speculative masonry to England, the true sources of Masonic history have been strangely neglected. Of the forty-nine members described in the 1670 list, only twelve were operative masons. One of the speculatives, and the Master for the year 1670, was a tutor and collector of the customs, and enjoyed the distinction of presiding in the lodge over four noblemen (the Earls of Findlater, Dunfermline, and Erroll, and Lord Pitsligo), three ministers, an advocate, a professor of mathematics, nine merchants, two surgeons, two glaziers, a smith, three slaters, two wig-makers, an armourer, four carpenters, and several gentlemen, besides the operatives and a few other tradesmen. Gould says that if this is not speculative Freemasonry, then he 'despairs of ever satisfying those who deem the proofs he has adduced to be insufficient'.

He admits it may be suggested that the register was not written in 1670, but asserts that objection carries no weight, since there is abundant internal evidence to confirm the document's antiquity. Furthermore, the styles of calligraphy and orthography, and the declaration of the penman, all confirm when the record was compiled. It is a *bona fide* register of the members of the Lodge of Aberdeen for 1670.

Gould assumes that at its inception, sometime before 1483, the Lodge of Aberdeen was a purely operative body. It follows that the predominance of the speculative element apparent in 1670 must have evolved over many years. Unless the operative masons of the Aberdeen Lodge were actuated by sentiments very different from those prevailing in other Masonic bodies of that early period, the admission of members not of their own class, except representatives of the nobility and gentry of the immediate neighbourhood, must have been viewed with extreme disfavour. Likewise the introduction of members of trades other than Masonry could not have been effected rapidly. He says we have no clues about the internal character of this lodge in the sixteenth century, yet, human nature being much the same everywhere, the operative masons must have slowly become reconciled to the expediency of such an innovation. Indeed the operatives affected might initially have termed it an invasion; they were allowing themselves to be outnumbered by members of other and possibly rival crafts.

The Geomatic masons making up the majority of the lodge in 1670 could not have been the first of their kind to be admitted to membership; otherwise the lodge would suddenly have been flooded with a speculative element. Gould concludes that the character of the lodge had been for many years much the same as is revealed by these early documents. And this means that the precise time when it became a body practising speculative Masonry cannot be even approximately determined.

One of the operative members, John Montgomery (No. 12), a Warden in 1686, contracted with the magistrates for the building of the present Cross, which is an ornament to the 'brave toun'. With rare exceptions, from 1670, the Master was elected from the gentlemen, or Geomatic, masons, while the Senior Warden was usually chosen from the Domatic, or operative, element until 1840. In 1700, when the number of noblemen and gentlemen and other professions and trades admitted as members caused accommodation problems, the brethren purchased the croft of Footismyre, where they built a house and held their lodge meetings.

Kenneth Fraser, who was Warden 1696–1708, and Master in 1709 (No. 5 of the apprentices, 1670), became the King's Master Mason. In 1688 he took down the bells from the great steeple of the Cathedral of St Machar. Two Wardens were appointed until 1700, when the *First*, or Senior Warden, was discontinued until 1737, when the old custom of having two Wardens resumed.

In the by-laws of 1853 there is a list of the masters and wardens from 1696, but an earlier one can be compiled from the notes subsequently inserted in the mark book of 1670. Many of the 'Authoires' held office in the lodge, and not a few occupied the Master's chair for many consecutive years, their names also appearing as Wardens.

The apprentice minute-book contains records from 1696 to 1779, but some of the admissions date from 1670. The elections are in one part of the book, and the entries in another. Here is a sample of these minutes

Aberdeine Massone Lodge.
Election 1696.
Att Aberdeine, the 27 of December, being St John's Day, 1696, thee Hone Lodge being convened hes unanimusly choysen James Marky, Maister.

> *John Ronald, Keneth Fraser* Wardens
> *William Thomsone*, Treasurer
> *Alex. Patersone and Geo. Gordone,* Key Masters

Another *minute* reads:

Aberdeine, the twentie-sext of July 1701,
The Honourable Lodge being conveined, hes unanimouslie received, admitted, and sworne, William Forbes of Tulloch, Mercht in Aberdeine, a brother in our fraternitie, and oblieges him to pay to the treasurer yierly twelve shillings (Scots) for the poor, as witness our hands, day and place forsaid, &c.

> Signed *Patrick Whyt, Mr William Forbes*

There are *numerous* entries of apprentices, and Gould quotes one example:

Aberdeine the third day November 1701,
The Honorable Lodge being conveined, hes unanimouslie
Received and admitted, John Kempt, brother and printise to
Alexander Kempt, Younger, entered printise in our fraternitie, and
by the points obliedges him during all the days of his lyf tyme (if
able) to pay the Treasurer of the Massone Lodge in Aberdeine
yierlie, twelve shillings Scots money for behoof of the said Lodge,
as witnesseth our hands, day and place forsaid.

Signed *John Kempt.*

On 11 February 1706 Ensign George Seatone was made a 'brother in
our fraternitie', and on 18 July William Thomsone (younger), 'a
sklaiter, was received a masoune brother'.

Gould reports that he searched for evidence of any rules that insist
on Candidates for Freemasonry being 'perfect in limb and body'.
Throughout the records, apart from the *Measson Charter*, of which
the spirit rather than the letter was accepted as a rule of guidance,
there is no mention of this 'perfect limb' legislation, which, of late
years, Gould said, had become so important in American
Freemasonry. And Gould maintained that he had searched vainly in
the records of those early times for a full specification of the twenty-
five Landmarks, which modern research claims to be both ancient and
unalterable.

Entries from 15 December 1715 describe five apprentices as
'lawfull' sons. Perhaps it may be inferred that candidates not born in
wedlock would have been ineligible (though in Scotland the stigma of
illegitimacy was removable by subsequent marriage, and it seemed to
Gould improbable that the status of a bastard entailed the same disabil-
ities as in England). Apprentices were sworn not to engage in any work
above £10 Scots money, under a penalty that the lodge should impose.
But when they were passed to fellow-crafts this rule was relaxed. The
annual subscriptions were 1s. sterling for operatives, and double that
sum for gentlemen; the money was for the use of the poor. Small as these
sums were, the early period of their fixing must be considered. Though
insignificant now to English ears, they were not insignificant to many of
the Scottish fraternity, and some lodges still refuse to impose any
annual contributions whatever upon their members.

The following minute of 1709 mentions fees charged to those
wishing to learn the 'Mason Word':

Att the Measson Hall of Aberdein, 20 of December 1709, the honorable lodge thereof being lawfullie called and conveined to setle ane compositione upon those who shallbe entered prenteises in our forsaid lodge of aberdeine, and all unanimouslie agreed that the meassones prenteises within the said lodge shall pay for the Benefit of the measson word twelfe poundes Scots at ther entrie, yr. to, with all necessarie dewes to the clerke and officer, with speaking pynt and dinner, and all those who shall be entered in our Lodge, who hath not served their prenteishipe therein, is to pay sixtein pounds Scots, with all dues conforme as aforesaid, and this act is to stand *ad futurem re memoriam*. In witness whereof wee, the Maister and Warden and Maisters of this honorable Lodge have signed thir presents with our hands, day and dait forsaid.

On 15 November 1717 George Gordon, 'Master of arithmetick in Aberdein [was] unanimously admitted a member of this fraternity, and with this minute Gould ends his extracts from these records. However, before leaving the subject, he expressed a hope, which will be shared by many students of the craft, that before long a complete history of the Aberdeen Lodge would be written by some one who rightly comprehended the extraordinary character of its ancient records.

Chapter 10

The Legend of Kilwinning

The Masonic Kights Templar

Gould reports a tradition among the Masons of Scotland that, after the dissolution of the Templars, many of the Knights fled to Scotland and placed themselves under the protection of Robert Bruce, and that after the battle of Bannockburn, which took place on St John the Baptist's day in the summer of 1314, this monarch instituted the Royal Order of Heredom and Knights of the Rosy Cross and established its chief seat at Kilwinning. It seems by no means improbable that from this Order the present Masonic Degree of Rose Croix de Heredom took its origins.

Gould says that, whatever may have been the origin and foundation of the Royal Order of Scotland, its claim to be the oldest Masonic Order of Knighthood is presumably valid. He notes that the separate Order of Knights Templar Masons was also instituted by Freemasons, but has nothing Masonic in its ritual.

Gould says that, with regard to the documented history of the Order, he has presumptive evidence that a Provincial Grand Lodge of the Royal Order of Scotland met in London in 1696 and indubitable evidence to show that in 1730, there was a Provincial Grand Lodge of the Order in south Britain, which met at the Thistle and Crown, in Chandos Street Charing Cross. Its constitution is described as being of Time Immemorial. In 1747 Prince Charles Edward Stuart, is said to have issued his famous Arras Charter, in which he claimed to be Sovereign Grand Master of the Royal Order.

Gould quotes Lawrie's *History of Freemasonry* as saying that Free Masonry was introduced into Scotland by those architects who built the Abbey of Kilwinning, and that the Barons of Roslin, as hereditary Grand Masters of Scotland, held their principal annual meetings at Kilwinning. He thinks it improbable that the popular belief in Hereditary Grand Masters, with a Grand Centre at Kilwinning, will ever be effectually stamped out although his tone suggests he would prefer this. He says that, as waters take tinctures and tastes from the soils through which they run, so Masonic customs, though proceeding from the same source, may vary according to the regions and circumstances where they are planted. And, to be sure, neither the traditions nor the usages of the Craft have come down from antiquity in a clear unruffled stream. Why the Masonic bodies of Scotland and England followed such different paths is for history to determine, for he says such a task lies beyond his immediate purpose, and so he leaves the problem to a historian of the future, but indicates these promising lines of inquiry.

The two legendary centres of Masonic activity, York and Kilwinning, were both within the ancient Kingdom of Northumbria. He quotes Disraeli as observing that:

The casual occurrence of the ENGLES leaving their name to this land has bestowed on our country a foreign designation; and – for the contingency was nearly arising – had the Kingdom of Northumbria preserved its ascendancy in the octarchy, the seat of dominion would have been altered. In that case, the lowlands of Scotland would have formed a portion of England; York would have stood forth as the metropolis of Britain, and London had been but a remote mart for her port and her commerce.

Gould speculates that the Italian workmen imported to Northumbria by Saints Benedict Biscop and Wilfrid, may have formed Guilds, in imitation of the *collegia*, which perhaps still existed in some form in Italy, to perpetuate the art among the natives, and hence gave rise to the legend of Athelstan and the Grand Lodge of York. But, unfortunately, Northumbria was the district most completely ravaged by the Danes, and again effectually devastated by the Conqueror, so the theory is impossible to prove.

Whether at Kilwinning or elsewhere, it is tolerably clear that the Scottish stone-workers of the twelfth century came from England. The English were able to send them, and the Scots required them. Also, it is a fair presumption from the fact of numerous Englishmen of noble birth having, at the instance of the King, settled in Scotland at this period, that craftsmen from the South must soon have followed them. Indeed, late in the twelfth century, the two nations seemed one people, Englishmen travelling at pleasure throughout Scotland and Scots, similarly, free to roam through England. Gould concludes, however, that it is quite impossible to decide when the Legend of the Craft, and other Masonic traditions that are enshrined in the Old Charges, were introduced into Scotland.

Conclusions to Part Two

This research by Robert Gould shows without doubt that Freemasonry originated in Scotland, and that it is documented as a Speculative Craft back to 1599 and had lodges in 1483. He adds evidence to support the assertions of William Preston about the role of King James VI and reproduces the statutes that William Schaw used to establish the modern lodge system. He quotes the Templar legend of Kilwinning but comments that there are two Masonic Orders that draw on the traditions of the Knights Temple: the Masonic Order of Knights Templar, and the Royal Order of Scotland. And he makes a case for the St Clairs of Roslin having held some type of hereditary overview of the Craft in Lowland Scotland, by citing the role of the Warden of Aberdeen.

This is dangerous material for the claim of the United Grand Lodge of England that it originated speculative Masonry in London in 1717. The strong case Gould makes for a Scottish origin for the Craft must have been extremely upsetting for the mandarins of the UGLE and the other founder members of Quatuor Coronati, who had already been their chosen mouthpieces before that lodge was formed. They must have been pleased that he could not resist the offer to help found a 'Premier' Lodge of Research with the ambit of UGLE. In the light of this it is perhaps not surprising that the emphasis of the later editions of his *History of Freemasonry* support the UGLE line far more clearly.

Interestingly Gould was promoted to Senior Grand Deacon of the United Grand Lodge of England before he published the version of *The History of Freemasonry* that included the ideas I have outlined above. He never got any more Masonic preferment.

Elsewhere in his pre-Quatuor-Coronati research Gould said that the symbols, metaphors and emblems of the Freemasons could be divided into three different species. First, those derived from the various forms of heathenism – the sun, the serpent, light and darkness. Secondly, those derived from the Mason's craft, such as the square and compasses. Thirdly, those derived from the Holy Land, the Temple of Solomon, the East, the Ladder of Jacob, etc. He claimed the first two could be found in the heritage of the kingdom of Northumbria. The third group, he felt, being of a crusading character, favoured a connection between the Freemasons and the Knights Templar. These secret societies borrowed their rites of initiation, their whole apparatus of mystery, from heathen systems he sourced to Northumbria, which was at the height of its power during the fourteenth century, when the Templars were disbanded. He did not investigate this idea in depth – after all, it would not be an area of research that would endear him to his new Brethren of Quatuor Coronati – but he did inspire two of his Masonic contemporaries to do so. The first set of these ideas I want to look are those of J. S. M. Ward, who looked for the origins of what are known as the Higher Degrees of Freemasonry and the links some of these degrees might have with the Knights Templar.

Part Three

JSM Ward
on
Freemasonry and the
Knights Templar

Chapter 11

The Higher Degrees of Freemasonry

John Sebastian Marlowe Ward

John Sebastian Marlowe Ward was born on 22 December 1885 in what is now known as Belize City, British Honduras. He was initiated into the Isaac Newton University Lodge while a student reading history at Cambridge in 1906. He belonged to the Royal Arch, Mark Masons, the Royal Order of Scotland, Masonic Knights Templar, Knights of Constantine and the Order of the Secret Monitor.

Ward served in the army and worked as a customs officer before he became a writer. He was always a progressive thinker (he wanted to admit women into Freemasonry) and also a mystic – he managed to get himself excommunicated from the Church of England for insisting that a second coming of Christ was due at any time. He wrote a large number of books on the history and spiritual meanings of Freemasonry and was a contributor to the *Encyclopaedia Britannica*. In addition, he created what he called the anthropological school of Masonic research, as a response to what Gould and Quatuor Coronati were then calling the authentic school of Masonic research. Ward felt it was better to look for similarities in ritual and try to see if there were common roots, rather than just rely on lodge minute books, as Gould did.

A Past Master of Quatuor Coronati, reviewing Ward's *Freemasonry and the Ancient Gods* in the Masonic press said:

Quite the most pretentious publication dubbed Masonic that has appeared in England for some time is 'Freemasonry and the Ancient Gods,' offered by J. S. M. Ward as the fruit of fourteen years of study and research and published in attractive form, with a copious bibliography and index. Patient industry the author certainly reveals in chapter after chapter, yet one cannot but regret that his energy has not been applied to matters of his own knowledge rather than wasted on subjects far better covered by others. . . . Brother Ward has produced a work of great length containing much curious information, but it is really of no value to the student of Masonic history.

(My own research has consistently suggested that the more damning the personal attacks mounted by members of Quatuor Coronati against a writer, the more interesting his work is likely to be.)

The ideas in the next section are my retelling of Ward's ideas on the origins of Freemasonry, as expressed in *Freemasonry and the Ancient Gods*.

What are the Higher Degrees?

There are a number of additional degrees in Freemasonry, and they are known by various terms, none of which is quite satisfactory. Usually they are called the Higher Degrees, but this annoyed some Brethren, so the alternative of the Advanced Degrees was suggested. Sometimes they are called Side Degrees, which was a suitable name when there was no supreme body controlling a particular degree, but now all the degrees have regular rulers.

Once many degrees were conferred haphazardly, in the way the Cork Degree is still. After a lodge meeting two or three brethren might ask, 'Would you like to be made a Secret Monitor?' The brother would then be taken to a quiet side room and have the degree conferred on him. The ritual was often simple, mainly consisting of grips, tokens, and words.

The degrees which started in this manner are the Secret Monitor, the Royal Ark Mariner, and St Lawrence the Martyr. Some degrees, however, were never this simple. The Rose Croix, for example, required elaborate ritual and symbolism to make its point.

The additional degrees fall into three classes. Firstly, degrees which extend the Craft system, secondly degrees based on the cross and *vesica piscis*, and thirdly side degrees of practical use. In the third group there are various degrees that have one feature in common: their ritual and symbolism is weak, and their chief object is mutual help and support.

The degrees of St Lawrence and the Royal Ark originated among operative Masons in the eighteenth century as a way separating real Masons from the new speculatives. As a form of self-help, they brought together genuine operatives who felt deprived of real fellowship and hesitant to ask a gentleman speculative for assistance if they got into difficulties.

The Secret Monitor started in the USA in the mid-nineteenth century, about the time of the Civil War. American Freemasonry was growing, but many brethren felt the old spirit of friendship and mutual help might die out unless it was somehow reinforced. The Secret Monitor was brought in to meet this need, and it soon had over four million members in the US. Modern Masons often have the same sort of worries. We meet three or six times a year in Lodge or Chapter, but hardly get to know each other; higher degrees give more opportunities to meet.

The Secret Monitor uses the old Aberdeen idea of an intender. Every brother is placed in the care of a Deacon, whose duty is to keep in touch between the meetings and report to the Conclave that he is well; should a brother have any problems he can apply to his Deacon for help. This scheme depends for its success on the diligence of the Deacons. If they fail, it collapses completely. (One of the problems Ward sees with many of the additional degrees is that the officers are appointed in rotation, whether they are suitable or not, instead of being appointed by merit.)

Since there are now few operatives left in Freemasonry, the degrees of the Royal Ark and St Lawrence have only the charm of their ritual, and their simple symbolism left to maintain them. However, Ward thinks, the Secret Monitor, when working well, provides much needed mutual aid and support.

There are two degrees in the Secret Monitor, and attached to it there are seven degrees of the Scarlet Cord. For a collector of degrees, there are nine to acquire under the auspices of the Grand Council of the Secret Monitor, and when Ward includes the Chair degree, it totals ten. The Royal Ark Mariner is a special Lodge attached to a Mark Lodge, rather as a Royal Arch Chapter is attached to a craft Lodge, and is ruled by the Grand Mark Lodge. The degree of St Lawrence is the first of the Allied Degrees.

Group 1 – Degrees of the Craft

Masonry can be divided into Christian and non-Christian Masonry: that is, Masonry that investigates the Cross, and Masonry that addresses the Nature of God. The Cross degrees are not in all cases essentially Christian, but the rule in England is that only Christians are allowed to take them. In one or two cases this creates a strange situation where degrees that are clearly not Christian can only be reached by Masons who have first taken Christian degrees. This applies in the case of the Red Cross of Babylon, which can only be taken by Masons who already hold the degree of St Lawrence the Martyr.

To Ward's mind, the ideal order of the non-Christian degrees would be:

Entered Apprentice	Royal Master
Fellow Craft	Select Master
Mark Man and Mark Master	Super-Excellent Master
Master Mason	Royal Arch
Past Master	Red Cross of Babylon
Most Excellent Master	Grand High Priest

When arranged in this order, the series takes a Mason in historical order through the Craft legend. It starts with the building of the Temple, explaining many interesting details of its construction, tells of the great tragedy when the secrets came to be hidden in the secret vault. It explains why the Temple was destroyed, why and how it was rebuilt, describes the rediscovery of the lost secrets, of the heroism of Zerubbabel, the Mason who won the approval of the King of Persia and completed the Second Temple. Finally, the series offers prophetic encouragement to become part of a new priesthood, the Order of Melchisedec. Ward thinks that, as an exercise in symbolism, this sequence would keep separate the study of the nature of Divinity from the study of the mystery of the cross. But historic events made this logical sequence impossible in England.

English Freemasonry gained a lot from the Union of 1813, but it also lost a lot. Ward claims that the Duke of Sussex held strong deist views and eliminated all Christian teaching from the craft degrees, and weakened the Christian degrees. As a direct result the Christian degrees fell into decay, many almost disappearing completely. He thinks that the fact some survived and prospered is a strong testimonial to their real spiritual worth.

When the formation of the United Grand Lodge of England forced these Christian degrees to fend for themselves, strange alliances were forged and new sovereign bodies created with little regard to a logical arrangement of their sequence. Those who are responsible are long dead and past blaming, but Ward says we should be thankful to those who saved so much from the wreck. He admits that what is done cannot be undone, and Freemasonry is left with a multitude of governing bodies where two or three at the most would have been far better.

The following sections cover, in turn, all degrees of the Cross that Ward knew about.

Group II – The Masonic Degrees of the Cross

The Eighteenth Degree of the Ancient and Accepted Rite is the most widely known Masonic degree of the Cross, but many of this body's intermediate degrees are clearly not Christian, neither is its thirtieth degree strictly Christian. The sequence of degrees is controlled by the Supreme Council of the Thirty-third Degree.

The Grand Priory confers the degrees of Knight Templar, the Mediterranean Pass and the St John of Malta.

The Grand Imperial Council controls the two degrees of the Royal Order of Scotland –Knight of Harodim and Knight of the Rosy Cross. They also control the Red Cross of Constantine, Knights of the Holy Sepulchre and of St John. Both these groups of degrees were set up in imitation of the Chivalric Orders of the Middle Ages, and there is also the Rosicrucian Society, which has nine grades.

These are the Masonic degrees that Ward could strictly associate with the Cross. St Laurence and the Knights of Constantinople are also Christian degrees, but they are bundled with the Grand Tylers of King Solomon and a version of the Secret Monitor under the control of the Council of the Allied Degrees.

Additional Degrees

The first additional degrees Ward recommends taking after the Third Degree are the Mark and Royal Arch. Some brethren say the Mark should be taken first, because its symbolism is so closely associated with the degree of the fellow-craft, but others will tell you that you should take the Royal Arch first, because it holds the genuine secrets of a Master Mason. Whichever order you take them in, Ward advises waiting until you have learned something of what they mean before taking more degrees.

The degree of Royal Ark Mariner is attached to the Mark Degree, but Ward believes it is an operative degree. It tells of the Masonic legend of the Flood. It is not connected with the Ark of the Covenant, which is dealt with in one of the cryptic degrees; neither is it similar to the Twenty-first Degree of the Ancient and Accepted Rite.

The Cryptic Degrees

You have to take the Mark degree and be a Royal Arch Mason before you can take the degrees of the Cryptic Rite. There are four of them, and they are usually given sequentially in one evening. The degree names are Most Excellent Master, Royal Master, Select Master, and Super-Excellent Master. They are governed by the Grand Council of Royal and Select Masters. The degrees claim to explain parts of the Royal Arch that would otherwise be difficult to understand. The degree of Most Excellent Master is not the same degree as the Scottish degree of Excellent Master; in Scotland the degree of Excellent Master is conferred on an English Royal Arch Mason who has not gone through the ceremony of passing the Veils. The passing of the Veils was at one time part of the Royal Arch, but in England is now worked in only Bristol, Yorkshire, Northumberland, and Lancashire.

Ward thinks the passing of the Veils is an important part of the Royal Arch degree, and in most parts of the United States an English Royal Arch Mason is placed in a similar position as he is in Scotland, in that he will not be admitted to a Chapter until he has passed the Veils. The four Veils symbolically represent the Wardens at the Gates in Amenti, and, until you have passed through the super-physical stages they symbolize, you cannot hope to approach the Light at the Centre.

Once you have taken the Cryptic Degrees, you will be well advised to take the Allied Degrees in order to obtain the Red Cross of Babylon.

The Allied Degrees

In theory the Council for the Allied Masonic Degrees control a large number of degrees, but only six are actually worked. These are St Lawrence the Martyr, Knight of Constantinople, Red Cross of Babylon, the Grand Tylers of King Solomon (or Mason Elect of Twenty-seven), the Secret Monitor and the Grand High Priest. To qualify to take the last degree, you must already have served as Third Principal in the Royal Arch, and also passed through the Mark. Only the officers of these degrees wear regalia, but there is a separate jewel for each degree.

Rose Croix

The qualification to take the Rose Croix degree is that you must be a professing Christian and have been a Master Mason for at least a year. It is administered by The Supreme Council, Thirty-third Degree.

Royal Order of Scotland

The Grand Lodge of the Royal Order of Scotland can only be held at Edinburgh in Scotland. In England its degrees can only be conferred at a provincial Grand Lodge. There is one at York, one at Windsor, one that covers London, one in East Anglia, one in the West of England, and one for the counties north of York.

To take the degree of the Harodim, or First Degree, a brother must have been a Master Mason for five years. This rule applies at York and Windsor, but the Metropolitan Provincial Grand Lodge will only admit members of the Thirtieth Degree of the Ancient and Accepted Rite. This is somewhat similar to the system used at the Apollo Lodge, Oxford, which admits only members of the University, although there is no by-law to that effect. Everyone knows that only members of the University will be admitted into the Apollo, and those who are not 'Varsity men apply to other Oxford Lodges. Similarly, London masons who are not members of the Thirtieth Degree of the Ancient and Accepted Rite know they must go to Windsor to join the Royal Order of Scotland.

Ward thinks these degrees are some of the most interesting in Freemasonry. The Royal Order has been worked in London since at least 1743, and, even at that time there were two Time Immemorial Chapters in existence. The ritual is a curious old rhymed verse, which shows every sign of great age, and the arrangement of the degree confirms him in his belief that, even in its present form, this ritual is extremely old.

The Windsor Chapter meets at the old Guild Hall in that town, and its proper title is the Provincial Grand Lodge of the Southern Counties of England.

The ritual is similar to parts of the Red Cross of Babylon, the Arch and the Rose Croix. During one part of the ritual the candidate has to go contrary to the sun, and this is why a Candidate must have passed the veils before being eligible for this degree. According to ancient Masonic belief, only beyond the darkness of the northern veil does the sun go from West to East.

The Masonic Knight Templars

The supreme body is the Grand Priory. In England the robes consist of a tunic and mantle of white, adorned with a Red Cross, a cap, sword-belt, cross-handled sword, black sash, star and jewel.

The Mediterranean Pass is treated as an intermediate step leading to the degree of Knight of St John of Malta. The distinguishing symbol of this degree is a jewel; there is a complete uniform, made up of a black mantle with a white cross and a red tunic, but it is seldom worn except by officers of the Priory.

This Templar degree is worked in Preceptories, while the degree of Knight of St John of Malta is conferred in a Priory. Strictly speaking, these are Masonic orders and not degrees, though the name degree is often loosely used. Ward likens the Templar degree to the Third Degree, but says the Knight of St John is symbolic and metaphysical, like the Royal Arch.

Only Christians are admitted to these degrees. In America they wear an apron and a cocked hat, while the Knight of St John of Malta wears an apron with a red cross in the middle. The ritual of St John of Malta is not given in full in the American way of working the degree: just the signs and words are communicated, after the brother has been made a Knight Templar. In England and Scotland it is worked in full, and Ward found it fascinating. But he said that it needs a large number of officers to carry it out well. For this reason it is usually conferred in a Grand Priory, but this can result in a lot of candidates taking it at the same time, which can detract from the work. Ward was glad that he was able to have it conferred on him in his own Priory.

The next degree for a keen mason is the Thirtieth Degree, which in practice is seldom given to anyone who has not served as a Most Wise Sovereign in a Rose Croix Chapter. The remaining three degrees are only given as a reward for Masonic service, and their numbers are strictly limited.

The other degrees left to take are Knight of the Red Cross of Constantine, after which you can continue to the Knights of the Holy Sepulchre and of St John.

The Rosicrucian Society has nine grades, and to become a Zelator, the lowest grade, you must first be a Master Mason. The groups are called Colleges and their purpose is to study the meaning of Masonry and its ancient mysteries. Promotion to the various degrees is by merit, and for the higher grades a member must qualify by reading a paper on some deep subject or render conspicuous service to the Society.

There is one other degree worth mentioning, the Illustrious Order of Light. It is worked only at Halifax and London, and requires a most elaborately decorated series of rooms for the correct performance of its ritual. Admission is usually restricted to those who have passed the fifth grade in the Rosicrucian Society. The degrees, which are based on the Egyptian and Indian mysteries, take a long time to carry out. It is an impressive degree, but Ward can find little authentic information as to its origin or history. [It is still worked in Halifax. RL]

Ward says that all the degrees so far discussed tell a sensible story if you take them in order. The sequence is: Old Testament, New Testament, and the Christian life in action.

The degree of Royal Arch Knight Templar Priest, still conferred in the north of England, is a genuine old degree. The Grand Council of Knights of the Grand Cross of the Holy Temple of Jerusalem, which has existed at Newcastle from time immemorial, has the power to confer it. They entered into a Treaty of Alliance with the Grand Council of the Allied Degrees on 1 January 1897.

Ward listed all the degrees of which he was aware and says are of undoubted authenticity that are worked in England. Excluding the intermediate degrees of the Ancient and Accepted Rite, which are not worked, and the various Chair degrees, and including the seven grades of the Scarlet Cord, he lists at least 45 degrees worked in England. If you include the various Chair degrees, and intermediate degrees such as the Mediterranean Pass, the Seventeenth Degree and Twenty-ninth Degree, you can nearly double the number. As Ward remarks, the earnest student of Masonic lore has plenty to study.

Having looked at Ward's ideas on the Higher Degrees of Freemasonry and their relationship to each other, I will now move on and look at his views on the links between Freemasonry and the Knights Templar. The legend of Kilwinning says that a contingent of Knights Templar who were based at the Masonic Lodge of Mother Kilwinning supported King Robert at the Battle of Bannockburn, and, as a reward for this action, the Masonic Royal Order of Scotland was created to reward them. Gould was sceptical of this story, and Preston does not mention it, saying only that at one time the Knights Templar Grand Masters were also Grand Masters of the Freemasons. Let us see what Ward has to say.

Chapter 12

The Knights Templar

Beginnings

In the year 1118 Hugues de Payens and eight other knights formed a league to protect the pilgrims who went to the Holy Land. They took vows before the Bishop of Jerusalem to live and fight for Jesus Christ in chastity, obedience and poverty. Their order grew quickly, and ten years later Hugues returned to the Holy Land at the head of 800 noble recruits from England and France. St Bernard of Clairvaux became their patron, and by his death the Order had spread throughout Europe. At the end of the twelfth century it was one of the most powerful organizations in the Christian world.

The Order had three classes: knights who fought, priests who prayed (both of whom had to be of noble descent) and serving brethren, who didn't have to be of noble birth. Entrants could take vows for a fixed number of years, or for life. One of the Order's rules called for its members to live in poverty, and its earliest badge showed two knights riding one horse, to denote humility and poverty. But these virtues did not last long. The Templars soon became established in large castles up and down the Holy Land, and their pride became proverbial. The King of Jerusalem, Baldwin II, gave them use of a building on Mount Moriah near the site of King Solomon's Temple, and from this they got their name of Knights of the Temple. When Jerusalem was taken by the Muslims they moved their headquarters to Castle Pilgrim at Acre. They were driven out of Acre in 1295 and then retreated to Cyprus.

They first came to England and set up a Priory at the Old Temple, near what is now Southampton House, in London, during the reign of

King Stephen. In 1185 they moved to the site of the Temple Church in Fleet Street, London. King Louis VII of France gave them a site in Paris that became famous as the Paris Temple. These headquarters in England and France were their chief recruiting stations, and they quickly started to acquire endowments of estates in England, Scotland, and France. At the time of their dissolution they owned more than 9,000 large manors. Their estates were scattered all over England, with 25 in Yorkshire alone.

During the fighting in Palestine many knights died, and they fought many hard battles to prove their devotion to the Cross. At the battle of Ascalon they routed Saladin, but the Grand Master and most of the brethren were left dead on the battlefield. There also appears to have been a close connection between them and the Assassins, or followers of the Old Man of the Mountains, and it is a tradition that two of the original nine founders of the Templars had been affiliated to the Assassins. (Ward says that 'assassin' did not always mean 'murderer', but was the name given to someone who took the drug hashish. This stimulant was one method that warriors used to motivate themselves before they went into battle.)

The Assassins were members of a mystic, pantheistic sect who Ward says were bitterly hostile to the Mohammedans [although they *were* Muslims – an Ismaili sub-sect opposed to the Sunni majority] and equally detested by them. The first association between the Templars and the Assassins was probably a mutual alliance against a common enemy. However, it ended with the Assassins having to pay tribute to the Grand Master of the Temple, and in 1249 their chief offered to become a Christian if the Templars would release his sect from this obligation.

Twenty years before the Templars were driven out of Acre, the Assassins were practically annihilated by the Saracens (their descendants are the Aga Khan and his followers). After Acre fell the Templar Grand Master and most of the knights were slain, and the Order regrouped on Cyprus. However, they did not try to recover Jerusalem, but got caught up in petty European squabbles instead; they seem to have abandoned their task of defending Christendom, and left themselves open to the attacks of their enemies. This hiatus in their activity might only have been temporary, but for the intervention of King Philip IV of France, who struck at them in 1307.

At that time the Templars numbered 15,000 active brethren, and close on 40,000 affiliates, but they had few friends in France. Their pride and wealth alienated the people, and their willingness to admit base-born men aroused the indignation of the nobility. The Templars combined arrogance with humble origins, attracting instant dislike, and the kings of Europe instinctively objected to a cosmopolitan Order that had taken over some of the finest estates in their kingdoms, and paid them no service or tax.

Even the clergy hated the privileges granted to the Templars by various Popes. They answered only to the Pope and were not subject to the authority of the bishops in whose dioceses their establishments lay, who therefore could not excommunicate them or control them in any way. When Pope Alexander III created the office of Knight Templar Priest within the Order, so that the Templars could confess to their own priests, they were able to totally ignore the parochial clergy. It became a Templar tradition not to confess to outside clergy without special permission; this was to keep the secrets of the Order inviolate, but it also allowed heresy to go unchecked. The last straw must have been when Pope Innocent III freed the Templar clergy from any duty of obedience to a diocesan bishop.

The Templars' absolute autonomy gave rise to suspicion, and charges of heresy and worse were brought against them. In some matters the Templars were unorthodox according to the ideas of their age. Thus, it is clear from transcripts of their trials that the form of confession and absolution they used was not the same as that used by orthodox clergy.

In the fourteenth century there were three important military orders: the Teutonic Knights, the Hospitallers and the Templars. The Teutonic Knights were doing useful work against the savage Slavonic tribes on the German frontier and, since they were concentrated there, they were difficult to attack. The Hospitallers were nowhere near as rich as the Templars, but were actively engaged in fighting the Turks in the Near East – and they had a wiser Grand Master (he received the same summons from Pope Clement V that Jacques de Molay got, but suspecting treachery, made an excuse not to go because he was too busy besieging Rhodes). Philip the Fair of France – or Philip the False, as his enemies called him – hated the Templars for many reasons, not least because they had refused to admit him into their Order. He also hated Pope Boniface VIII, and when Pope Clement V took charge demanded an inquiry into Boniface's life and actions. Clement was in a weak position, because his papal throne had been the gift of the King of France, and when Philip accused Boniface of atheism, blasphemy and immorality, Clement was willing to placate him to prevent the scandal of a public investigation. At that time the Pope was living on French territory, at Avignon, where he had been forced to stay by the French King, so it was to France that Clement summoned the Grand Master of the Templars to discuss a new crusade.

Jacques de Molay went to France and on 13 October 1307 was arrested on Philip's orders. He was taken from the Paris Temple together with sixty knights. Philip accused them of heresy, idolatry and degrading vices. The king had previously sent out sealed orders to all the provincial governors, who, at dawn on Friday the thirteenth, arrested every member of the Order in France.

Philip based his charges on the evidence of two witnesses – Noffo de Dei, and Squin de Florian, both of them expelled from the Templars for serious crimes, and men whose word could not be trusted. But Philip relied on something more effective than the word of two scoundrels. He employed the most diabolical torture. His Grand Inquisitor, William Imbert, was supported by the Dominicans, who already detested the Templars. Skilled torturer that he was, Imbert almost always succeeded in extracting confessions from his unfortunate victims. Some knights were asked, 'Do you wish to defend the Order?' They answered, 'Even unto death,' and most who answered so were burnt at the stake.

In November 1307 the Pope issued a Bull stating that the heads of the Order had confessed the truth of the crimes of which they were accused, and he sent instructions to Edward II of England to arrest all the Knights Templar in his kingdom. The English King refused, saying that the Templars were faithful to the purity of the Catholic Faith. However, Edward was in the middle of settling a marriage with Phillip's daughter, Isabella of France, and his future father-in-law put such pressure on him that Edward ultimately gave way and seized Templar property, though he would not arrest or torture them. This delay enabled many of the knights to escape into obscurity, warned of the fate that threatened them by what was happening in France. It is from these Knights that the Masonic Templar succession must derive, if there is a real link.

A Papal Commission arrived in England in September 1309 and insisted that Templars were arrested and taken to London, Lincoln and York for trial. Many escaped, particularly in the north, where the Sheriff of York was reprimanded for allowing them to wander throughout the land.

At that time Scotland was nominally under English rule. Scotland and Ireland were included in the same instructions, and Templars from both countries were taken to Dublin for trial. It is unlikely that many Scottish Templars were captured, and in these circumstances the tradition of the Royal Order of Scotland, as well as the Scottish Masonic Templar Preceptories, may well have a solid foundation. It is probable that these Scottish knights would join the Scottish rebels in 1314 at the Battle of Bannockburn to fight against the English Government that was persecuting them. Indeed, what else could they do? They were fighting men. If they could not fight against the Infidel, nor for Edward II, why not fight for his opponent, King Robert of Scotland?

King Edward eventually surrendered the accused knights to ecclesiastical law, but until March 1310 nothing was done. At that time torture was not permitted in England, and unsurprisingly no confessions were obtained. The Pope warned Edward II that he was imperilling himself by hindering the Inquisition, and even offered the king remission of all sins if he would help. This was too tempting for Edward to resist, and in 1311 he allowed torture to be used. Three of the accused confessed, but the results were unsatisfactory from the Pope's viewpoint. The prisoners admitted they were guilty of heresy, and agreed to do penance. They spent the rest of their lives in various monasteries, but received good pensions; William de la More, Master of the Order in England, received two shillings a day, and ordinary members four pence (quite a tidy sum then). The king gave most Templar estates to his favourites, but some passed to the Knights Hospitallers.

In Italy an inquiry at Ravenna decided all the Templars were innocent, even those who had confessed under torture, but in Florence torture succeeded in getting many to confess to loathsome crimes. In Castile the Templars rose in arms and took to the mountains. Legend says they became anchorites and were so holy that when they died, their bodies remained uncorrupted. (The existence of such a tradition indicates that in Castile they were not thought of as evil men.) In Aragon they were acquitted and pensioned, but in 1317 a new Order was founded, which Ward names as L'Ordre des Chevaliers de Notre Dame de Montesa. It adopted the Templar rule and clothing with the approval of Pope John XXII. These knights were a great asset to Aragon, which was involved in constant war with the Moors and could not have managed without them.

In Majorca the Templars were pensioned, and in Portugal, King Dinis also overcame his difficulty by founding a new Order in 1317, which was really a continuation of the Templar Order but was called the Society of Jesus Christ. It was formally approved by Pope John XXII in 1318, and many Templars joined it, often keeping their original rank. Their castle at Belem, near Lisbon, retained its exterior shields showing the Templar Cross.

In Germany the Templar knights convinced the nobility that they were innocent, and the majority escaped with their lives. Many joined the Teutonic Order, and did good service in Prussia against the Slavs. In Bohemia the Templars retained their estates and were allowed to bequeath them to their heirs.

Only in France were they treated with cruelty and gross injustice. Phillip made no attempt to give the knights a fair trial. A Bull issued by Clement on 12 August pretended to give the results of an examination that was not held till 17 August. It also claimed that the confessions were spontaneous; this was an absolute lie. Ward quotes one example to demonstrate the brutality of the persecution and the King's treachery. In 1310 Clement called on the Order to defend itself and say why it should not be suppressed. Five hundred and thirty six knights volunteered to defend the Order, and Philip promised that they would be exempt from danger. They duly appeared before the Papal Commission in Paris and related their sufferings. (One knight showed the Commissioners the small bones of his feet, which had dropped out when he was tortured by fire.) But, once the knights were in his power, Philip broke his word and ordered them to be prosecuted. As some had already confessed to heresy under torture, their defence of the Order was treated as a relapse, for which they could be burnt at the stake.

Phillip showed no mercy. The Templars were burnt in batches, and accounts of their sufferings are awful. Fifty-four were burnt by Philip de Marigni, Archbishop of Sens, and, despite their screams of anguish, not one recanted as he burned. However, seeing what awaited them, many of the other knights withdrew their defence. Aymeric de Villars le Duc was hauled before the tribunal on 15 May, three days after he had seen the 54 taken to the stake, and he told the Commissioners that under torture he would swear anything they required. He even admitted that he had slain the Lord Himself.

Many different methods of torture were used. Wood splinters were driven under fingernails, or into finger-joints, teeth were pulled out, heavy weights hung from the dangly parts of the body, fire was set under the soles of the feet, which were first rubbed with oil. Almost every torture later used by the Spanish Inquisition was tried and tested on these men who, before 1307, had been the champions of Christianity against the Turks. Even the dead were not allowed to rest. Philip ordered the remains of a former Treasurer of the Order, who had died a hundred years before, to be dug up and burnt.

Ward hurries over the rest of the story of the Templars' persecution and the seizure of their property, and briefly discusses the death of their Grand Master. He says that Jacques de Longvy de Molay was of noble birth and joined the Order at Beaune in 1265. He was a valiant soldier and was elected Grand Master in 1298.

During his torture he confessed and wrote a letter advising other knights to do the same, saying they had been deceived by ancient error. He admitted the denial of Christ, but denied giving permission to practice vice. On 22 November 1309 he came before the Papal Commission in Paris, and was asked if he wished to defend the Order. He said that this was the sole reason he was there. On Wednesday 26 November he came before the Commission again and listened as they read his confession. He said he was amazed at what it contained, and he wished to God that the law of the Saracens and Tartars was observed against such evil ones as sat on the Commission, for they either beheaded such calumniators, or sawed them asunder. On 29 November the Commission accused the Order of paying feudal homage to Saladin. Molay denied this. He was sent back to prison until 1314, when the final act of the tragedy took place.

The Pope delegated authority to three cardinals, who condemned de Molay to perpetual imprisonment. However as he left the hall, along with the Master of Normandy, both of them cried out to the listening crowd that the Order was innocent of all the charges. This gave Philip an excuse to condemn them to death by fire as relapsed heretics. On 11 March 1314, therefore, they were brought to a little island in the Seine, between the King's Palace and the Augustine Monastery. There Molay made a last speech, declaring there was no truth in his confession, which had been wrung from him when the torture of the rack had reduced him to such a state that he did not know what he was doing. He said the confession was a lie, and not even to save further torture and death would he add a second lie. He insisted the Order was guiltless of the foul charges.

That evening Jacques de Molay died in agony amid the flames. To the last he protested the innocence of the Order, and, as he was dying, he cursed Clement the Pope and Philip of France, summoning them to meet him before the Throne of God within a year. Philip gloated over the scene from the wall of his palace garden. But the summons was confirmed by a Greater King: two months later Clement died of lupus, and eight months after Molay's death, Philip also died from a fall from his horse. (They were not the only ones summoned by their victims. Another Templar burned at the stake ordered his Inquisitor, Guillaume Nogaret, to appear with him eight days later before the Throne of God. Within the set time Nogaret passed to his last judgment.)

This is the tale of the destruction of the Templars. Ward says he could give more terrible details, but he has said enough to show that neither justice nor good faith nor yet mercy were shown to the unfortunate victims in France. He says this story is one of the blackest in the records of Christianity.

What did the Templars believe?

Nine main charges were eventually brought against the Templars. These were:

1. That they denied Christ and defiled the cross
2. That they worshiped an idol
3. That they used a perverted form of the sacrament
4. That they carried out ritual murders
5. That they wore a cord around their waist that had a heretical meaning
6. That they performed a ritual kiss
7. That they changed the ritual of the Mass and made use of an unorthodox type of absolution
8. That they were immoral
9. That they were treacherous to other divisions of the Christian forces

Ward thinks that, in some sense, charges 1, 5, 6, 7 and, to a limited extent, 8 were true, but that 2, 4, and 9 were baseless. Charge 2 he suspects possibly arose out of their practice of venerating some relic, which was exaggerated and garbled by ignorant and hostile critics.

As the Templar's ritual of initiation was secret, the evidence used to frame the charges could only have been overheard by eavesdroppers and was likely to have been misunderstood. The charge of denying Christ could have been part of a dramatic section of the ceremony of initiation whose meaning might not have been fully understood by the participant. Petrus Picardi, a Templar knight said it was part of a test of religious fidelity, and, if he were brave enough to refuse to deny, he would have been worthy to be sent to the Holy Land at once. The Preceptor of Poitou and Aquitaine, a knight named Gonavilla, said that the threefold denial was done to impersonate St Peter and his three denials of Christ. Another knight, Johannis de Elemosina, yielded when pressed and made the denial. He reported that his initiator was scornful and told him, 'Go, fool, and confess.' Many knights said the denial was '*ore non corde*': coming from the mouth, not the heart. They explained the spurning of, or spitting on, the cross in the same way, saying the spitting was '*juxta, non supra*' (beside it, not on it). It was similar to a medieval miracle play, particularly one called *The Festival of Idiots*, in which a player acts the part of an idiot soul who spits on the cross. (However, there was at the time a Gnostic heresy held by the Cathars, which said that, since the cross was the means of killing the Saviour, it was not an emblem to be reverenced but should be loathed. The Cathars were bitterly persecuted for this.)

The evidence suggests that the ritual cross was painted or carved on the ground. This would mean that the ceremony involved a ritual step. The proper manner of advancing from West to East in a certain Masonic degree involves tracing out, through the proper steps, a Latin cross. Most Masonic candidates do not realize why they in turn face North, South and finally East.

In one sense, Christian Masons can interpret the spurning of the cross as being similar to the three regular steps in Freemasonry. Those steps ritually symbolize an act of trampling on the cross of our passions, to represent the phallic cross that caused the death of our Lord. Of course, this is giving the ritual an esoteric meaning. It might also have had an exoteric purpose: as a trial of the candidate's submission to the instructions of his superiors (in other words, a test of the relative strengths of his obedience and his religious fidelity). During the ceremony of denial and spurning the cross with the feet, knights with drawn swords threatened the candidate; this is like the old Masonic Templar ritual of the Cup of the Skull, in which the candidate is threatened if he hesitates to drink.

The Templar Knights made a case that they adored and worshipped the cross three times a year, in September, in May and on Good Friday. Ward does not believe this act with the cross could have been anti-Christian. He says it must have had some deep symbolism and inner meaning. When asked why they did it, many knights said it was the custom of the Order. This is an answer that most Masons, too, would give if asked why we did so many strange things in our ritual.

The second charge, of adoring an idol, has been linked to the name Bathomet or Mahomet. This name is derived from a Greek word meaning Baptism of Wisdom. Much of the evidence says that the collect of the Holy Spirit was used during the Templar ceremony of initiation, and this suggests that an infamous Head they were supposed to venerate in their secret rituals could have been a figure of the Holy Ghost. Many Gnostic sects lay great emphasis on Holy Wisdom, whereas the Latin Church has traditionally neglected the third section of the Trinity. Some of the knights described the head as being that of an old, bearded man. Ward was reminded by this description of the Gnostic symbol for the Manifested Deity Abraxas, but thinks it is more likely that it was a reliquary shaped in the form of a head, and probably contained a skull.

Ward has little doubt the Templars were affected by the ideas of Gnosticism, probably ideas acquired while serving in Palestine. He says that even the shape of their churches is symbolic. The round, or octagon-shaped, Templar churches remind us of the veneration for the octagon that is part of present day operative Masonic tradition. The Templar cross forms an octagon if the points are joined together, while the circle comes from the pre-Christian religions, not Latin or Greek Christianity. There may also be a symbolic and esoteric reason for the Order calling its churches Temples; the Masonic legend that the shape of these churches was copied from the church built by the Empress Helena to hold the true cross may have some significance.

Ward rejects entirely the idea that the Templars carried out a perverted Sacrament, and likewise rejects the charge of ritual murder. The fifth charge may simply have referred to a Cistercian Cord of Chastity, for the use of such an item was laid down in the regulations drawn up by St Bernard. The Inquisitors thought it was proof of heresy, because they associated it with the Cathars and the Assassins, both of which groups wore a red girdle to which they attached great importance. Today Muslim dervishes invest the novice with a girdle. It is just possible that the idea of wearing a red cord was imported from the East and had a heretical meaning, but the monastic use of the girdle was so well known at that time that Ward concludes it was nothing more than a Cistercian Girdle of Chastity. The inquisitors did not accept this, however, saying that their girdles were evidence of their heresy.

It seems well accepted that a ritual kiss was used. What is unusual is that it is said to have been given on the backside. Ward suggests that its object was to instil humility. He points out that in the Prussian Knight degree the candidate had to kiss the pommel of the principal officer's sword to show his humility. The posterior kiss could well be a variation of the original concept. In the thirteenth century people were coarser than now, and Ward views this ceremony as similar to the treatment a new boy at school may receive from a bully. He says it is not a reason to suspect there was anything immoral in this kiss. Neither does it do much to support the charge of 'giving permission for unnatural vice' (part of charge no. 8). With regard to sexual morality, the Templars were probably no better or worse than the orthodox clergy of the day. Whatever the truth of it, the charge of unnatural vice was never pursued.

No substantive evidence of treachery was produced. It was said that occasionally the Templars might not have used all their energy to support their rivals, the Knights of St John, or even some of the Christian princes in the Holy Land.

That left the charge of changing the ritual of the Mass and making use of an unorthodox type of absolution. Ward says the evidence about the form of any alterations is conflicting, but it is clear that the form of Mass they used was definitely orthodox. If the Templars were celebrating an unacceptable variation on the Mass, then the case for heresy was made. Every knight would try to play down the importance of any variations he had noticed, but each twist of the rack would encourage him to add something new to his confession. The service of Mass was conducted by the Templar priests, and any heresy would depend on the view these priests took of how the ritual should be performed. They were educated men, who had enough spare time to think, reflect and meditate, but they were subject to no restraining influence from bishops and the usual Church hierarchy. In such circumstances they were free to think for themselves, to speculate and to use their speculations to develop knowledge and insights picked up from the heretical sects of the East. Doubtless some Templar priests would go further than others, and there would be genuine differences between the Preceptories. The knights, on the other hand, were fighting men, mainly ignorant and ill-educated; they would have to take on trust what their priests told them. They confessed to Templar priests, and so had no chance to comparing what their own priests taught with the ideas of the clergy outside their Order. They might not even have been able to understand the slight differences between two Latin sentences, so that the orthodox liturgy and heretical Latin prose would sound little different to their untutored ears. (Despite this power and responsibility, though, the Templar priests were not persecuted; it was the knights whom the Inquisitors targeted.) And the differences in the words of the Mass were slight. The evidence showed that the Canon of the Mass was left intact, though some priests omitted the words 'This is My body' from the consecration – hardly a burning issue.

The absolution, however, was unorthodox. Although the detail of the evidence varies, Ward says that one fact stands out. A Preceptor named Radulphus de Gisisco said that he was given the following absolution in French: 'Beau segnurs freres, toutes les choses que vous leyssuz a there pour la honte de la char ou pour justice de la maysson, tei pardon come je vous fayit je vous en fais de beau tour de bonne volente: et Dieu qui pardona la Maria Magdalene ses pechiez, les vos pardoient,' etc. A Templar knight from Catalonia, Garcerandus de Teus, reported the same form of absolution, but his version was in English. 'I pray God that He may pardon our sins, as He pardoned St Mary Magdalen and the thief on the cross.' [But the French and English versions Ward offers are by no means 'the same form of absolution'. The French one is not only longer, it makes no reference to the thief.]

From this Ward suggests that these words might be a quotation from Christ's words to the thief who was crucified alongside him. But he then relates that Garcerandus went on to report how the reference to the thief had been explained to him:

> The thief meant Jesus, or Christ, who was crucified by the Jews, because he was not God, though he called himself God and the king of the Jews, which was an outrage on the true God, who is in heaven. When Jesus had his side pierced with the lance of Longinus he repented that he had called himself God and king of the Jews, and he asked pardon of the true God. Then the true God pardoned him. It is for this reason that we apply to the crucified

Christ these words: 'As God pardoned the thief who was hung on the cross.'

Now, Ward tell us, if this belief was generally held by the Templars, then there is no question that they were heretics; in the view of the fourteenth-century Church they were not even Christian. If they held these views, then their denial of Christ and the spurning of the cross are proof that the Templars were non-Christians. But, Ward asks, was this statement just a personal view taken by a single unlearned Templar knight? He found no evidence that such a view was held generally. A Templar knight called Trobati said that he had been ordered not to worship a God who was dead and claimed that instead he had been told to put his faith in an idol. But his testimony is the only one amid hundreds of statements that supports this anti-Christian belief.

It is Ward's opinion that the Order did not hold non-Christian beliefs, although he does not think its form of absolution was orthodox. It accepted that laymen could absolve sins in certain cases. The support for this idea comes from England, where the knights were not questioned under torture, and where they denied most of the charges but admitted to mild heresy and offered to do penance to make amends.

But there was an important underlying religious issue at the time. It was clear that the Crusades were a failure. Jesus had failed to support the defenders of His faith against the Infidel. Seeing this, many thoughtful minds could not but question whether a faith in Christ was really the direct Revelation from God that they were told it was. During the Crusades they had encountered devout men who did not believe it – and those followers of another God had won. They also met Gnostic Christians, who explained the story of Jesus in a very different way to the Latin Church. It seems highly likely that some of the knights were led into new lines of thought that diverged from the strict orthodoxy of the day.

Ward reminds us of the Gnostic belief that Christ was not crucified and that it was Simon, the man who was said to have helped Him carry His cross, who died in His place. The Masonic Templar tradition of the two Simons may allude to this. Ward says that in the USA the skull used in some Masonic rituals is often called Old Simon. Some Gnostics held a still more extraordinary view: they claimed that the world was created by Lucifer, and the man hung on the cross was a Messenger of the God of Justice, whose mission was to inflict a hard and impossible code of law. In this world view Lucifer had slain Jesus to protect men from His oppression. Many strange and wild doctrines thrived in the Near East, and the Templar knights could not have avoided hearing them. But Ward thinks it is unnecessary to follow this idea much further. He had already said the average knight was a straightforward warrior and was unlikely to have bothered about such subtleties. Perhaps a knight might have been interested in the phallic significance of the cross but he was unlikely to adopt the more extreme views.

Ward says he is aware that the Turkish dervishes use a method of initiation that resembles the Masonic system quite closely. And he speaks of a tradition that Freemasons could have got their ritual from them via the Templars and Richard Coeur-de-Lion. He does not want to suggest that this is the real and only origin of Masonic ritual, but he thinks it is very likely that a new flood of ideas entered Western European thought when the Templars were brought into close touch with a European guild of operative builders called the Comacine Masons at that time. The pointed Gothic arch, based on the *vesica piscis*, appeared at the same time as the Crusades, and Ward feels that the speed with which it spread through Western European architecture suggests that a well-organized body was promoting it. Other Eastern customs also spread to the West: for example, the nun's wimple was just a European form of the veil of the Mohammedan woman.

Ward is of the opinion that some of the Templars' secret ritual could have been copied from the rites of the Dervishes or the Assassins, for it is well known that they were closely associated with both. Ward says that to his personal knowledge the Druze are the probable descendants of the Assassins and have at least one Masonic sign, and a similar system of degrees. He goes on to add that there are various theories that the Templars did not perish but took refuge in Freemasonry and survive today in modern Masonic Templar Preceptories.

Chapter 13

Templar Transmission Theories

A Choice of Ways

Ward says there are three possible routes by which the Templars could have become part of Freemasonry – French and English, Scottish – and each one seems to be independent of the others.

The Templars were split into three classes: (1) Knights, (2) Templar Priests, and (3) Serving Brothers, with the last subdivided into two (a) men-at-arms, and (b) craftsmen. Many of the servants, particularly the craftsmen were quite wealthy, and after 1307 they were in a position to help their former masters. Neither the serving brothers nor Templar priests seem to have been persecuted; King Philip concentrated his fury on the knights.

There certainly were some masons among the craftsmen, for the Templars were great builders. One Templar, called Frere Jorge la Macon, who was a Comacine Mason, was expelled from the Order for misconduct. Comacine Masons at this date were not illiterate workmen; a surviving existing contract says that 'John Wood, Masoun, was allowed borde for himself as a gentilman and his servant as a yeoman'.

The Templars were a self-contained body. They had their own priests and their own Masons, neither of whom were persecuted by King Philip. Moreover, the Order had many concealed estates scattered around Europe, and thousands of knights escaped the purge. A simple way for them to disappear would be to enter the Masonic brotherhood, with the help of their former servant craftsmen. With the threat of a cruel death hanging over them, Ward is sure they would have quickly swallowed their pride and become convinced of the advisability of joining the Craft.

Four possible representative bodies might have transmitted Templar knowledge to the Freemasons. These are:

1. The knights of the Society of Jesus in Portugal, and their sister body in Spain. This group are certainly descended from the Knights Templar, but they were purged of heresy, if there had ever been any heresy in Spain or Portugal. However, this Order has never been connected with Freemasonry, and has remained completely Roman Catholic.

2. The traditional history of the Continental Masonic Rite of the Strict Observance says there was a group of knights who accepted Pierre d'Aumont as the successor of de Molay. This Masonic Order once had a strong following in Germany and Scandinavia, but has now almost died out.

3. There is a group of French knights who accepted Jean Marc Larmenius as the successor to de Molay.

4. A group of English and Scottish knights who acknowledged neither of these successors but were already established in Britain.

Ward looked at the third group first but said he believed that, even if it were a genuine Templar survival, this did not prove that modern Masonic Templar degrees are descended from the old Order. The main information about this group comes from a document known as the Charter of Transmission. Ward says that Bro. F. Crowe discovered this document and presented it to the Grand Priory of the Temple in England, and it currently hangs in the Council room at Mark Masons' Hall.

The French tradition was that Jacques de Molay decided to carry on the Order secretly, despite the Pope ordering its suppression. While he was held in prison before his execution in 1313 he assigned his power and authority to a successor, Johannes Marcus Larmenius. When Larmenius, grew old he drew up the Charter of Transmission and appointed Theobaldus his successor. Thereafter each succeeding Grand Master added his name to that original document, until 1804, when the Templar Grand Mastership passed to Fr Bernard Raymond. The document's Latin is abbreviated and medieval in tone, and part of it is in cipher. There is also a post-1804 section in French, which was added to until about 1840. The signatures vary considerably in style and wording. Ward translated the document into English thus:

> I, Brother John Mark Larmenius, of Jerusalem, by the Grace of God and by the most secret decree of the venerable and most holy Martyr, the Supreme Master of the Knighthood of the Temple (to whom be honour and glory), confirmed by the Common Council of the Brethren, being decorated with the highest and supreme Mastership over the whole Order of the Temple, to all who shall see these Decretal letters, I wish health, health, health.
>
> Be it known to all both present and future that, my strength failing on account of extreme age, having taken full account of the perplexity of affairs and the weight of government, to the greater glory of God and the protection and safety of the Order, the brethren and the Statutes, I the humble Master of the Knighthood of the Temple have determined to entrust the Supreme Mastership into stronger hands.
>
> Therefore, with the help of God, and with the sole consent of the Supreme Assembly of Knights, I have conferred and by this decree I do confer for life on the eminent Commander and my dearest Brother Theobald of Alexandria the Supreme Mastership of the Order of the Temple, its authority and privileges, with power according to conditions of time and affairs, of conferring on another brother, having the highest distinction in nobility of origin and attainments and in honourable character, the highest and Supreme Mastership of the Order of the Temple, and the highest authority. Which may tend to preserving the perpetuity of the Mastership, the uninterrupted series of successors, and the integrity of the Statutes. I order, however, that the Mastership may not be transferred without the consent of the General Assembly of the Temple, as often as that Supreme Assembly wills to be gathered together, and, when this takes place, let a successor be chosen at the vote of the knights.
>
> But, in order that the functions of the Supreme Office may not be neglected, let there be now and continually four Vicars of the Supreme Master, holding supreme power, eminence and authority over the whole Order, saving the right of the Supreme Master; which Vicars should be elected among the Seniors, according to the order of profession. Which Statute is according

to the vow, commended to me and the brethren, of the very holy our abovesaid Venerable and most blessed Master, the Martyr, to whom be honour and glory. Amen.

I, lastly, by the decree of the Supreme Assembly, by Supreme authority committed to me, will, say and order that the Scots Templars deserters of the Order be blasted by an anathema, and that they and the brethren of St John of Jerusalem, spoilers of the demesnes of the Knighthood, on whom God have mercy, be outside the circle of the Temple, now and for the future.

I have appointed, therefore, signs unknown, and to be unknown to the false brethren, to be orally delivered to our fellow-knights, and in what manner I have already thought good to deliver them in the Supreme Assembly.

But these signs must only be revealed after due profession and knightly consecration according to the Statutes, rights and uses of the Order of fellow-knights of the Temple sent by me to the above-said eminent Commander, as I had them delivered into my hands by the Venerable and most holy Master the Martyr (to whom honour and glory). Be it, as I have said, so be it. Amen.

I John Mark Larmenius gave this Feb. 13, 1324

I Theobald have received the Supreme Mastership, with the help of God, in the year of Christ 1324

I Arnald de Braque have received the Supreme Mastership with the help of God AD 1340

I John de Clermont have received the Supreme Mastership with the help of God AD 1349

I Bertrand Guesclin &c. in the year of Christ, 1357

I Brother John of L'Armagnac &c. in the year of Xt. 1381

I humble Brother Bernard of L'Armagnac &c. in the yr. of Xt. 1392

I John of L'Armagnac &c. in the yr. of Xt. 1418

I John Croviacensis [of Croy] &c. in the yr. of Xt. 1451

I Robert de Lenoncoud &c. AD 1478

I Galeas Salazar a most humble Brother of the Temple &c. in the year of Christ 1496

I Philip de Chabot . . . AC 1516

I Gaspard Cesinia (?)

Salsis de Chobaune &c. AD 1544

I Henry Montmorency (?) . . . AC 1574

I Charles Valasius [de Valois] . . . Anno 1615

I James Rufelius [de] Grancey . . . Anno 1651
I John de Durfort of Thonass . . . Anno 1681
I Philip of Orleans . . . A.D. 1705
I Louis Auguste Bourbon of Maine . . . Anno 1724
I Bourbon-Conde . . . AD 1737
I Louis Francois Bourbon-Conty . . . A.D. 1741
I de Cosse-Brissac (Louis Hercules Timoleon) . . . A.D. 1776
I Claude Matthew Radix-de-Chevillon, senior Vicar-Master of
the Temple, being attacked by severe disease, in the presence
of Brothers Prosper Michael Charpentier of Saintot, Bernard
Raymond Fabre, Vicar-Masters of the Temple, and Jean-
Baptiste Auguste de Courchant, Supreme Preceptor, have
delivered these Decretal letters, deposited with me in unhappy
times by Louis Timoleon of Cosse-Brissac, Supreme Master
of the Temple, to Brother Jacque Philippe Ledru, Senior
Vicar-Master of the Temple of Messines, that these letters in
a suitable time may thrive to the perpetual memory of our
Order according to the Oriental rite. June 10th, 1804
I Bernard Raymond Fabre Cardoal of Albi, in agreement with
the vote of my Colleagues the Vicar-Masters and brethren the
Fellow-Knights, have accepted the Supreme Mastership on
November 4th, 1804

Ward does not consider the French portions, for he says that the
genuineness, or otherwise, of this document depends on the sections
before 1804.

Ward says that Bro. J.G. Findel, [author of an 1869 *History of
Freemasonry*] rejects the Charter on the grounds that he considers it
to be worthless. Findel claims:

1. That the Latin is not typical of the fourteenth century
2. That no Grand Master could nominate his successor
3. That the deed is unnecessary
4. That the institution of four Vicars-General was unnecessary
5. The level of hate shown against the Scotch Templars show it
   to be an eighteenth-century work aimed at the higher Masonic
   degrees
6. The signature of Chevillon leads to the same conclusion, for
   this deed was without any doubt prepared under the rule of
   his predecessor, Cosse-Brissac (1776–92); it must have been

delivered over to Chevillon in the hottest fury of the Revolution of 1792, when everything like aristocracy, and these Templars into the bargain, were suffering persecution. If this document, and all the signatures accompanying it, were genuine, then because France had seen many tempora infausta since the fourteenth century, these would have afforded those Grand Masters (as well as Chevillon at the time of the Revolution) the chance to add any remark they chose to their signatures. But this was not the case, for each signature is the counterpart of the other, Chevillon's alone excepted; and that and Brissac's being the only genuine signatures the very deviation of these from the counterfeit signatures proves them genuine

The manner in which the names of these Parisian Templar Masters succeed each other is incorrect.

Ward then says that Findel goes on to point out other supposed discrepancies, such as:

Bertrand du Guesclin, 1357–81, Constable of France, certainly did not sign his name, for it is a well-known fact that he could neither read nor write.

Ward says none of Findel's arguments have any merit and refutes them point by point.

1. The Latin is abbreviated and might easily be fourteenth-century. Sir George Warner, Keeper of the Manuscripts of the British Museum, and a great expert on the subject, examined the original. Findel did not. Sir George believed the Latin was written in a fourteenth-century style, but he thought the illumination was probably fifteenth-century. Findel based his arguments on a copy made by the Masonic historian Claude Antoine Thory, never bothering to decipher or even look at the original, and Thory's Latin translation is not correct.
2. In the Charter Larmenius it expressly says: 'and with the sole consent of the Supreme Assembly of Knights I have conferred,' etc.
3. If this document is real it was created at a time when the Templar Order was in a highly disorganized condition. Under

these circumstances a charter such as this would have been useful to prove to any brother that the holder was entitled to the office of Grand Master. Before 1307 there would have been no doubt as to who was elected, but once the Order was pushed into secrecy, a charter of this type would be needed.

4. The Order was dispersed and there was a real danger that the Master might be found and killed by its persecutors. In these circumstances having four Vicars would be a prudent precaution. In these dramatically changed circumstances the Order would have to adopt new ways.

5. That a reference of Scottish Templars dates the charter to the eighteenth-century is the worst kind of a priori argument and simply an assumption. Findel produced no evidence. Ward feels that this statement 'that Scots Templars deserters of the Order be blasted by an anathema' could just as likely prove the genuineness of the document, if those Scottish knights were the men who helped Bruce and then joined Scottish Freemasonry, as the tradition of the Royal Order says they did.

For his point No. 6, Ward says that Findel has no evidence, just assertions. If he had looked at the original document he would have seen that all the previous signatures are not distinctive. Ward tells of an old family Bible he has dating from the start of the eighteenth century, in which his forebears wrote the births, marriages and deaths of the members of the family. The entries are terse. Mary marries Norman, has a son Gerald, who marries Hilda, with dates. And so it goes on. But one old lady in the later nineteenth century decided to fill two valuable pages with a long-winded account of her husband's funeral and a long list of his virtues. Ward makes the point that Findel would use this to demonstrate that all the previous entries must be forgeries. He would say that there had been other funerals, and earlier husbands had done good deeds. Why were these not recorded? His answer would be that all the brief entries had been forged. So his point about Chevillon is farcical. The French Revolution was probably the worst time the nobility had ever experienced and Chevillon was garrulous.

The main thrust of Ward's line of reasoning is that Findel's arguments are valueless because he failed to use a true version of the text, and relied on a flawed translation by Thory. Ward thinks the document is genuine, although he realizes that most Freemasons have been encouraged to believe it is forged. While Ward studied history at Cambridge University, he does not rely on his own authority to declare the document genuine, although he believes it looks just as genuine as many other fourteenth- and fifteenth-century manuscripts that nobody doubts. He feels the view he quotes of Sir George Warner outweighs those of Masonic students who say it is forged. Ward cannot help but wonder if such students have been overwhelmed by a fault characteristic of many English Freemasons: a fear of even suggesting that anything connected with Freemasonry might be older than the eighteenth century, lest they fall out of favour with the United Grand Lodge of England. He maintains that many English Masons prefer to declare any evidence on the other side as forged or based on imagination than to court the displeasure of UGLE.

Ward hopes this blinkered attitude will not survive, and that a new Masonic generation will be able to look beyond the destructive rumour that Speculative Masonry was created in London in the eighteenth century. But he admits that, even if this document is genuine, it does not prove that the Masonic Templar degrees come from the Ancient Order. It might, though, help in understanding certain Templar traditions and influences that he finds in Freemasonry. Admittedly these are mainly on the Continent, but it is not unreasonable to think that Continental Masonry might have influenced the English version, and the Auld Alliance means that Scottish Freemasonry would be particularly susceptible to French traditions.

Any successors to the Paris Templars have become extinct, as far as Ward can trace, though he is uncertain exactly when this happened. But he is sure that this body was still in existence up to about 1850, and that was not Freemasonic. Between 1804 and 1850 it fell into undesirable hands. But Ward is convinced it is now extinct – otherwise why would Brother Crowe be able to purchase its greatest treasure, the Charter of Transmission? And why, he asks, was it sold as a Knight Templar Certificate, when it would have been far more valuable as the Charter it really is?

The doctrines taught by the Paris Templars between 1804 and 1850 would appear to him to have been simply a vague form of Pantheism. But, whatever they taught in their final days, Ward believes that the tale told in the Charter is perfectly reasonable. If the remnants of the Templars in France wanted to carry on the Order as a mystical secret society, the method described in The Charter seems the best possible.

Ward reports that it has been said the cross that decorates The Charter is the cross of the Knights Templar combined with that of Knights Hospitaller, and hence the Charter must be of a late date. But he says this is not necessarily correct. The flared cross now called Templar was adopted by the English Templars, but Bro. Crowe seemed to regard only this cross as Templar. However, the Templars also used the Maltese cross [which is now used by the Hospitallers and St John Ambulance] and the ordinary Latin cross. An Irish brother showed Ward an old Irish Masonic Templar apron, and it had a simple Latin cross upon it. Also, Ward tells us of an old English Masonic Templar Apron with an ordinary Latin cross upon it in Great Queen Street Library. Frater Ladislas de Malcrovich of Budapest said that the cross pattéÈ, the flared Templar Cross, was first used towards the latter part of Templar history, and earlier they had used a plain Latin cross.

When Ward examined the round churches of the Templars he found that the space within the columns forms an octagon. (He points out this can easily be seen in the Temple in London.) The ritual manner of advancing from West to East in the Masonic third degree is to make a cross, with the emblems of mortality at its centre. However, some Operative Lodges still perform the ceremony of passing through the octagon, and when doing so they must trample on the cross. Returning to the confessions of the Templars, the expression *passait par-dessus* was used when talking about trampling on the cross. Ward say that, if we see this ritual act as a ritual step, then it is one that we still use in our lodges.

Ward believes that the Templars used many different crosses, and it was the colour, red on white, that identified a Templar cross, not the shape. Simple cross shapes would be used on architectural details and clothing, while more ornate ones would be used in manuscripts and seals. He says Bro. Crowe is wrong in suggesting there was a single and peculiar Templar cross

The Knights of St John had a white cross on a black ground, and they used forms of the eight-pointed cross as well, and also the cross pattéÈ. The Maltese cross only became exclusively associated with the Hospitallers after the Templars had been suppressed. In the early Middle Ages things were much more fluid, but the disappearance of the Templars, the Hospitallers' only rivals to the title of Knights of the Cross, left the latter in undisputed possession of this symbol.

Ward says that the Maltese cross has a cosmic symbolic meaning.

It symbolizes the points of the compass and the limitations of matter within the infinity of spirit. It is, he says, a symbol of matter made out of triangular symbols of the spirit.

Chapter 14

The English and Scottish Knights Templar

Templar Links to Freemasonry

Ward considered how the English and Scottish Knights Templar could have been involved in the beginning of modern Freemasonry. He began by looking at the many symbols that today are associated with Freemasonry and are found on the tombs of old Knights Templar. He pointed out that similar Freemasonic emblems are found carved into the walls of Templar buildings.

One of the most common symbols is the interlaced double triangle known as the Seal of Solomon or Star of David. Ward says he saw in Germany the grave of a Templar knight who died well before the destruction of the Order, and on the gravestone were a number of Masonic emblems, including square, compasses, the pentalpha, a celestial globe and various pointed stars. He also commented that it was noticeable, when reading through the transcripts of the trials, that many of the phrases used by the knights sounded Masonic.

Out of 15,000 knights who were active members of the Order in 1307, only 800 are named as killed or imprisoned. It is, of course, always possible that many names of the executed and imprisoned may not have been recorded, but that still leaves many thousands who simply disappeared. What happened to them? Did the missing knights survive?

Ward found a clue in the actions of the Templar Preceptor of Lorraine, who, when he heard the verdict of the French Commission, released all under his command from their vows and ordered them to shave their beards and remove their robes. This would help them to escape, as at the time the Templars were the only Order whose members let their beards grow.

In the Masonic degrees of the cross, Ward says there are two influences. One is hermetic and mystical, whilst the other is Templar. This suggests two possible lines of transmission:

1 The Mother Kilwinning Scottish legend, associated with King Robert Bruce; and
2. The Emigrant French legend, associated with the Highlands and Aberdeen (see Chapter 16).

The Legend of Kilwinning says that King David I introduced the Templars into Scotland before 1153, and gave them an estate called Temple on South Esk; by the time of their dissolution the Templars owned estates all over Scotland. When they were suppressed, King Robert Bruce was trying to raise a Scottish Army to fight Edward II of England, and when an English Inquisition, ordered by Edward, was held at Holyrood in 1309 only two Templars turned up. All the others were said to have joined Bruce's army, which was by then advancing against the English.

Ward reports that the general regulations of Royal Arch Masonry in Scotland say that the war saved the Templars in Scotland. He adds that the Duke of Antin, in a speech made in Paris in 1714, said that the knights who agreed to support Bruce were made Freemasons at Kilwinning and took James, the Lord Steward of Scotland, as their Grand Master.

On St John the Baptist's Day 1314 Bruce routed Edward II at the Battle of Bannockburn. According to the traditional history of the Royal Order of Scotland, King Robert conferred the rank of Knights of the Rosy Cross on those Masons who had helped him win. Ward says that, if the Charter of Transmission is genuine, the hostility of Larmenius in 1324 to Scottish Templars is explained. If the Masons were really Templars who, without the authority of the rightful successor of Jacques de Molay, based the ceremonies of their new Order on the old reception ceremony of the Templars, then they were not legitimate in Larmenius's eyes. The dates make this story plausible. But what happened to any Templar knights who supported King Robert, after the fighting ended? Did they receive estates? Was some of the old Templar property given to them personally? Did others receive lands taken from the supporters of Edward II? Ward says that, if they did, then many would have married and passed their estates on to their descendants. But would the secret Templar ritual, its detail changing as time went on, also have been passed on to their descendants and friends? The legend connecting Kilwinning and Templary says they were. And that legend is persistent. It crops up all over Europe and is found in the ritual of many different degrees.

The openly Templar lands were passed mainly to the Knights of St John, Ward says. Numerous Templars in Britain joined the Hospitallers, and in a few cases they were ordered to do so. Ward reports that the Knights of the Order of St John referred to their lands as 'Terree Templarioe' despite edicts being issued to the contrary. During the Reformation some Hospitallers turned Protestant, and those who did were given title to their Order's lands, as private property, by the King. But others remained Catholic and elected David Seaton as their Head. Ward quotes Alexander Deuchar, then Scotland's leading expert on the history and rituals of Freemasonry, as saying that the Templars had incorporated themselves into Freemasonry as early as 1590. If Deuchar had any substantial proof of this, the matter would be settled definitely. But Ward says it may yet be possible to check out the claim, because the Reformation took longer in Scotland than in England, so many monasteries survived up to 1588.

A Chapter of 'Cross-legged Masons', was part of the Lodge at Stirling as early as 1590, Ward reports. 'Cross-legged Masons' is a name for Masonic Templary, and Stirling Lodge is known to have worked many higher degrees, including Rose Croix, Royal Arch, and Knight Templar before the formation of the Scottish Grand Lodge in 1736.

In a description of the Lodge of Perth, written in 1638 by a Bro. Adamson, Ward found this verse:

For we are Brethren of the Rosie Cross,
We have the Masons' word and second sight.

He believes this shows that there were speculative Masons in Perth in 1638, for Adamson was an MA, not an operative mason. It also shows that the Rose Croix degree was known and worked as a degree in the Royal Order. And, finally, it shows the Freemasons of this time had a secret, mystic word and claimed occult powers.

Lodge Mother Kilwinning worked Templary up to 1799, Ward

reports, because their minutes for that year say that they granted a charter to the Irish Kilwinning Lodge to work the Royal Arch and Knight Templar degrees of Freemasonry. But by 1813 they stopped working these higher degrees, and went as far as to deny that they ever had. The reason, he says, is simple: in 1800 the Grand Lodge of Scotland threatened that any Lodge which worked these higher degrees would lose its charter. The loss of their Grand Lodge Charter at this time would have left the members of Mother Kilwinning liable to prosecution under the Secret Society Act of 1799, because the exemption made in favour of Freemasonry would not have covered them if their own Grand Lodge had struck them off its list. Hence, they gave up their higher degrees rather than their Craft. The politics of the time account for their rejection of Templary in 1813, despite the fact they had granted a charter to work it to another Lodge early in 1799, before the Secret Society Act became law.

The creation of the United Grand Lodge of England caused the higher degrees to be attacked and driven out of Freemasonry, despite a clause in its Constitution that expressly permitted Lodges that already worked the chivalric degrees to continue. The same attitude carried over into Scotland, and hostility to the higher degrees encouraged many lodges to deny that they had ever been connected with such degrees as that of Masonic Knight Templar. But in Ward's opinion this false denial in no way invalidates the proofs that they formerly worked these speculative degrees. He points out that the lodges which worked the Higher degrees were speculative lodges. Mother Kilwinning had the Earl of Cassilis as its Master in the seventeenth century, and in the Lodge of Aberdeen – which dates from 1541, although its written records only go back to 1670 – more than half the members were non-operatives, among them earls, ministers, doctors, lawyers.

Ward confirms that the Aberdeen Lodge met in the open, in remote fields, and says that for a Templar encampment this was natural, but it was not a common practice for an Operative Lodge. He says there are many other accounts of Lodges or bodies of Masons in Scotland who met in the open who also worked the higher degrees. Lodges Kilwinning, Stirling, Aberdeen, Perth and Renfrew, all worked higher degrees and were all either in, or near, the locations of ancient Templar Preceptories.

The same thing happened in England. Lodges at Bristol, Bath and York, which have Masonic Templar Preceptories, are sited close to where mediaeval Templar Preceptories once stood. And all three cities are remote from the central Government in London, and therefore, Ward says, Templar knights were more likely to survive in these places.

Chapter 15

The Auvergne – Mull Templar Transmission Theory

The Grand Master of Auvergne

Ward recounts a Masonic legend that says that the Templar Grand Master of Auvergne, Pierre d'Aumont, fled to Scotland in 1307. He was accompanied by two commanders and five knights, and they landed on the Isle of Mull, where they disguised themselves as operative Masons. On the summer St John's Day* 1313 they formally re-established their Order and elected d'Aumont their Grand Master. Since their local cover depended on their being taken for Masons, they called themselves Freemasons and adapted their Templar rituals to make use of the tools of a Mason's Craft. They moved to Aberdeen in 1361, and from there Freemasonry spread throughout Europe. Ward found this story in the rituals of the Masonic Rite of Strict Observance.

He says that if a contingent of nine Templar knights fled from France to Scotland they would certainly have strengthened the local Templars, and this could account for why Larmenius took against them in the Charter. Naturally he would be more upset by French knights who deserted their fellows than by Scottish Templars who struck out on their own at a difficult time.

But Ward is concerned that all the transmission theories and legends talk only about the knights. What of the Templar priests? Surely they would try to preserve some the secret Templar mysteries and it would be easier for them to escape than it was for the knights.

*There are two per year: St John the Baptist's day on 24 June, near the summer solstice, and St John the Divine's day on 27 December, near the winter solstice.

The priests of the Templar Order were used to working with operative Masons. When Templar churches were being built or altered, it would have been the Templar priest who supervised the work. And it would have been a perfectly natural step to talk to the Masons responsible for the carving about the inner meaning of the symbols being set in stone. The Templar priests would have been well equipped to discuss the Masonic symbolism with the Operatives, and this shared interest could have led to better understanding. When the Order was dissolved in 1313 some Templar priests might well have seen a way of saving their ritual and mysticism. If such a movement had started amongst the Masons it would have grown and a wandering lodge of Operative Masons would now have known the secrets and signs to test other surviving Templar priests. As more disposed Templars were discovered they could be taken into the new Society of Freemasons.

There were many kinds of secret and mystical societies in the Middle Ages, and in such an environment an early lodge of speculative Masons working some of the Templar rites could flourish. But, Ward asks, how much of our present Masonic ritual can be shown to have originated with these ancient Templar priests?

Templar Symbolism

Masonic mantles, sword-belts and tunics are like those worn in the Middle Ages, but they were adopted in comparatively recent times. Perhaps they look right because the individual who designed them drew on historical knowledge of the Templars. When Ward looked at early Masonic Templar regalia he found the Brethren wearing aprons and sashes. The cross of the Templar Order changed several times. The flags flown in modern Preceptories are the old ones, but when were they revived? They might have been passed down through the ages, but they were never secret. If anyone wanted to revive the Order of the Temple it would not be difficult to get the flags right. Certainly the black-and-white banner has an esoteric meaning. And Ward adds that his study of stellar symbolism shows it to have a cosmic significance. The symbolism of light and dark, day and night, suggests the range of the solar system is bounded on its outermost limit by the sphere of Saturn, to which is assigned the colour black. The inner sphere is that of the moon, whose colour is white. So the black and white banner signifies the linking of Heaven and Earth or the unifying of Man and the Universe. A red cross on a white field was the other Templar banner and this symbolism of the cosmic cross, Ward says, shows the material world enfolded within the spiritual world.

The Templar seal shows two knights riding one horse. Ward says its exoteric meaning is that the knights were so poor and humble that they could afford only one horse between them, but he offers another interpretation. The less innocent story says that two Templars were riding one horse to battle, and the one in front commended himself to Christ, whereas the knight behind commended himself to him who best could help. The first knight was wounded, while the other escaped unhurt. The latter was a demon, and told his human companion that, if the knights would only believe in the powers of evil, the Order would flourish. In this way heresy entered the Order. Ward thinks that this story is an invention of the Templar's enemies. He feels that the seal may have been a reference to the twins who really represent the duality of the human soul: the stellar characters of Castor and Pollux.

This seal was later replaced by the Winged Horse, which is a symbol of illumination. The Agnus Dei was another emblem the Templars used. At one time this had been a symbol of Mithras – the ram and the sword, or cross – but the fact that it was adopted by Christians easily accounts for its use by an avowedly Christian Order.

Traces of Templar Ceremonies in Masonic Templar Rituals?

Ward thinks some parts of Masonic regalia and ritual have been made up from facts commonly known about the Templars. He cites the seal, the banners and the uniform, and he says that any clever archaeologist could have recreated the old Templar ceremony from the Regulations and the Confessions. Much more interesting to him, though, was the Masonic Templar ritual. He remarks on how it is full of curious anachronisms that mix old with modern ideas. The ritual is divided into three sections to match the three stages in a knight's career: novice, esquire, knight.

The kiss on the posterior is similar in intent to the ritual used in the degree of Prussian Knight of the Ancient and Accepted Rite, when the pommel of the superior's sword is kissed. The Meditation of that degree has the feel of old ritual, but the Anathema [drinking from a cup not made by human hands] remains a peculiarly unpleasant ritual, which only recently changed. Before this some versions called on the former owner of the skull to haunt any breaker of the oath sealed by drinking from it. This flavour of medieval necromancy does not seem to be eighteenth-century work. (Ward does, however, decry the fact that English ritual has been revised at least five times, and the changes may well have destroyed many valuable clues to a possible Templar origin of the rites.)

Ward expands on the ritual toast 'to all those valiant', which was once drunk from a skull; any candidate for Templarism who hesitated to drink was threatened with the swords of the surrounding knights. He says this is still done in the USA. But, he asks, whose skull does the cup represent? Some rituals refer to Simon the traitor. Who was this traitor? Does it refer to the Simon who carried Jesus's cross, or to the Simon whom the Gnostics say died on the cross in place of Christ? The skull appears for a third time on the altar, along with the crossed thigh bones which make up the emblems of mortality. Why is this? Is it to remind us that there is an exoteric meaning within the story of Calvary, or is it hinting at a medieval Templar legend that is mentioned in the records of the Templar trial?

Ward tells the story as follows:

A great lady of Maraclea was loved by a Templar, a Lord of Sidon; but she died in her youth, and on the night of her burial this wicked lover crept to the grave, dug up her body, and violated it. Then a voice from the void bade him return in nine months' time, for he would find a son. He obeyed the injunction, and at the appointed time opened the grave again and found a head on the leg bones of the skeleton (skull and cross-bones). The same voice bade him 'guard it well, for it would be the giver of all good things,' and so he carried it away with him. It became his protecting genius, and he was able to defeat his enemies by merely showing them the magic head. In due course it passed into the possession of the Templar Order.

This tale reminds Ward of the charges of worshipping a head which were brought against the Templars. Many knights said that some sort of head existed, and a few commented that they thought it was in the form of a skull. The Papal Commissioners in Paris found a skull when they searched the Paris Temple.

But what do these legends of a magic skull mean? Ward thinks they might be garbled accounts of some initiation ceremony repeated by ignorant eavesdroppers and made horrible by vulgar minds. He explains how the Egyptian mystery legend of Osiris tells how Isis found the dead body of Osiris and had intercourse with the corpse. From this union Horus, the avenger of Osiris, was born. To prevent anything like this ever threatening him again Set, Osiris's murderer, hacked the body into pieces and scattered it throughout Egypt.

Ward suggests that a Templar ceremony could represent such a mystic marriage, using it as a symbol of reaching a state of divine union. It encompasses death and the tomb, with rebirth following the tomb. The body, which is female, dies, but the spirit, which is male, rejuvenates it, and begins a new life. Displayed in the room where this mystical journey is enacted are the age-old emblems of death, a skull and cross-bones. But in all the mystery traditions of the world these emblems of death lead to a new birth, and so they are also emblems of life. Ward asks, is modern Masonic Templar ritual a last relic of the old ceremony? Is the name Simon just a corruption of the title of the legendary Templar Lord of Sidon?

He points out that the penal sign of the Masonic Templar degree has a double significance, and it refers to the penalty of the Order. The scorching rays are the fire which will not be quenched, implying that the soul shall not have rest until the Judgment Day, while the second part of the penalty fixes the head between earth and heaven, rent like an unfortunate spirit, who in medieval legend wanders in the void, unable to enter Hell or Heaven.

Ward also relates an interesting story he heard in a town in Hungary. In this town there is an old hall that once belonged to the Templars. The peasants told a strange story of the ghost of a Templar who used to appear in this hall from time to time, and had been seen by some of them. The ghost always appeared in a peculiar position. The peasants described the position and, Ward says, when he was made a Masonic Templar he realized that the position taken by the ghost was the same as that shown to him by the Preceptor as the Grand Sign of the Order.

Now, he asks, what possible explanations are there for this legend? English Masonic Templary does not exist in Hungary. Ward suggests two:

There was a ghost that appeared just as reported. If so, the old Templars used the Masonic Templar sign and attached great importance to it.

Templar tradition lingers in this part of the world, and dim remembrances of the ritual and the sign survive among the peasants, some of whom may be descendants of Templar serving brethren.

Either way, the result is the same. It implies this sign is derived from medieval Templary, and such a sign would be regarded as heresy, if not blasphemy, by the Inquisitors. They would have used it as proof of the charge of mocking the cross. Its esoteric meaning among the knights is that that all men suffer as He did, on the eternal cross of the human race. But such a posture would have been rank heresy in the eyes of the medieval Papacy. Symbolically it implies that it is by suffering that humanity will attain perfection, rather than by a vicarious sacrifice. This is a most damnable heresy to the Papal Curia.

Ward explains how during their initiation the medieval knights were deprived of everything except their underclothing. He reports how Thomas Walsingham, in his life of Edward II, said: 'In the reception of Hugo de Buris, he removed all the clothes he was wearing, except his underclothing,' but Geraldus de Pasagio said 'he took off the coloured clothes he was wearing behind the altar except his shirt, breeches, socks and boots ... and put on a garment of camel's hair'. Johannis de Turno and William de Raynbur, speaking during their trials, also said that this was the common procedure for initiating a Templar Knight. During the ceremony the Preceptor would dress the candidate in the robe of the Order, and place a *birretum*, a type of cap, on his head. After this investment with the regalia the secret ceremonies were carried out.

This ceremony took place just before dawn, and the Temple was lit by two candles. It was guarded by two guards armed with drawn swords at the door, and a third placed on the roof outside. The Temples were round buildings and from the rooftop the guard sentry could see all round the outside and so stop any eavesdroppers. Ward believes that the name of Tyler, used for the Masonic outer guard, derives from this Templar sentry. And he says the number three plays a major part in Templar ceremonies. A new knight took a threefold vow of Chastity, Obedience and Poverty, and the Ritual Kiss and the Symbolic Denial each had three parts. A knight was allowed to keep three horses and was sworn not to give ground to up to three enemies. He ate meat three times a week and gave alms three times a week when he attended Mass, and three times a year all the knights met for a ceremony of the Adoration of the Cross.

Masonic Templar ritual has a similar emphasis on the number three, and Ward detects many other small points of resemblance with the original medieval ceremony, so far as he has been able to recreate it. The Continental Templar degrees of the Ancient and Accepted Rite traditionally commemorated Jacques de Molay and the other martyrs in drinking the Cup of Vengeance. Ward suspects this has been cut out of English ritual in recent times.

Many crusaders brought back Eastern customs and the Templars were no exception. The old Templars were the only Order to wear beards at a time when all other European lay knights avoided them. Ward thinks they picked up the custom from the Near East and also took up the idea that to pluck out their own beards was a way of showing distress. (It also gave them the opportunity to tear out handfuls of another man's beard when they were angry with him.) The Royal Order of Scotland uses a certain word that alludes to this practice, and it also occurs in the English Templar ritual – yet there seems to be no particular reason for it, so why is it included? Ward says that, if the tradition of the Royal Order is right, and its degrees were reorganized by Bruce and the Templars, then this usage makes sense.

In England, Ward tells us, the Masonic Templar Order is known as the United Order of the Temple and the Hospitallers. He is doubtful whether any of the present ritual of the St John degree comes from the real knights. They existed up to the last years of the eighteenth century, and an honorary body still exists in Rome, its membership confined strictly to Roman Catholics of noble lineage, and one of its last Grand Masters being a Hapsburg. The Order of Hospitallers was strictly orthodox. From 1300 to nearly 1800 they waged a stubborn rearguard action supporting their faith, and year after year they fought on against the Turkish conquest, initially from Rhodes. When Rhodes fell, Malta was granted to them by Charles V in the early sixteenth century.

Among the modern Masonic officers there is one whose name is a puzzle: the Turcopolier. Ward says this title was given to the leader of the Turcopoles, a Eurasian class that grew up in the Near East, the offspring of European merchants by Asiatic women. Ward says that everyone knows the legend of Gilbert and the Saracen princess who followed him to London, and whose son was Thomas à Becket, the fierce, martyred Archbishop. He says that although modern historians are sceptical of this pretty legend, there is no doubt that the ordinary Turcopoles existed.

The Hospitallers were concerned for these half-caste children and undertook to care for all unwanted boys, whom they brought up as Christians and trained to be men-at-arms and light cavalry. They wore turbans to be distinguished from the true knights of the Order, because they were not of noble descent, and so could not become full knights. They were commanded by an officer called the *Turcopolier*, and this office was always given to an Englishman. The Turcopoles fought many a bloody battle, and excelled themselves during the siege of Rhodes.

After the retreat to Malta, the Knights Hospitaller reorganized and fought the Turks on the high seas. This culminated in a tremendous struggle for Malta, during which the Turks besieged the island for three years. Ward says it always saddens him, when he reads the account of the siege, that in such an hour of need no English knights took their stand beside those of other nations. He says this was because between the fall of Rhodes and the siege of Malta the Reformation took place in England, and Henry VIII dissolved the Order. Henry made no serious charges against the Order, and gave its Prior a generous pension, although that knight never touched a penny of it. He died the day after he received the news that the Order was suppressed.

There were no English knights at the siege of Malta, but when Don Juan defeated the Turkish fleet and relieved the knights, Queen Elizabeth ordered a solemn *Te Deum* to be sung in old St Paul's for the victory of Christendom over the infidel. (The crypt and chancel of the Hospitallers' great Priory Church of St John of Jerusalem, in Clerkenwell, still stands. A narrow alley close by is known by the name of Jerusalem.)

After securing Malta the Knights Hospitaller were not idle. They took to policing the Mediterranean. Their galleys patrolled the seas around Malta in a never-ending battle against the Algerian Corsairs, a group of pirates who plundered shipping and sometimes raided the southern coasts of Europe. When the last Hospitaller knights passed away the French were forced to invade Algiers to stop these raids.

Throughout the seventeenth and eighteenth centuries, the Knights

Hospitaller adopted new methods to adapt to changing conditions. Then Napoleon's ships appeared before the walls of Valetta. The island could not have stood a long siege, and the British fleet was racing to the rescue, but the Grand Master of the Order surrendered. When the British arrived they drove out the French; their military took over the forts of the Knights, and the policing of the seas was taken over by the British fleet. The descendants of these Knights Hospitaller of St John of Jerusalem survived in Rome, but, Ward says, they had lost their purpose and their glory.

About 1825 a revival of the Order took place in England, and George IV became its head. The knights met in the crypt of St John of Jerusalem, Clerkenwell. They set themselves the work of helping the wounded or injured. Ward claims that the Red Cross [this seems unlikely] and the St John Ambulance are offshoots of this Order. The St John Ambulance ran the first ambulances on the streets of London, and during the Great War a dozen great motor-ambulances could be seen any day near the priory gate of St John of Jerusalem. But this Order has no connection with the Masonic Order of the Knights of Malta.

The ritual of the Masonic Knights of Malta reveals a most interesting drawing on an octagonal table. While parts of the ceremony may be based on traditions of the Order, it seems to Ward that the degree itself is late eighteenth-century. The Hospitallers were orthodox through all their history, and used no secret initiation ceremony. The official ritual of the old knights is still used by the Order in Rome, and the ceremony of the Order at St John's, Clerkenwell, closely follows the ancient ritual and does not resemble the Masonic one.

But, says Ward, the Templars were different. They had a secret ceremony, and, if they carried it on inside the Order of St John after their suppression, or independently as Masons, it could easily have survived the dissolution of the Hospitallers because of its esoteric and symbolic meaning.

[The French Templar Transmission Theory will be discussed in Part 4, in the context of the ideas of A. E. Waite]

Chapter 16

Other Chivalric Degrees in Freemasonry

Legends of the Cross

So far Ward has considered the main degrees of Templary, which are taken in Masonic Preceptories. These are Knight of the Mediterranean Pass, Knight Templar and Knight of Malta. He also talks about three more degrees, which, for all practical purposes, constitute one Order with three sections in its ritual. These are the Knight of the Red Cross of Constantine, the Knight of St John, and of the Knight of the Holy Sepulchre.

The ritual draws on medieval legends of the cross. These include the vision of the cross that led Constantine the Great to adopt Christianity after seeing a vision in the sky, and the legend of the discovery of the true cross by his mother Helena.

Ward noticed several interesting things about the regalia, for example the jewel of the Knight of St John is placed within a lozenge, which he believes represents the *vesica piscis*. A Commander of St John wears a jewel of four tau crosses (T-shaped), with four equal-armed crosses spaced within the taus; the eight tau crosses combine to create a single symbol of a cross, so totalling nine crosses in all. Ward says he believes this is to symbolize the nine months of the legend of the Templar Lord of Sidon and the skull.* The jewel also

*This legend says the Templar Lord of Sidon was in love with a woman who died. He was so distraught that he opened her grave and raped her as she lay dead. As he finished his gruesome action he heard a voice telling him to return in nine months' time. When he did he found a skull and a pair of crossed thigh bones in the grave which he then took away as relic. This symbol of the skull and cross bones is used in the modern Craft as the emblems of mortality shown on the Third Degree Tracing Board.

includes a phallic cross of creation [by which Ward means the Latin cross of the Roman Church – see Figure 2] and the cross of suffering and rebirth [which Ward says is the tau cross]. These crosses are used in the jewels of the Red Cross of Constantine and the Knights of St John and Holy Sepulchre. Ward says it shows the fourfold phallic cross of matter within the circle of eternity, and this forms the heart of the fourfold tau cross within the lozenge, or *vesica piscis*. The eagle of St John is a symbol of the four compass points, and signifies the spirit soaring towards God.

The ritual of this Order is impressive. While Ward is not sure if any parts are genuinely old, he says that they are certainly interesting. This degree was imported from Malta around 1880 by Brother R. W. Little, but all he did in fact was to revive it when it almost died out. It was being worked as far back as 1780 by Major Charles Shereff. William White, Grand Secretary from 1780, and other prominent Masons were members, and in 1796 Lord Rancliffe became Grand Master of these degrees, he also became Grand Master of the Masonic Knights Templar. He was succeeded by Judge Walter Rodwell Wright in 1804, and after him the Duke of Sussex was installed Grand Master for life.

Ward says that Sussex did his best to destroy these degrees, as he did all the Christian degrees. This was Sussex's only motive for taking supreme office in most of them. They had been safeguarded by the clause in the Act of Union that permitted those lodges that already worked chivalric degrees to continue working them. Sussex did not quite succeed in destroying them, but when the degrees were revived much of the ritual had to be obtained from USA, where the degrees survived his onslaught. In America these degrees are associated with a body called The Thrice Illustrious Council of the Cross, which also works two degrees not used in England. These are the Knights of the Christian Mark and Guardians of the Sacred Conclave, and the Knights of Three Kings.

The sashes of the Grand Imperial Council, which grants the right to work these degrees, have four fleurs-de-lis in place of the crosses of the Commander. The fleur-de-lis is the emblem of the Blessed Virgin, and Ward believes it symbolizes the Cross of Calvary on which Christ paid the price for the sins our passions cause. He says the symbols remind us that this would not have been possible but for Mary's act of giving birth. It therefore represents the cross and the *vesica piscis*. The radiated triangle within two squares* is to remind us of the divine spark within man. He is placed in a material world, which is set in the limitless spaces of eternity, depicted by the circle. For the jewel of knights and commanders, who are not members of the Grand Imperial Council, one of the squares is replaced by a parallelogram.

Ward says that the quadruple tau, which is the type of cross used in this degree, is linked to the city of Jerusalem; it symbolizes Mount Calvary and the Sepulchre. The body that suffered on the cross of our passions is represented by the four taus of animal matter. As it was raised to life on the third day the tomb symbolizes the womb of the new life. The triangle of the Divine Spirit revives the square of matter and expands it to the circle of the infinite.

And what of the cross that Constantine saw in the sky? Ward says he saw the sun make a huge red cross across the sky one evening while he was in Burma.

> Behind the cross, which fell upon slight clouds gathered around the sun in the west, the sky itself turned green like turquoise, blue as sapphire, purple as amethyst. It reminded me of the sash of a knight of this degree. As the sun sank into the west, it seemed as if a purple curtain came down fold by fold, then the purple turned to black of an almost velvety texture. Next stars rushed out while that emblem of Islam, the crescent moon, swam into view. The great Buddhist Shwe Dagon Pagoda stood black and solemn, its golden sheath no longer reflecting the glory of the sun. The voice of the grasshoppers failed, and the stillness of a tropic night fell on the world, broken only by the lapping of the waters of the lake.

A cross in the sky is a symbol of the Cosmic Christ, Ward says. It is a symbol of humanity, which suffers in order to rise out of matter into the circle of eternity. It is a cross of the four cardinal points, a cross within a circle, symbolizing matter within eternity. The ritual statement 'in this sign thou shalt conquer' is more than a record of an historic incident. Suffering enables matter to triumph and be illuminated by the light that comes from the sun, which is an emblem of the

*A Masonic symbol consisting of an equilateral triangle with the Sun's ray shining from it, set within two squares, rotated by forty-five degrees to form an eight-pointed star. It is often set with a circular jewel.

Supreme Being. As the cross descends from the sun, it spreads in all directions to cover the whole Earth. It is a sign that each man shall raise himself, by that ladder of light which is within him, to be one with God. The cross is synonymous with light, for the cosmic cross is not only made of light, it is light. From the centre point of the circle it radiates till it touches the circumference. It is not even bounded by the circle of heaven; it stretches out North, East, South and West beyond the limits of the limitless. It is a seal of salvation, placed on the forehead of every human being.

The Cross, the Vesica Piscis and Masonic Astrology

The symbols of the Cross and *vesica piscis* are to be found in the higher Masonic degrees, particularly the Rose Croix and the Royal Order of Scotland, Ward says. Traditionally there have always been ten greater mysteries. The seven lesser mysteries are represented in Freemasonry by the Craft, Mark, Arch, Cryptic and similar degrees. The ten greater mysteries are mysteries of the cross, and they are represented by the Rose Croix, the Royal Order, and the degrees of the Ancient and Accepted Rite. For example, the Knight of the Brazen Serpent is pre-eminently a cross degree.

Cross degrees are quite distinct from the chivalric degrees, which involve the symbolism of the cross but are not hermetic degrees. The Knight Templar and its rituals of the Mediterranean Pass and the Knights of Malta are avowedly Christian, as are the Red Cross of Constantine, and the Knights of the Sepulchre and of St John. But they all claim to arise from chivalric orders of the Middle Ages. But the symbolism of these degrees is separate from the hermetic degrees.

The symbols of the cross and the *vesica piscis* are found within the higher degrees, and they also appear in craft masonry. (Ward thinks this is due to a blending of craft and higher-degree work during the eighteenth century, or possibly earlier.) In the first degree of the Craft there is a limited reference to the symbolic lessons of the cross. The purpose of the craft degrees is to teach about the nature of God and the earthly duties of man, these being the subject of the lesser mysteries. The greater mysteries teach what happens after death, and this is part of the mystery of the cross. But, Ward tells us, the cross also has a phallic or creative aspect.

Figure 1 – Astrological Symbols of the Planets, as drawn by Ward

One Masonic organization, the Rosicrucian Society, studies the cross and the rose. It does this by investigating the occult and mystical side of Masonry, of philosophy, the Cabbala and the ancient wisdom. Its ritual venerates Christian Rosencreuz, the mythical founder of the medieval Rosicrucians.

Masonic ceremonies show the universal nature of the cross, symbolizing the four cardinal points of the compass as well as the mystic cross of the universe. They contain astrological lore, and explain the astrological use of the cross and circle as symbols of the planets. The wheel cross, or the cross within the circle, represents the Earth and refers to the mystic crucifixion of the saviours of the world. All traditional astrological symbols are based on the cross and circle.

The cross above the circle represents Mars, and symbolizes man's passionate nature. The Martian type is forceful and generous, but rash and impetuous. In his heedless rush he often ignores the rights and feelings of others. So the cross above the circle symbolizes animal passions that have not been brought under control by the spiritual nature symbolized by the circle. The circle when shown without the cross but with a point at its centre represents the sun. This is the emblem –the point within the circle symbolizing the Divine Spirit in Man.

The cross beneath the circle stands for Venus, and symbolizes passions subdued and controlled by the Divine Spirit of Love. Venus is called the planet of love. This is the divine love which passes all understanding, but which may be degraded into sexual passion. Just as Mars has a good side, so Venus has bad aspects.

Mercury is represented by the half-circle, a symbol of the fickle moon, above a full circle, representing the Divine Spirit. The moon, which takes its light from the sun, was thought by the astrologers to represent the soul of man – the soul being half material, half spiritual, neither good nor bad, but responding to good or bad influences around it. The cross beneath the circle says the passions have been subdued by the Divine Spirit, but not completely, as with Venus. The moon symbol has an instability and a variability of character that leads astray those who are under the influence of Mercury. Mercury, however, is the giver of adaptability, desire for travel, and commercial ability.

The sign of Jupiter is the half-circle and the cross. Those who fall under the influence of this planet are just and true men, of sound judgment and good understanding, generous in word and deed, not over-rash in giving nor yet grudging by nature. The benign influence of Jupiter lends a happy balance to their lives. The cross of the Redeemer bends the moon symbol to its benign aspect, and a final peace is at hand.

Saturn is the opposite of Jupiter. Its symbol is the cross above the sign of Luna. It is the Tempter, the Satan, or perhaps the Tester. Saturn chastises and tames primitive unruly passions. A man who has Saturn in his ascendant will bear many crosses in his life, find countless obstacles and suffer many disappointments. His cross of suffering is raised aloft, and the changeful moon takes its colour from it. The man who suffers Saturn's influence will emerge strengthened by trials and purged of faults. Saturn, at its best, builds a cautious and careful nature.

Life will be hard for anyone for whom Mars is set at the angle of the cross or square with Saturn. But, as lessons are learned, the square will disappear, and a new benign influence will replace it. Saturn, when it is square with any other planet, can spoil good influences: for example, when crossed with Venus it changes divine love into carnal lust. But all evil things pass in time, as only good is eternal. This, Ward explains, is what the Craft teaches about the lore of the astrologers, that their system involves not fortune-telling but character analysis. And from a man's character they could deduce his likely actions in different circumstances.

Uranus and Neptune are new planets, and were unknown to most of the Western astrologers, although Ward notes that Indian astrologers claim they knew about them long before they were observed through a telescope. These planets are so far away that they only influence men who have achieved great heights of spirituality.

They did not influence many men before the nineteenth century, because they were not sufficiently spiritually evolved. One exception was Jesus Christ, a typical Neptune man of the exalted type. Neptune and Uranus are mysterious planets, and their effects little understood. At present they affect only a few individuals, their influence being most powerful with mystic and psychic people (Neptune affects mystics and Uranus psychics). Their influence on ordinary people is generally unpleasant, but their benign side comes into play for spiritual people.

Uranus's symbol, a cross between two half-circles resting on a circle, combines the symbols of Mars, Jupiter and Luna. This combination explains why Uranus may affect the spiritual-psychic-soul plane, the body plane, or the earth plane. At its worst it brings worldly disaster, but its better aspects offer a love of the old and the occult. The symbol of Neptune combines two half-circles and the sign of Mars: the half-circles are poised on the ends of the arms of a cross. The half-moons are raised to mark Neptune's mystical influence. In the symbol of Uranus they are placed halfway down to show that the Uranian types are psychics and occultists, not true mystics. The double moons show the great variability of the influence of these two planets.

Ward feels that, whatever you may think of astrology as a practical art, it has a higher aspect, which is the analysis of character, and the symbols help in this study. He says the planets are outward and visible signs of great spiritual forces, and in the lore of Masonry symbolize angels or attributes of the Deity.

Ward has so far mainly talked about the phallic cross, or the cross of our passions. But he goes on to explain that there are two types of cross in the symbolism of Freemasonry: the tau cross, which is shaped like a T and represents the old phallic cross of creation, and the Latin cross (see Figure 2), which is a symbol of suffering. The two aspects of the symbolism of the cross blend and often cannot be separated. For example, although symbolically Christ was crucified on the cross of passions, pictures and sculptures of the event usually show the cross of suffering. The two thieves are generally shown on tau crosses, often with their arms bent over them. This emphasizes different aspects of the cross, and such oversights show that the old knowledge of cross symbolism has been lost.

The Tau Cross

Ward considers that originally the tau symbol was inverted, ⊥, and in this form is just a symbol of the phallus and a primitive way of representing the male creative function. So it is a symbol of the Creator of All. In the same way the *vesica piscis*, is a simplified form of the female productive principle in God. A mother preserves life and brings forth a child. She then suckles it and sustains it until it can stand alone. So the symbol of the *vesica piscis* became associated with the Saviour. But Ward notes that the Hindu symbol of the Rose and Cross is a lingam (that is, a phallus) surrounded by a yoni, (which is a vagina); it symbolizes the union of male and female principles in one God.

Ward says that phallic worship is ancient, and the phallus was a symbol of God. It remains so today in India, where the lingam is revered by millions of perfectly moral people who hold the strictest views on sexual morality.

In the story of Osiris, who was cut into pieces and scattered throughout the land of Egypt, his member was missing when Isis reassembled his body, and she made a wooden substitute. This is a double symbolism making the phallus and the cross one symbol. The risen Osiris had no more need for his member, and the legend is a lesson to encourage us to control the passions that torment our soul. Symbolically Osiris, minus his member, is cleansed of all passions and is now fit to go to the mansions of bliss.

This tau cross also appears as the symbol of the axe (see Figure 2). The axe is a symbol of rule, particularly the double-headed axe, which retains the tau shape. This symbol goes back to the Neolithic, when a haft was split and bound, and the stone axe head passed through it, making a butterfly or tau shape. The stone axe can also be seen as a hammer, which is the symbol of Jupiter, Indra, Thor and the kings of the Pantheon. When bronze replaced stone the substitution of the double axe restored the ancient symbol. The stone war hammer retained the T-shape.

The axe or hammer has been a symbol of rule and authority among both men and gods since very early times. The axe, called Neter, was a symbol for God among the ancient Egyptians. It is also the symbol of Indra, who was a king of the gods in India. In Knossos there is a temple called the House of the Double Axe. This is because the temple contains an altar of three cubes on which are carved a number of double axes. The arrangement of this ancient building reminded Ward of a modern lodge-room:

There is a stone throne for the Worshipful Master, round the sides are stone benches for the columns, and in the centre an altar formed by a treble cube adorned with these ideograms of axes, one on each side of each cube. Probably the god thereby referred to is Zeus, or at least his prototype.

Ward says that the Norse god Thor had the axe as his symbol, and the Egyptians associated the axe with Ptah. The axe was also a symbol of authority among Greeks and Romans, and for the Anglo-Saxons it had the same significance, which Ward believes derived from the axe of Thor.

The symbol of the tau cross dates back to Neolithic times. Ward tells how he saw the excavation of a Neolithic grave in England that held the skeletons of a man and his wife. She had been slain at his burial and her body laid in the grave with her feet against his side so together their bodies formed a tau cross.

The hammer, or its modern Masonic equivalent the gavel, and the tau were once identical, Ward explains. This shows a natural evolution of symbolism. The tau cross evolved from the phallus, as a symbol of God the Creator, the Father. Once mankind evolved the axe symbol the patriarchal age arrived, and who else, he asks, should wield authority as the father of the clan but the earthly representative of the Heavenly Father?

The Latin Cross

The Latin cross (see Figure 2), is a cross of suffering and redemption, Ward tells us. Its symbol has a different origin from the tau. It evolved when the two poles of Boaz and Jachin were crossed to divide the heavens into four quarters. This cross is an important symbol in the solar cult, with the swastika being an early form of it. Both versions are symbols of the sun on its journey round the earth.

This Latin cross is the one on which the cosmic Christ is forever being crucified. There are many pre-Christian forms of this cross. The most common has all arms equal and is found all over the world.

This cross was found by early explorers among numerous races in Africa long before any missionaries could have brought it. It was also am important symbol for the Druids. Among native Americans, the Hurons tattooed themselves with a cross or a serpent on the thigh, while in Africa the Baratonga tattoo a cross and a square side by side. But ancient Egypt had more variations on this cross than any other country. The Teutonic cross was a symbol worn by the gods; Bes and Nefer-Hetep are both shown wearing it. Moreover, the equal-armed cross is often found with characters cut into the arms, and, looking at these symbols Ward was struck by the fact that if the characters had been Hebrew instead of Egyptian, he would had taken it for the jewel of the Most Worshipful Sovereign of the eighteenth degree. He says that these Egyptian characters, making up an *ankh*, stand for a holy name.

The symbol of the *ankh* was an Egyptian emblem of eternal life. The cross of suffering and redemption is distinguished from the phallic, or tau cross, by the presence of a fourth arm, or headpiece. The *ankh* is a form of cross of redemption, as the loop forms a head-piece, but it really combines the emblems of the tau and *vesica piscis*, so symbolically uniting both male and female aspects of the cross in one. This makes it the most venerated of all crosses. Ward reminds us that among the Hebrews, the tau was regarded as a sacred symbol and is associated with both the upward and downward pointing triangles.

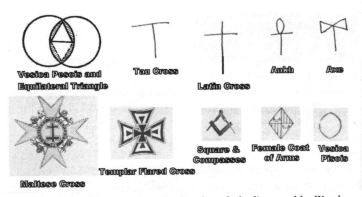

Figure 2 – The crosses and related symbols discussed by Ward

The Crosses of the Craft

Ward says that both cross symbols can be found in the Craft, but the tau cross is the most important. Think about the shape you make as you take the first regular step, he asks. What is it? Now you know where the tau cross fits into Freemasonry. Consider this step in relation to the anti-Christian charge made against the Templars: that they trampled on the cross. The meaning of the act is perfectly clear if that cross was the tau cross, for it is the ritual of the first regular step in Freemasonry. This symbolizes that as Entered Apprentice Freemasons we must learn to trample our animal passions underfoot. Unless our animal passions are brought under control as we continue through each degree, we cannot find the centre of the circle. This step uses not the symbol of the Latin cross of suffering, but the older phallic cross. Ward is sure that the lessons of the steps are unobjectionable, once their symbolism is understood.

But, Ward says, the symbol of the tau cross is evident in the gavels of the officers of a Craft Lodge. They are T-crosses and combine the symbols of the hammer (the sign of rule), and the T-cross (the symbol of the male creative side of the Deity). Likewise a T is placed on the apron of the Master of the Lodge, to show the symbol as a square, and also to bring out its phallic meaning. If this were not intended, why not use a single square, the form used on other occasions in Lodge? The officers who hold the gavels are the Master, Senior Warden and Junior Warden. They are the rulers in the Lodge, but they also represent three aspects of the Deity When their three tau crosses are united, as they are in the Royal Arch, the triple tau, the symbol of a single God, is formed. The Deacons represent the mothering and preservative side of the Craft, and they never hold gavels.

The symbol of the Latin cross, or cross of suffering, is only seen in two places in a Craft Lodge. These are the shapes of the Tyler's sword and the Inner Guard's dagger.

The First Degree of the Craft is a degree of birth, Ward says. It serves to remind us of the suffering of the mother who gave birth to us. The ritual reminds us of the pain that we and she felt when we came from darkness into light. The proper manner of proceeding from East to West in this important craft degree is in a series of Latin-cross steps. But the Latin cross is really part of the ritual of the higher degrees, such as the Rose Croix, and the Templar degrees.

The Mark is also a craft degree, and in it we find the T-cross disguised as the symbol of the Lewis. This is a metal cramp used to join pieces of stone together. The ritual also tells us that a Lewis is the son of a Mason, and a support in old age.

In the Royal Arch the triple tau is described at length. Its form symbolizes the threefold nature of the Deity, who is one and yet three. Each of these three Persons has attributes of the other two. God the Creator is also the Preserver and the Destroyer, and in India the phallus is the symbol of Shiva the Destroyer. The creative act brings with it a death that ends time. The cross of birth is also the cross of death, and its symbol is the Latin cross. Christianity completes the triple Tau by showing us that because God the Preserver was slain on the cross, we shall be born again to salvation.

Ward comments that the tau was a popular Masons' mark in medieval times, and a particularly well-cut one can be seen on one of the pillars in the chapel in the White Tower at the Tower of London. It is contemporary with the column, and cannot be later than 1080.

Chapter 17

The Vesica Piscis

The Symbol of Woman

Ward says that the *vesica piscis*, (), symbolizes the passive, female principle. It is found in India and China, being placed behind the gods or the Buddha, but its use is universal. In India it is called the yoni, and is associated with the phallus to form the lingam stone, which is an object of veneration in Hindu temples. The original Egyptian Divine Trinity was Father-Creator, Mother-Preserver, and Son-Destroyer. In the Christian Trinity Jesus represents the destroyer of death, while the Holy Ghost takes the place of the Divine Mother. There was a sect of Eastern Christians who regarded the Virgin Mary as the second person of the Trinity, so reverting to the ancient Egyptian Trinity.

The *vesica piscis* has always been associated with the preservative side of the Deity, and Vishnu is often depicted standing in it. The Buddha is similarly depicted, and in medieval Europe the saints, and particularly the Virgin, were also placed in it. Because the Church was said to be the Bride of Christ ecclesiastical seals were surrounded by a *vesica piscis*. The seals of the nobility were never placed in this symbol, but in a circle.

The symbol of the *vesica piscis* is the basis of most medieval architecture. The pointed arch and the rose window are based on it. The basis of architecture is geometry, and the *vesica piscis* appears in the first proposition of Euclid, where it is used to form an equilateral triangle. Ward tells us that this triangle has long been used as a Masonic emblem of God Himself.

The equilateral triangle formed by the intersection of two circles is a proposition of great practical use to medieval Masons. It carries a deep mystical lesson in its simple symbolism. The symbol of the Royal Arch and the cryptic degrees is the reversed equilateral triangle, ▽. It extends to the lozenge, or diamond shape, ◊, which is the form a woman was allowed to use for the shape of her personal coat of arms (see Figure 2).

In ancient Egypt the *vesica piscis* was associated with the tau cross to form the *ankh* (see Figure 2), which is a symbol of eternal life. Ward says that the earliest rituals used by the Rose Croix and the early Greek Christians shows that they understood the esoteric significance of this symbol of womanhood. But, he adds, as men hesitated to call a spade a spade, a number of synonyms grew up to stand for the symbol of the *vesica piscis*. The most common was the rose, which went on to develop new and fanciful meanings that obscured its original meaning. It came to represent the five wounds of Christ, and of Hiram Abif. It was said that red roses show the colour of the victim's blood, and white his innocence. In Christian times the rose was linked to Jesus, as the Rose of Sharon and the Lily of the Valley. So the white lily was substituted for the white rose. In Jacobite times the white rose was associated with King Charles I, known as the White Martyr. In this way the white rose became a badge of the Jacobites.

The symbolism of the rose has swamped the *vesica piscis*, Ward says, but it survives in Craft Lodges in the form of one of the most ancient and mystical symbols of Freemasonry.

The Vesica Piscis in the Craft

The craft has always honoured the square and compasses, and it is within these ancient tools that we find the *vesica piscis*. A woman was not allowed to have her coat of arms in the shape of a shield, which was considered to be suitable only for male warriors, so the lozenge was substituted. But why, Ward asks, was it not a square or any other shape?

Ward says that the *vesica piscis* is a symbol derived from the distinguishing aspect of the female anatomy in the Middle Ages. In heraldry it is stylized and disguised to suit the fastidious, but its symbolic origin is clear. He notes that the lozenge shape is easily constructed by arranging the square and compass into the mystic sign, so uniting the meaning of the *vesica piscis* with Masonic implements. When the Candidate takes his Obligation over the square and compasses, the gavel (or phallic tau cross) is also on the Master's pedestal. So the cross and the *vesica piscis* come together to form the third great light in Masonry. The cross represents the active, or male influence in the Lodge, which the Master uses before taking any action. The female symbol is passive and only becomes active when the square and the compass are separated.

Ward explains how the obligation is taken inside this lozenge emblem. The candidate is admitted on the cross of the inner guard's dagger, ruled by the tau cross, and obligated within the *vesica piscis*. The first lesson he learns is how to make the first regular step in Freemasonry, and so publicly declares his intention of trampling underfoot the primitive and animal passions that attack his soul. The lozenge is the symbol of the preserver, and by making his obligation on it the candidate promises to preserve the secrets of the degree and so is saved from the fate that would befall a cowan.

Having been admitted in the First Degree on the dagger cross, the first half of the *vesica piscis* is presented to his naked left breast as he makes his obligation. In the Second Degree he is admitted on the square, and it is raised above his head, before it later plays its important role in his second obligation. In the Third Degree he is admitted on the compasses, which are also raised over his head, but they play no part in the third obligation.

In this ritual sequence, Ward explains, the Candidate passes through the *vesica piscis* in two sections, and this symbolism is twice emphasized during his obligations. These acts have exoteric and esoteric meanings and invoke the female or passive principle of the Deity, just as the creative or masculine is brought to mind by the tau cross.

The candidate is reminded that, just as he enters the material world through the *vesica piscis*, so he must enter his life of initiation by the same road. Only after he has done this will he be able to see the light at the Centre. The *vesica piscis* is the female or preservative principle of God, without which we cannot exist, nor hope to be preserved from the powers of darkness and evil that threaten our spiritual journey.

Ward insists that the cross and *vesica piscis* are to be found in Craft Lodges, and thinks it would be strange if they were not, considering how old they are, and how essential they were to the initiatory rites of the ancient mysteries. He reminds us that the lozenge symbol of the *vesica piscis* is found all over the world; ancient Egyptians, Maya in Central America, and Druids in Great Britain and Ireland all used it in their rituals.

He notes two further instances of this symbol in the craft: first, in the collars of the officers, and, second, the rosettes on the Master Mason's apron. All full members of the Lodge have three roses on their apron to remind them that their duty is passive, to obey the commands of the Worshipful Master. The Master, as a symbol of his active role, wears three taus on his apron instead of the three rosettes.

Conclusions to Part Three

Ward trained as a historian at Cambridge and was initiated into the Isaac Newton Cambridge University Lodge, No. 858. He looked closely at the possible ways in which the rituals of the Knights Templar could have been passed into Freemasonry and made a case worth considering, and perhaps even reinvestigating with the tools of modern data retrieval.

It is perhaps not surprising that Ward has never been taken seriously in the pages of Quatuor Coronati's house journal. Here is an example of the esteem in which he is held by the self-professed 'Premier' lodge of research:

> Curiosity about the many odd characters who figure in the development of 'Fringe Masonry' in the Victorian era has grown rapidly, but there has been little attempt to consider their motives or to bring the tools of reputable scholarship to the study of their enthusiasms . . . The reason for this neglect is an understandable wish on the part of the authentic school to distance itself from the more lunatic pronouncements on Masonic history and traditions that have been made by representatives of the 'esoteric school'. By the 1920s papers reflecting the 'esoteric' approach had virtually disappeared from the Proceedings and Transactions of Study Circles and Research Lodges, all of which were anxious to retain the academic respectability that the work of the authentic school had given to Masonic research . . . But if the work of the Esoteric School was denied access to Masonic research publications, it faced no such restriction in the outside world. During the inter-war period books based upon the esoteric approach

appeared in profusion, their authors (e.g. JSM Ward . . . *et al.*) making claims and drawing conclusions that would have been far less extravagant and outlandish had their authors previously received the benefit of reasoned debate and scholarly criticism of their theories within the confines of this research lodge.

But Ward had no real chance of any of his ideas being accepted by any arm of the United Grand Lodge of England. He was raising the whole question of where did Freemasonry start? And his work could not be scholarly by the standards of Quatuor Coronati, because he was not concluding that it started in London in 1717.

The paragon of reasoned debate and scholarly criticism who wrote the extract quoted above, held a Diploma in Public Health, while Ward had been awarded an upper second-class honours degree in history from the University of Cambridge. But one was a Grand Officer of the Premier Grand Lodge of the World, whilst the other was not. If UGLE does not like your ideas, then, as Ward himself pointed out, English students of Masonic history who seek Grand Lodge honours fear even to suggest that anything connected with Freemasonry might be older than the eighteenth century. To do so is to ensure that they fall out of favour with the United Grand Lodge of England. So the reasoned debate and scholarly criticism of Quatuor Coronati would, as Ward said, always prefer to declare any evidence of an origin of Freemasonry earlier than 1717 as forged or based on imagination.

One particular idea of Ward's, however, struck a chord with my own research. He saw a link between the lozenge symbol and Freemasonry. Ward could not have been aware of the extreme antiquity of the lozenge symbol,* but he certainly recognized its significance and explained the symbolism clearly.

However, the case he makes for a Templar link to Freemasonry raises many questions worthy of further debate, so the next writer whose ideas I decided to revisit is another anti-hero of Quatuor Coronati, AE Waite.

It dates back over 70,000 years, but this evidence was only found in 2001. It is the earliest symbol known to have been carved by humans, as I explained in Turning the Hiram Key (2005), and produces a measurable emotional effect on the human perception system.

Part Four

A. E. Waite
on
Freemasonry, the Secret
Tradition and the
Knights Templar

Chapter 18

The Secret Wardens

Arthur Edward Waite

Arthur Edward Waite was a highly original mystic thinker. He was born in New York in 1857, to an English mother and an American father; his mother, who was not married to his father, brought him to live in England when he was two. As a young man he studied theosophy and magic, spending many hours in the Reading Room of the British Museum. He wanted to write fiction, but never quite made it as a novelist. In 1896 he became a member of the Hermetic Order of the Golden Dawn, went on to join the Societas Rosicruciana in 1902, and in 1910 published the famous Waite-Rider deck of Tarot cards. He then started a whole new field of Masonic research when he wrote a two-volume book, *The Secret Tradition of Freemasonry* (1911).

He was not initiated into Freemasonry until he was in his forties, when he entered Runymede Lodge, No. 2430, in Wraysbury on 19 September 1901. He was raised at St Marylebone Lodge, No. 1305, in London in 1902 and went on to become Master of Runymede Lodge in 1910. Once he was raised Waite became a keen collector of Masonic degrees and a prolific joiner of side orders. In 1902 he created what he called a Secret Council of Rites with the sole objective of working rituals that were not always recognized by the United Grand Lodge of England. He also visited Scotland to take the degrees of the Early Grand Rite. In 1902 Waite attended some meetings of Quatuor Coronati Lodge but was not impressed by the scholarship there, saying of its members:

These people know not whither they are going. These are not brethren; they are simulacra – antic figures which a juggler dances.

When Waite published his *Secret Tradition of Freemasonry* and the later *New Encyclopedia of Freemasonry*, the Quatuor Coronati lodge followed its normal policy of attacking his ideas and rubbishing him personally. One of its members said in a review of Waite's *Encyclopedia*:

What particular advantage or abilities does Bro. Waite claim to possess which enable him to take a position superior to that of earlier writers? . . . Can he be so set down in ignorance, or is this book to be understood as yet another deliberate flight into the realms of fantasy?

The writer was rewarded in the usual Masonic manner for his attack on somebody prepared to question the theory that Freemasonry started in London in 1717; he was first made Master of Quatuor Coronati and then a Grand Deacon of the United Grand Lodge of England. Realizing that there was Masonic preferment to be earned by attacking Waite, other members of Quatuor Coronati joined in the hue and cry. One reviewer, who remarked that 'Waite had an inordinately high opinion of his own scholarship, and a correspondingly low one of the more usually recognized Masonic scholars', also became a Master of Quatuor Coronati lodge, and in due course Grand Sword-bearer to the United Grand Lodge of England. Waite was made a Senior Grand Warden of the Grand Lodge of Iowa for his Masonic writing, but was never honoured by the United Grand Lodge of England. Even so, he is still remembered by Quatuor Coronati, witness a recent published comment by another lodge member:

During his lifetime Waite was castigated, and with justification, for his peculiarities of style, for his frequent errors of historical fact and for his cavalier attitude and contemptuous references to his contemporaries.

Waite's attitude to facts is demonstrated in the comments he made in the introduction to his translation from the French of the works of Alphonse Louis Constant:

The History of Magic, by Alphonse Louis Constant, written – like the majority of his works – under the pseudonym of Eliphas Levi, is the most arresting, entertaining and brilliant of all studies on the subject with which I am acquainted. So far back as 1896 I said that it was admirable as a philosophical survey, its historical inaccuracies notwithstanding, and that there is nothing in occult literature which can suffer comparison therewith.

I have to admit that Waite's writing style can be ponderous, but his ideas about the Secret Tradition that inspires Freemasonry remain interesting, which is why I have summarized them in the fourth part of this book.

The Wardens of the Temple of Sion

Waite reports that a Holy Order called the 'Temple of Sion' existed in 1464, which he thinks may be the first instance of a form of speculative Masonry, though he is not sure that it is conclusive evidence for a separate existence of symbolical Masonry. This and the Regius manuscript are the basis of his idea that some Hermetic fraternities played a part in the development of the speculative Craft. He believes that it was the mystic ideas of a Kabbalistic section of what he called Wardens of the Secret Tradition that transformed Freemasonry. He says their work is traceable in the Craft legend, which represents a reflection of Zoharic preoccupations that began in England with Robert Fludd and Thomas Vaughan, were continued through Henry More, and are in evidence in both France and Britain around the time of the French Revolution.

Waite says that the Kabbalistic preoccupation with the mystery literature came before symbolic Masonry, just as the Baptist came before the Christ. He draws on an authoritative body of Jewish writings known as the Sefer Zohar, which, he says, offers scholars proof that the Secret Tradition of Israel was the most powerful engine for bringing about a general conversion. They believed that the Zoharic Messiah was literally their own Messiah, and that Kabbalistic doctrine foretold the idea of the Christian Trinity. When they found that there was a legend of loss in Israel, and that something was expected to be restored, they believed that restoration would be Christ.

He says that we Masons also know of a loss, and must therefore look towards Kabbalism as the likely root-matter of our mystery. Christian High Grade Masonry restores our loss in Christ, and he is inclined to think that the Craft was designed to dissolve into Christian Masonry.

Enter Chevalier Ramsay

Waite says that Chevalier Andrew Michael Ramsay laid the foundation of the Christian High Grades of Freemasonry in 1737. Ramsay held a French Masonic office of Orator and Grand Chancellor, and his intervention took the form of a discourse to the Provincial Grand Lodge of England, which he delivered from his lodge in Paris. Ramsay's lodge dated from 1730 and had applied for a constitution as a Provincial Grand Lodge in 1735; when Ramsay delivered this oration the lodge was newly authorized.

His words may be summarized briefly:

1. The Crusaders created the Order of Freemasonry in the Holy Land during the period of the Christian Wars in Palestine.
2. Its objective was to unite individuals of every nation
    (a) To restore the Temple in the city of Jerusalem and maintain and extend the true religion there and
    (b) To return to the basic principles of the sacred art of architecture.
3. The Masonic mystery is a continuation of the mysteries of Ceres, Isis, Minerva, Urania and Diana.
4. The Masonic mystery is a continuation of the old religion of Noah and the patriarchs.
5. Freemasonry comes from remote antiquity and was restored, rather than started, in the Holy Land.
6. To thwart Saracen spies the Crusaders agreed secret signs and words to recognize each other.
7. They adopted symbolic ceremonies to initiate candidates and advance members from lower Grades.
8. When kings, princes and lords returned from Palestine to their own countries they established Masonic Lodges.
9. This is how Lodge Mother Kilwinning was formed in 1286.
10. The main order of chivalry was St John of Jerusalem.

Waite notes that Ramsay's words imply that the Lodge of Kilwinning is important to the beginning of Scottish Freemasonry; that Freemasonry was a universal Order from the start, as its first lodges were formed by returning Crusaders; and that the Masonic mystery has its roots in the religion of Noah and the Patriarchs. These simple affirmations soon became articles of faith.

At this time the Craft was a new introduction to the continent. Only in 1725 was the Lodge of St Thomas founded in Paris, under a warrant from the London Grand Lodge to John Ratcliffe, Earl of Derwentwater. But Ramsay's Oration gave the Order a claim to date from time immemorial that was imposed on its own authority and only explained by legend. Ramsay, although a licensed spokesman, put forward his personal views in the language of certainty, and they were accepted blindly. An example of this is his claim that unknown superiors granted patents to Lodges from a Holy House in Great Britain. The romantic association with the Crusades inspired the continental imagination. And Waite says that Ramsay hinted at Jacobite connections within French Freemasonry to enhance the attraction of his ideas.

Ramsay's discourse drove the evolution of the High Grades, and, although he is credited with the introduction of a Rite, Waite rejects this idea on the basis of his own research and also on the authority of Gould. However he admits that Ramsay's ideas gave rise to a Masonic tradition known as the Ecossais, or Scots, Lodges, saying that lodges claiming to inherit this tradition manipulated their Craft Grades to fit Ramsay's hypothesis and also added High Grades to their rituals. Waite says it is from this source that the St Andrew degrees, the Knightly degrees, and the Templar degrees sprang. Ramsay kindled a passion for Grades, and more and more degrees were invented as system grew out of system.

The year 1754 marks the foundation of the Rite of the Strict Observance, although Waite thinks it had earlier roots in the mystic Rite of Martines de Pasqually and the Chapter of Clermont. The name of Baron von Hund is closely linked to the Strict Observance. He was received into Masonry in 1742. A year later he said the Earl of Kilmarnock created him a Knight of the Temple.

Waite notes a gap of some seventeen years between Ramsay's statements and the start of the Strict Observance in 1754. But in this period isolated Grades were formed. These were the Petit Elu, or Lesser Elect (known as the Kadosh Grades) in 1743, the Primordial

Rose-Cross Jacobite Chapter of Arras in 1747, and the Jacobite Grade of Ecossais FidèËles in 1748. Finally, in 1750 the Mother Scottish Lodge of Marseilles was founded.

Ramsay was born at Ayr, in Scotland, in 1668, and when he delivered this discourse in 1737 he was nearly seventy. Waite says this is not an age at which considerable Masonic or other activity might be expected. The Oration was Ramsay's last public intervention in Masonry (he died in 1743), and Waite thinks that his Masonic influence ended with his discourse, and that he probably had no intention of producing the effect on Masonry that appeared after his death. He believes that the Rit De Bouillon and the Rite of Ramsay are figments of French imagination, created more than half a century later.

He says that the first degrees of these Grades are initially the same as the first three degrees of the Craft. Their higher grades, as listed by Waite, are:

(4) Scottish Master
(5) Novice
(6) Knight of the Temple – also called Knight Levite of the Tower, and Knight of the Tower.

This structure compares with the Rite of the Strict Observance whose first three degrees are the ordinary Craft Grades. They are followed by

(4) Scottish Master
(5) Novice
(6) Knight Templar, or Knight of the Temple. This degree is divided into *Eques*, *Armiger*, *Socius* and *Eques Professus*.

Waite thinks that the Rite of Ramsay is an imaginary antedated version of the Rite of the Strict Observance, which originated in Germany with Baron von Hund. There is doubt and confusion about Hund's background, some saying he was initiated at Strasbourg when it was part of France, others that it was in Frankfurt-am-Main. But Waite insists that both rites are manifestly Templar, and that the Strict Observance just amplifies Ramsay's theory.

Waite rejects the theory that Ramsay is the father of the idea of Masonic chivalry, and that the Ecossais Grades follow his ideas, because the Kabbalistic Tradition is at the root of the symbolism of Craft Masonry, and the Kabbala has no place in Scotland either in Crusading times or later. As to the claim that Ramsay's theory covers just the operative side of Masonry, Waite prefers to accept the Building Guilds in Great Britain as the source for this body of symbolism. He does not accept that Palestine was its inspiration. He said that, for all he knew and cared, Kilwinning might be the head and fountain of the operative Craft, but he went on to conclude that idea that Masonic chivalry originated in the Holy Land of Palestine came out of Chevalier Ramsay's head.

The Chapter of Clermont was formed by Chevalier de Bonneville in Paris in 1754. This Chapter was instituted to confer only the High Grades, and it recognized three:

(a) Knight of the Eagle.
(b) Illustrious Knight or Templar.
(c) Sublime Illustrious Knight.

It was a Templar system. Baron von Hund is said to have taken these grades in Paris before he set up the Strict Observance; a branch of this Chapter existed in Berlin in 1760. In 1758 the Chapter in France renamed itself the Council of the Emperors of East and West.

In 1750 the Scottish Mother Lodge of Marseilles was founded, reputedly by a wandering Scotsman. Its rite consisted of eighteen Degrees:

1. Apprentice
2. Companion
3. Master
4. Perfect Master of St Andrew
5. Grand Ecossais
6. Knight of the Black Eagle
7. Commander of the Black Eagle
8. Rose Croix
9. True Mason
10. Knight Argonautic
11. Knight of the Golden Fleece
12. Apprentice Philosopher
13. Knight-Adept of the Eagle and the Sun
14. Sublime Philosopher

15. Knight of the Phoenix
16. Adept of the Mother Lodge
17. Knight of the Rainbow
18. Knight of the Sun

Waite records that this lodge was founded in Marseilles as a Lodge under the patronage of St John of Scotland. Around 1762 it claimed to be the Scottish Mother Lodge of France, and by 1765 had branch lodges at Paris and Lyons, in Provence, the French colonies, and even in the Levant.

The Council of the Emperors of East and West, which grew out of the Chapter of Clermont, had twenty-five degrees. Waite lists them as:

1. Apprentice
2. Companion
3. Master
4. Secret Master
5. Perfect Master
6. Intimate Secretary
7. Intendant of Buildings
8. Provost and Judge
9. Elect Master of Nine, or Elect of the Nine
10. Elect Master of Fifteen, or Elect of Fifteen
11. Illustrious Elect, or Chief of the Twelve Tribes
12. Grand Master Architect
13. Knight Royal Arch, or Royal Axe
14. Grand Elect, Ancient Perfect Master, or Grand Elect Ancient
15. Knight of the Sword, or of the East
16. Prince of Jerusalem
17. Knight of the East and the West
18. Rose Croix
19. Grand Pontiff, or Master *ad vitam*
20. Grand Patriarch Noachite, or Grand Patriarch
21. Grand Master of the Key of Masonry, or Grand Master of the Key
22. Prince of Libanus, Knight Royal Arch, or Royal Axe
23. Knight of the Sun, Prince Adept, Chief of the Grand Consistory
24. Illustrious Chief, Grand Commander of the White and Black Eagle, Grand Elect Kadosh

25. Most Illustrious Prince of Masonry, Grand and Sublime Knight Commander of the Royal Secret, or Commander of the Royal Secret

The Council of Emperors was also known as the Ancient Rite, the Rite of Heredom or the Rite of Perfection. The holders of its highest Grades were called Substitutes-General of the Royal Art and Grand Wardens of the Sovereign Lodge of St John of Jerusalem.

Waite tells of a legend that Prince Charles Edward Stuart placed the Rite under the care and patronage of Frederick the Great in 1786. Frederick is said to have increased the number of degrees to thirty-three. Another story says that in 1761 the Council granted a patent to a Stephen Morin to promote the system in America, and that Morin took the system to Charleston, at the beginning of the nineteenth century. Eight further grades were then added to make up the rite now know as the Ancient and Accepted Scottish Rite. The Degrees said to be added to those of the original Council were:

1. Prince of Mercy
2. Grand Commander of the Temple
3. Chief of the Tabernacle
4. Grand Scottish Knight of St Andrew
5. Prince of the Tabernacle
6. Inspector Inquisitor Commander
7. Knight of the Brazen Serpent
8. Sovereign Grand Inspector-General

Despite its position and influence Waite thinks that Ancient and Accepted Scottish Rite is inchoate. He says it preserves several Grades that have no value, symbolically or otherwise. The Candidate is continually testifying his obedience to the New Covenant while returning to an obedience of the Old Law. The ritual jumps about in time. It is in the time of Solomon, then late in the Middle Ages, and then once again in Israel under the rule of Solomon. As only three out of thirty-three degrees are worked, Waite thinks a more logical arrangement should be adopted.

He sums up the legend of Chevalier Ramsay by saying that Ramsay explained the origins of Masonry as an evolution of a symbolic art of building that grew out of the material art and skill of the stonemason. He inspired Templar grades of Freemasonry, which have become

known as the Rite of Ramsay. Ramsay offered this rite to the English
Grand Lodge and when they refused it returned to France, where it
became an enormous success.

Gould believed that Ramsay's story was a sequence of idle fictions,
and Waite agreed that the Templar Masonic hypothesis could not
have begun with Ramsay. He says Ramsay's grades were not known
before the setting up of the rite of Strict Observance. The growth of
the Mason High Grades owes nothing to Ramsay's personal influence
but draws greatly on his speculative ideas. Gould claims that the idea
of Rite of Ramsay first appeared in 1825, but Waite says there are
traces of the legend some thirty or forty years earlier. The idea of such
a collection of rituals explains the rise of the Masonic Grades of
Chivalry in general and the Templar Grades in particular. Waite is
certain that no Masonic Templar Grades existed before the founding
of the rite of Strict Observance. But, he adds, there is an extrinsic
Templar claim that depends on the Charter of Larmenius.

Waite thinks the Ecossais Grades of Masonry are of great
symbolical importance. Below is a synopsis of three, which, he says,
offer a representative view of Scottish Masonry.

(1) Apprentice Ecossais. The candidate is told to wash his hands –
like Christ and His Apostles before the Last Supper. He then
makes the Sign of the Cross on his forehead, with the water.
This is a Masonic baptism, carried out on himself of his own
free will. It symbolizes his change of allegiance from the Old
Law to the New. Next seven gifts of the Spirit are given to him,
symbolizing the Christian rite of Confirmation. Then the
Master strikes seven light blows on his forehead with a gavel.
These signify the Candidate's acceptance of the mystic
responsibility of Christian Masonry. Finally, the Candidate
receives a symbolic Eucharist from the Master. This
completes the grade's reflection of the three sacraments of the
Church. Then there is a further ceremony in which the
Candidate kneels on the ground before a Blazing Star
embroidered in the carpet of the Temple. The letter G is placed
at the centre of the five-pointed star while the candidate
prostrates himself on his elbows, bows his head to the ground
and kisses the letter G. The ritual says he has now received the
Spirit of the Father through the channel of the Eternal Son via
the manifestation of His appearance on earth.

(2) Companion Ecossais. As the Candidate is introduced into the Temple he sees a great altar lit by eighty-one candles. The lights spell out the Divine Name in the four words of Jewish theosophy. Behind the Altar is an image of the glory of the Grand Architect surrounded by the seven intelligences of heaven. The Trinity is shown as a central triangle. It also shows the Ark of the Covenant covered by the wings of the cherubim; the Lamb seated by a book sealed with seven seals; the Brazen Sea, the Seven-branched Candlestick, the Altar of Burnt Offerings and the Table of the Shewbread.

The candidate is told to take off shoes as he is about to enter the Holy of Holies. The tomb of the Master Builder is in the middle of the Temple. The candidate enters the tomb, which is usually drawn on a floorcloth or an embroidered carpet, and is told that his destiny is to take the place of the Master. As a Companion Ecossais he takes on himself the burden of the Christ-life.

(3) Master Ecossais. The arrangement of the Temple is the same as for the previous Grade, but four twigs of acacia now surround the tomb of the Master. The venue is still the Temple of Solomon, but it has undergone a great transfiguration, because the symbolism shows that Word of the Christ now fills the Holy Place. The Candidate washes in water, confesses his sins, and questions are put to him. If he makes satisfactory answers he is admitted to the work of completion of the Living Temple. Next he reads the Obligation of the Grade, and the paper it is written on is burnt before him. He is next appointed Intendant of the Buildings and is called Moabon. He becomes responsible for the progress of the spiritual Temple. A Masonic ordination follows making him a priest of transcendental Masonry. He is anointed on the forehead, the right eye and the heart with oil. He receives another Eucharistic Rite before being sent forth as member of the Order of Melchisedec to preach to every nation.

According to the ritual of the Grade there are three Covenants: (a) That of Mount Sinai; (b) That of the Death and Passion of Jesus Christ; (c) That of the Divine Alliance. These three are one, even as three angles form one triangle.

Waite says he does not think the erudite and spiritual mind of Andrew Michael Ramsay would lose anything of its lustre if he were the author of these Grades. They might even have been worthy to pass under the chivalrous patronage of Godfrey de Bouillon, but the first Christian King of Jerusalem was not mentioned in Ramsay's oration.

Chapter 19

The Influence of
Chevalier Ramsay

Ramsay's Oration

Waite makes an important point about Ramsay. He says that many
writers have been content to follow vague reports of his Masonic
discourse rather than refer to the text; but most of those who have
seen it have failed to notice one important statement in it. Before
discussing his point I have reproduced the text of Ramsay's Oration
below for reference:

> The noble ardour which you, gentlemen, evince to enter into the
> most noble and very illustrious Order of Freemasons, is a certain
> proof that you already possess all the qualities necessary to
> become members, that is, humanity, pure morals, inviolable
> secrecy, and a taste for the fine arts.
>
> Lycurgus, Solon, Numa, and all political legislators have
> failed to make their institutions lasting. However wise their
> laws may have been, they have not been able to spread through
> all countries and ages. As they only kept in view victories and
> conquests, military violence, and the elevation of one people
> at the expense of another, they have not had the power to
> become universal, nor to make themselves acceptable to the
> taste, spirit, and interest of all nations. Philanthropy was not
> their basis. Patriotism badly understood and pushed to excess,
> often destroyed in these warrior republics love and humanity
> in general. Mankind is not essentially distinguished by the
> tongues spoken, the clothes worn, the lands occupied, or the

dignities with which it is invested. The world is nothing but a huge republic, of which every nation is a family, and every individual a child. Our Society was at the outset established to revive and spread these essential maxims borrowed from the nature of man. We desire to reunite all men of enlightened minds, gentle manners, and agreeable wit, not only by a love for the fine arts, but much more by the grand principles of virtue, science, and religion, where the interests of the Fraternity shall become those of the whole human race, whence all nations shall be enabled to draw useful knowledge, and where the subjects of all kingdoms shall learn to cherish one another without renouncing their own country. Our ancestors, the Crusaders, gathered together from all parts of Christendom in the Holy Land, desired thus to reunite into one sole Fraternity the individuals of all nations. What obligations do we not owe to these superior men who, without gross selfish interests, without even listening to the inborn tendency to dominate, imagined such an institution, the sole aim of which is to unite minds and hearts in order to make them better, and form in the course of ages a spiritual empire where, without derogating from the various duties which different States exact, a new people shall be created, which, composed of many nations, shall in some sort cement them all into one by the tie of virtue and science.

The second requisite of our Society is sound morals. The religious orders were established to make perfect Christians, military orders to inspire a love of true glory, and the Order of Freemasons, to make good men lovable men, good citizens, good subjects, inviolable in their promises, faithful adorers of the God of Love, lovers rather of virtue than of reward.

Polliciti servare fidem, sanctumque vereri
Numen amicitiae, mores, non munera amare.

Nevertheless, we do not confine ourselves to purely civic virtues. We have amongst us three kinds of brothers: Novices or Apprentices, Fellows or Professed Brothers, Masters or Perfected Brothers. To the first are explained the moral virtues; to the second the heroic virtues; to the last the Christian virtues; so that our institution embraces the whole philosophy of sentiment and the complete theology of the heart. This is why one of our worshipful brothers has said:

Freemason, illustrious Grand Master,
Receive my first transports,
In my heart the Order has given them birth,
Happy I, if noble efforts
Cause me to merit your esteem
By elevating me to the sublime, The primeval Truth,
To the Essence pure and divine,
The celestial Origin of the soul,
The Source of life and love.

Because a sad, savage, and misanthropic philosophy disgusts virtuous men, our ancestors, the Crusaders, wished to render it lovable by the attractions of innocent pleasures, agreeable music, pure joy, and moderate gaiety. Our festivals are not what the profane world and the ignorant vulgar imagine. All the vices of heart and soul are banished there, and irreligion, libertinage, incredulity, and debauch are proscribed. Our banquets resemble those virtuous symposia of Horace, where the conversation only touched what could enlighten the soul, discipline the heart, and inspire a taste for the true, the good, and the beautiful.

O noctes cœnæque Deum . . .
Sermo oritur, non de regnis domibusve alienis
. . . sed quod magis ad nos
Pertinet, et nescire malum est, agitamus; utrumne
Divitiis homines, an sint virtute beati;
Quidve ad amicitias usus rectumve trahat nos,
Et quæÊ sit natura boni, summumque quid ejus.

Thus the obligations imposed upon you by the Order, are to protect your brothers by your authority, to enlighten them by your knowledge, to edify them by your virtues, to succour them in their necessities, to sacrifice all personal resentment, and to strive after all that may contribute to the peace and unity of society.

We have secrets; they are figurative signs and sacred words, composing a language sometimes mute, sometimes very eloquent, in order to communicate with one another at the greatest distance, and to recognise our brothers of whatsoever tongue. These were words of war which the Crusaders gave each other in order to guarantee them from the surprises of the Saracens, who often crept in amongst them to kill them. These signs and words recall the remembrance either of some part of our science, or of some moral virtue, or of some mystery of the faith. That has happened to us which never befell any former Society. Our Lodges have been established, and are spread in all civilised nations, and, nevertheless, among this numerous multitude of men never has a brother betrayed our secrets. Those natures most trivial, most indiscreet, least schooled to silence, learn this great art on entering our Society. Such is the power over all natures of the idea of a fraternal bond! This inviolable Secret contributes powerfully to unite the subjects of all nations, and to render the communication of benefits easy and mutual between us. We have many examples in the annals of our Order. Our brothers, travelling in divers lands, have only needed to make themselves known in our Lodges in order to be there immediately overwhelmed by all kinds of succour, even in time of the most bloody wars, and illustrious prisoners have found brothers where they only expected to meet enemies.

Should any fail in the solemn promises which bind us, you know, gentlemen, that the penalties which we impose upon him are remorse of conscience, shame at his perfidy, and exclusion from our Society, according to those beautiful lines of Horace

> *Est et fideli tuta silencio*
> *Merces; vetabo qui Cereris sacrum*
> *Vulgarit arcanum, sub iisdem*
> *Sit trabibus, fragilemque mecum*
> *Salvat phaselum. . . .*

Yes, sirs, the famous festivals of Ceres at Eleusis, of Isis in Egypt, of Minerva at Athens, of Urania amongst the Phenicians, and of Diana in Scythia were connected with ours. In those places mysteries were celebrated which concealed many vestiges of the ancient religion of Noah and the Patriarchs. They concluded with banquets and libations, and neither that intemperance nor excess were known into which the heathen gradually fell. The source of these infamies was the admission to the nocturnal assemblies of persons of both sexes in contravention of the primitive usages. It is in order to prevent similar abuses that women are excluded from our Order. We are not so unjust as to regard the fair sex as incapable of keeping a secret. But their presence might insensibly corrupt the purity of our maxims and manners.

The fourth quality required in our Order is the taste for useful sciences and the liberal arts. Thus, the Order exacts of each of you to contribute, by his protection, liberality, or labour, to a vast work for which no academy can suffice, because all these societies being composed of a very small number of men, their work cannot embrace an object so extended. All the Grand Masters in Germany, England, Italy, and elsewhere, exhort all the learned men and all the artisans of the Fraternity to unite to furnish the materials for a Universal Dictionary of the liberal arts and useful sciences, excepting only theology and politics.

The work has already been commenced in London, and by means of the union of our brothers it may be carried to a conclusion in a few years. Not only are technical words and their etymology explained, but the history of each art and science, its principles and operations, are described. By this means the lights of all nations will be united in one single work, which will be a universal library of all that is beautiful, great, luminous, solid, and useful in all the sciences and in all noble arts. This work will augment in each century, according to the increase of knowledge, and it will spread everywhere emulation and the taste for things of beauty and utility.

The word Freemason must therefore not be taken in a literal, gross, and material sense, as if our founders had been simple workers in stone, or merely curious geniuses who wished to perfect the arts. They were not only skilful architects, desirous of consecrating their talents and goods to the construction of material temples; but also religious and warrior princes who designed to enlighten, edify, and protect the living Temples of the Most High. This I will demonstrate by developing the history or rather the renewal of the Order.

Every family, every Republic, every Empire, of which the origin is lost in obscure antiquity, has its fable and its truth, its legend and its history. Some ascribe our institution to Solomon, some to Moses, some to Abraham, some to Noah, and some to Enoch, who built the first city, or even to Adam. Without any pretence of denying these origins, I pass on to matters less ancient. This, then, is a part of what I have gathered in the annals of Great Britain, in the Acts of Parliament, which speak often of our privileges, and in the living traditions of the English people, which has been the centre of our Society since the eleventh century.

At the time of the Crusades in Palestine many princes, lords, and citizens associated themselves, and vowed to restore the Temple of the Christians in the Holy Land, and to employ themselves in bringing back their architecture to its first institution. They agreed upon several ancient signs and symbolic words drawn from the well of religion in order to recognise themselves amongst the heathen and Saracens. These signs and words were only communicated to those who promised solemnly, and even sometimes at the foot of the altar, never to reveal them. This sacred promise was therefore not an execrable oath, as it has been called, but a respectable bond to unite Christians of all nationalities in one confraternity. Some time afterwards our Order formed an intimate union with the Knights of St John of Jerusalem. From that time our Lodges took the name of Lodges of St John. This union was made after the example set by the Israelites when they erected the second Temple, who whilst they handled the trowel and mortar with one hand, in the other held the sword and buckler.

Our Order therefore must not be considered a revival of the Bacchanals, but as an order founded in remote antiquity, and renewed in the Holy Land by our ancestors in order to recall the memory of the most sublime truths amidst the pleasures of society. The kings, princes, and lords returned from Palestine to their own lands, and there established divers Lodges. At the time of the last Crusades many Lodges were already erected in Germany, Italy, Spain, France, and from thence in Scotland, because of the close alliance between the French and the Scotch. James, Lord Steward of Scotland, was Grand Master of a Lodge established at Kilwinning, in the West of Scotland, 1286, shortly after the death of Alexander III, King of Scotland, and one year before John Balliol mounted the throne. This lord received as Freemasons into his Lodge the Earls of Gloucester and Ulster, the one English, the other Irish.

By degrees our Lodges and our rites were neglected in most places. This is why of so many historians only those of Great Britain speak of our Order. Nevertheless it preserved its splendour among those Scotsmen to whom the Kings of France confided during many centuries the safeguard of their royal persons.

After the deplorable mishaps in the Crusades, the perishing of the Christian armies, and the triumph of Bendocdar, Sultan of Egypt, during the eighth and last Crusade, that great Prince Edward, son of Henry III, King of England, seeing there was no longer any safety for his brethren in the Holy Land, from whence the Christian troops were retiring, brought them all back, and this colony of brothers was established in England. As this prince was endowed with all heroic qualities, he loved the fine arts, declared himself protector of our Order, conceded to it new privileges, and then the members of this fraternity took the name of Freemasons, after the example set by their ancestors.

Since that time Great Britain became the seat of our Order, the conservator of our laws, and the depository of our secrets. The fatal religious discords which embarrassed and tore Europe in the sixteenth century caused our Order to degenerate from the nobility of its origin. Many of our rites and usages which were contrary to the prejudices of the times were changed, disguised, suppressed. Thus it was that many of our brothers forgot, like the ancient Jews, the spirit of our laws, and only retained the letter and shell. The beginnings of a remedy have already been made. It is only necessary to continue, and to at last bring everything back to its original institution. This work cannot be difficult in a State where religion and the Government can only be favourable to our laws.

From the British Isles the Royal Art is now repassing into France, under the reign of the most amiable of Kings, whose humanity animates all his virtues, and under the ministry of a Mentor, who has realised all that could be imagined most fabulous. In this happy age when love of peace has become the virtue of heroes, this nation [France] one of the most spiritual of Europe, will become the centre of the Order. She will clothe our work, our statutes, and our customs with grace, delicacy, and good taste, essential qualities of the Order, of which the basis is the wisdom, strength, and beauty of genius. It is in future in our Lodges, as it were in public schools, that Frenchmen shall learn, without travelling, the characters of all nations, and that strangers shall experience that France is the home of all peoples. *Patria gentis humanæ*.

Waite's Thoughts on Ramsay's Oration

Waite says that Ramsay implies that the Masonic Grades begin under the Law of Israel and end under the Law of Christ. This poses a curious dilemma for him. He says it follows from this statement that Ramsay refers only to the three Craft Grades, or that the Third Degree of his period was not the same as it is now, or else that there were some supplements and extensions attached to the Craft which correspond to the present use of the expression High Christian Grades.

The inference of the first alternative can only be that the Craft Grades have been edited to hide certain elements. Waite has no difficulty in accepting that an alteration took place, and he suspects the Duke of Sussex of influencing the matter and hints that a study of the Duke's actions will cast an unexpected light upon some buried episodes in the Masonic past of England.

He goes on to say that his second alternative implies that High Templar Grades were worked in the Craft before 1737. He questions this, except possibly in the case of the Grade of Heredom of Kilwinning, which he thinks is important. Then he adds that Ramsay's Oration remains a profound influence on higher Masonic developments.

Chapter 20

The Strict Observance

The Unknown Superiors

Waite thinks that much about the origin of the Rite of the Strict Observance remains dubious, but he thinks it was formed in 1754. He says it is the first Masonic system to claim its authority from Unknown Superiors, who claim absolute jurisdiction and obedience without question. He thinks that while the Unknown Superiors of the Observance may have been a real governing body, they may only have stood for Baron Karl Gotthelf von Hund and his followers.

Waite reports that Hund claimed that in 1743 he attended a convention at Altenberg at which he was received into the Order of the Temple in the presence of Charles Edward Stuart, the Young Pretender, and was referred for further instructions to C.G. Marschall von Bieberstein, Grand Master of the German Templar Province. On his reception, Hund was made the Grand Master's successor-designate, but did nothing till his sponsor's death in 1750 when he found that Marschall von Bieberstein had destroyed his records with the exception of the list of Grand Masters, showing the perpetuation of the Order, and the Roll of his Provinces.

Hund then took on the position of Provincial Grand Master and carried on the Order on his own authority. In this way the honour of von Hund was saved, the Knights Templar were perpetuated, and the role of the Unknown Superiors and of the partition of Europe into nine great Provinces of the Templar Order merged back into the realm of mystery.

The story of Hund's reception as a Knight Templar rests on his word alone, as does his claim that Prince Charles Edward and the Earl of Kilmarnock founded a continuing Order of the Temple. But Waite thinks there are other possibilities.

1. In 1682 a small private society was established within the court of King Louis XIV for the pursuit of scandalous vices. It was called, *Une petite Résurrection des Templiers*. The king promptly crushed it, leaving no record, and its members pursued their tastes individually. Waite says that the enemies of the Templar claim in Masonry always press this story into their service.

2. In 1705, during the minority of Louis XV, Philip of Orleans tried to restore the Order of the Temple, and took into his council the Italian Jesuit and antiquary Father Bonanni, who drew up the Statutes and obtained the famous Charter of Larmenius, being the Roll of Grand Masters from the time of Jacques de Molay to that date. There was an attempt to obtain recognition from the Order of Christ in Portugal, which is the actual successor of the old Knights Templar in that country. The experiment was a failure. The prince's emissary was thrown into prison then deported to Africa, where he died. The Order continued in France under the name of the *Society of the Sirloin*. In 1792 its Grand Master was the Duc de Cosse-Brissac. He was succeeded in 1804 by Doctor Fabre-Palaprat.

   Unlike Ward, Waite does not believe that the Charter of Transmission is a genuine document, but he admits that, if he is mistaken in this, then there is a real possibility that the Masonic Templars could have included the Young Pretender and his followers in their ranks.

3. The Strict Observance depends for its warrants on grounds of romance and tradition, Waite says. It claims that four foundations were made by Jacques de Molay on the eve of his martyrdom, but the Charter of Larmenius is indirect evidence. Waite points out that these rival Templar claims are not mutually exclusive – something that the revival based on the Charter recognized when it condemned the alternative claims as spurious. The Templar Grade of the Strict Observance does not exist in England, except as part of the dual Masonic Grades of Novice and Knight Beneficent of the Holy City of Jerusalem.

4. The Rite of the Strict Observance was not part of the Templar revival of 1743. But Waite does not believe that the story told by von Hund to the High Grade Masons at Altenberg is entirely false. He admits it is a vague story but thinks that von Hund was mistaken

about the identity of Prince Charles Edward Stuart. He says that von Hund failed to remember the name of the Lodge or Chapter where he was received, and he never said where it was. But there is nothing that suggests he did not undergo some ritual initiation. At that time the Grades of Chivalry were being created, and among them there may have been a design for a Templar foundation. Hund may have been shown documents that conferred some form of Masonic knighthood. Waite says that the form of Masonic Templar Knighthood now known as the Military and Religious Order is of considerable antiquity, and so such a Lodge might have existed in Paris. English Masonic Templarism has never claimed to hold titles showing a list of Templar Grand Masters, and it has never been divided into provinces. But none of this changes the fact that the Templar revival under the aegis of the Charter of Transmission gives no justification to the Strict Observance. Waite thinks that the connection of the Young Pretender with Masonry arose from the Jacobite interest in Continental Lodges, and is part of an attempt to interpret the legend of the Master Builder in terms of the ordeal and martyrdom of King Charles I. The story of the Young Pretender's initiation may have been part of an attempt to turn the popular legends of the Masonic aim of building a New Jerusalem [as promoted in the writings of William Blake] into pseudo-Masonic Grades.

5. Waite explains that a major written source for the legend of the Strict Observance is the dramatic poem *The Sons of the Valley* by German Romantic writer Zacharias Werner. This tells how Jacques de Molay founded four secret Masonic lodges to continue the suppressed Order of the Temple, and how Aumont, a prior of the Temple, carried the rite of Templarism to Scotland. There is a passage in the poem that is identical with a speech made by the Eminent Preceptor in the modern Ritual of the Military and Religious Order. Waite notes this but does not try to explain it.

6. There is unquestionable evidence that the Order of the Temple existed in Great Britain in 1779, when a reception took place in Aberdeen. There are not enough details of the ritual for Waite to form an opinion of its nature, or the source from which it was derived, but he has no doubt that some form of the Military and Religious Order was well established in Scotland before that period. He says that the Order appears in Ireland about the same time. A Templar grade was also conferred at Plymouth in 1778.

7. Waite points out that when Ramsay first put forward his thesis about the revival of Masonry in Palestine during the Crusades, he also put forward a thesis of transmission into Freemasonry. He said it did not come through the Order of the Temple, but was revived in the East, because in those parts some form of the ancient mysteries had persisted since the days of Noah and the Flood. Ramsay's Oration attempted to marry the rituals of symbolical Masonry to rites surviving from remote periods of antiquity. When people like Hund revived Templary they attempted to link the old chivalry with the secret tradition of the Temple of Sion. This link, Waite says, still accounts for the talismanic attraction of Knight Templary in occult circles in France and England.

The Levitikon

Waite describes how a forged heretical gospel called the *Levitikon* was found by Dr Fabre-Palaprat, who used it to transform the orthodox and Roman Catholic foundation he led into a centre for a new Johannite Christianity [a version of Christianity focused on St John the Divine]. The foundation split from its orthodox Christian members, who soon disbanded. The heretical branch promoted occultism and its Johannite focus, to develop a complete thesis of what lay behind both the original establishment of the Templar Order in the twelfth century and its revival. Waite explains that this idea came from the French writer Eliphas Levi, in his *History of Magic* [which Waite had originally translated from the French under the title of *Transcendental Magic, its Doctrine and Ritual*].

Waite says that Levi's Johannite theory of the Knights Templar claimed that they were a body of conspirators who came together to protect Christians visiting the Holy Places in Palestine, but they also had a concealed objective: to rebuild Solomon's Temple on the plan of Ezekiel. (Jewish mystics in the early Christian centuries had prophesied this secret dream of the Eastern patriarchs.) Once the Temple of Solomon was rebuilt, Waite claimed, it would be consecrated to Catholic worship and become the metropolis of the universe, with the patriarchs of Constantinople becoming masters of the papacy. It is maintained that the title of Templars cannot be explained by the fact that a house was allotted to the knights near the Temple of

Solomon, for this it had been destroyed, just as the Temple of Zerubbabel had been, and thereafter it would have been too difficult to identify its site. Their house was near the spot where the armed emissaries of the Eastern patriarch were to rebuild the Temple.

Waite goes on to explain that the Templars took as a model the military masons of Zerubbabel, who worked with the sword in one hand and the trowel in the other. They were part of an Oriental sect of Johannite Christians, who were initiated in the deep mysteries of Christianity and were the only ones who knew the true history of Jesus Christ. They considered the Gospel accounts to be allegory and had their own interpretation, which drew from Jewish traditions and the Talmud. They believed Jesus was initiated by the Egyptian priests of Osiris and recognized Him as the incarnation of Horus. This tradition, Waite says, was attributed to St John the Evangelist, who they said founded their secret church. The grand pontiffs of this Church of the Secret Tradition were called by the title 'The Christ', and the holder of this office at the time the Templars were founded knew Hugues de Payens. When de Payens became the first Grand Master of the Templars he was initiated into the mysteries of this secret Church and became the next 'Christ Designate'. From the beginning the Templars were the Wardens of the Secret Tradition, and their designs were hidden in profound mystery, although externally they were unimpeachably orthodox. They were surface Roman Catholics, but in their secret ceremonies they were Johannite. However, their ambition carried with it the seeds of destruction. They were discovered by the Pope and King of France, who overwhelmed them in one masterstroke. But their plan survived, for Waite tells us that when the Knights Templar were destroyed occult Masonry, the continuing tradition of the Temple of Sion, grew on the ruins.

This, Waite explains, is what can happen to the history of High Grade Masonry when it falls into the hands of an occultist like Eliphas Levi. He says that out of Levi's malicious stew, written in 1860, arose the idea that the Masonic Knights Templar were the force behind the French Revolution. Waite thinks that Levi's account is not history, nor is it decent fiction. In *The Secret Tradition of Freemasonry*, he calls Levi's work the idle and dishonest invention of someone who made up history according to his mood of the moment. Yet, as I noted in the opening to this section, Waite had still been prepared to translate and publish Levi's writings.

Rituals of the High Grades

There were no manuscripts of the rituals used by the Order of the Strict Observance still available to Waite, but he found summaries of the ritual for the reception of a Scottish Master, the reception of a Secular or Lay Novice, and that of a Scottish Knight. He compared them with the rituals of the Grades of St Andrew and with those of Novice and Knight Beneficent of the Holy City of Jerusalem and found a general similarity. He noted that everywhere in these rituals obedience to the Order, fidelity to its Superiors and unconditional silence is stressed.

The list of Grand Masters of the Strict Observance that the Order is supposed to have preserved has been never made public, and so Waite had no chance to compare it to the succession recorded in the Charter. But all its rituals confirm that the Master who succeeded Jacques de Molay was the Prior of Aumont.

The provinces of the Order were supposed to cover Northern Germany, Southern Germany, Auvergne, Bordeaux, and Great Britain, which was the location of the Rite's Unknown Superiors and of the veiled Grand Master of all. Waite says this scheme is an imitation of the old Knights Templar, whose possessions and connected Preceptories were divided into the provinces of Jerusalem, Tripoli, Antioch, Cyprus, with western provinces of Portugal, Castile and Leon, Aragon, France and Auvergne, Normandy, Aquitaine or Poitou, Provence, England, Germany, Upper and Central Italy and finally Apulia and Sicily.

Chapter 21

Mysteries of Dates and Origins

The Chapter of Clermont

Waite says that the active spirit in the formation of what he calls the super-Masonic Rituals is a romantic one. The various systems of rites range from the unintelligible deeps of the mysteries of St Clair, to the peculiar set of moral qualities that characterize the Craft Degrees. The Craft Grades are dramatic in form, covering a deep and ancient mystery. This, he says, is part of their greatness. But the High Grades are like the first editions of anonymous books that have appeared without an imprint; there is no date on their titles, so their dating is speculative.

Waite found difficulty in dating the rite of the Strict Observance to 1754. But he also found it difficult to account for the decade or so between the date on which Baron von Hund said he received the Order of the Temple from the Earl of Kilmarnock and the date when he appeared as Provincial Grand Master of his Rite in Germany. He says the Chapter of Clermont, too, was formed in 1754 – though he adds that, if it were possible to put this date back ten years, he would be able to account more simply for Hund's story. However, he thinks that the mysteries of dates and origins involve playing with fire. The Chapter of Clermont worked certain rituals, and if it were this body that received Baron von Hund into the Order of the Temple, then it must have had a Templar Ritual. But no one has seen this ritual, any more than they have seen the chivalrous grade of the imaginary Rite of Ramsay. Waite says there could be no difficulty about the Hund communicating with the Chapter; if he became its accredited representative in Germany, then he would have had its rituals. But from his own account he lost touch with his initiators, and failed to recontact them. In the end he set up his rite in Germany. If this is true, then Waite says he can understand how von Hund's theory of Unknown Superiors governing the rite came about. He agrees with von Hund's defenders, who believe that he was anxious to find them again. This story that von Hund was mysteriously initiated by someone he scarcely knew and then founded his own version of the Order in his own country is credible, says Waite. However, when von Hund says he was accredited in Germany by Marschall von Bieberstein, who was German Provincial Grand Master but held no records and was unable to disclose anything, Waite becomes a little suspicious. He concludes that it seems unlikely that Hund received his ritual from the Chapter of Clermont.

But what degrees did this Chapter confer when Chevalier de Bonneville founded it in 1754? Waite says the grades were recorded by Claude Antoine Thory in 1815, and they were:

1. Knight of the Eagle
2. Chevalier Illustre, or Templar
3. Sublime Illustrious Chevalier

But in 1825 an American expert on the High Grades named them as:

1. Novice
2. Ecossais
3. Knight of the Temple

Waite says he has found additional variations:

4. Scottish Master Elect
5. Knight of the Eagle
6. Illustrious Templar

To which are added later:

1. Sublime Knight or Maître Ecossais
2. Maître Elu
3. Maître Illustre
4. Maître Sublime

Waite also noted that the archives of the Grand Lodge of Brunswick say that Chapter of Clermont also worked the Craft Degrees. But he adds that the same archives say that the rite was founded by Adam, flourished under the aegis of Moses, who brought it from Egypt, and passed into the custody of Solomon, from whom it descended to the Templars. This claim makes the Chapter heir to all the ages, but it only seemed to work the Grades concerned with the periods of Solomon and the Knights Templar.

Waite explains that the rite spread to Berlin in 1758, when it fell into the hands of an unfrocked pastor named Philip Samuel Rosa, who reduced it to three Grades and took it in this form to Brunswick in 1762. From this confusion Waite tried to extract a tenable proposition. He says that the Clermont Chapter may have had a Templar Grade, but he thinks it unlikely. However if this was the case, and Hund was received into it, then it must have existed before 1754. He is quite certain the Strict Observance used its own rituals, so there would have had to have been two separate Templar Grades at work concurrently. He rejects that idea. This leaves the Chapter of Clermont with only the Ecossais Grades to work, unless there was a Degree of Chivalry of which Waite says he knows nothing, except that it could not have been Templar.

Council of Emperors of the East and West

If the Craft had not been taken to the Continent of Europe in the eighteenth century, Waite thinks there would never have been a High Grade Masonic movement. He says its impulse derives from Scotland, in the person of the Chevalier Ramsay. But, soon after the introduction of the Craft into France, the Masonic mind of that country needed something stronger than the fragmentary Craft story. That was a legend of a quest driven by an emblematic loss, and to satisfy the French it needed a sequel – the mystic legend of the Craft and the great meaning behind it was incomplete. The French were all Christians and believed that the missing Word was divine in its character. For them there was one name only that could put a crown upon the work. This was the name of Christ, and so the Christian Grades came into existence.

One suggestion Waite makes is that the Chapter of Clermont was merged into the Strict Observance. But he thinks it more likely that, after an existence of four years, the Chapter was taken over in 1758 under the title of the Emperors of the East and West. If so, then the Council of Emperors must have taken over the Grades worked by the Chapter, and yet in the whole sequence of its 25 rituals there is no Templar Grade.

The ritual of the Emperors of the East and West seems to Waite to be later than that of the Royal Arch, as known in England under the Craft Grand Lodge, but also contains elements that suggest that the Secret Tradition depends on wisdom reposing in Paradise. Those who possess its degrees discover the secret of the Sacred Delta, which contains the sum of the quest of Masonry. In this manner its Candidates become true Master Masons and share the hidden knowledge possessed by the prophet Enoch before the Flood. That knowledge was conveyed in a vision and afterwards reduced to writing and placed in a crypt built by Enoch. On the site of that vault Solomon erected the First Temple, and the preparation of the foundations led to the discovery of the secret vault. In this chamber the Sacred Lodge – made up of Solomon, King of Israel, Hiram, King of Tyre and Hiram Abif – had hidden the mysteries of Masonry. This story is mainly compatible with that of the Craft Legend.

The 23rd Grade is that of Knight of the Sun or Prince Adept, and it has been called the Key of Masonry. Its period represents Eden; the Master personates Adam, and the seven officers of the Grade are termed Cherubim, the unofficial members are Sylphs. Waite thinks its symbolism as a whole represents the perfect day of creation, ruled by the sun, depicted in the centre of a triangle, or delta, about which are congregated the angels of the planets.

The 24th Degree is called the Degree of Kadosh. In its original form it commemorates the abolition of the Templars and the murder of Jacques de Molay. Waite says that at one period the Candidate was required to trample on a crown and tiara, although he does not think this report is true. The formal execution of Philip, Clement V and the traitor Noffo de Dei is symbolized in the ritual by plunging a dagger into the symbolic heart of a traitor. The candidate climbs a mystic Ladder, of which one side represents the seven virtues and the other the liberal arts and sciences. The candidate learns that the Kadosh sword and dagger are symbols of wisdom and intelligence that are used to attack intolerance, ignorance and bigotry. On this understanding, he tramples symbolically on the crown of Philip the Fair, which signifies tyranny, and thereafter on the papal tiara, representing superstition and imposture.

The 25th Grade is Sublime and Valiant Prince of the Royal Secret. It is set in an encampment in which tents are allotted to the Knights Rose-Croix, Knights of the Brazen Serpent, Knights Kadosh, and other chivalries, including the Princes of the Grade. Its symbolic time is during the Crusades, but Waite thinks it is a grade of Templar heritage with traces of a revolutionary motive. The candidate is married to the Order and becomes a prince. The Grade includes an elaborate description of the Encampment, in which the degree is set, and a symbolical and a historical explanation of the preceding degrees.

The Masonic Order of the Temple

Waite reports that the Templar revival in Masonry has three possible lines of transmission from the original Knights Templar. One is via the Rite of the Strict Observance, and another through the so-called Charter of Larmenius. The Strict Observance survives as the Masonic grade of Beneficent Knighthood of the Holy City of Jerusalem, but its rival has died out. Independent of both there is the Military and Religious Order of the Temple, in Great Britain. Two living Masonic successors to the Templars remain, but neither has any knowledge of the other. Nonetheless, Waite says, they are both part of the legitimate ritual of Masonry.

The Military and Religious Order of the Masonic Temple is entered in England from a Chapter of the Royal Arch. But Waite maintains the Grade of Knight Templar has not always been a Masonic Order; there was a time in England when it was communicated to non-Masons.

He says the Templars were the prototype of Masonry, as their Temple was erected above all in the heart. This is Waite's first answer to those who say that the Masonic links to the chivalric Order are artificial, but he adds that it does not justify a claim to a chivalrous pedigree for Masonry, nor does it say that the Order of the Temple has survived into modern times. He thinks the three possible lines of transmission that he lists are exclusive of one another.

According to the Rite of the Strict Observance, the last recognized Grand Master of the Templars, Jacques de Molay, created four Metropolitan Lodges. These were Naples for the East, Edinburgh for the West, Stockholm for the North, and Paris for the South. These traditional centres remained hidden under the veil of Masonry until the upheaval that resulted in the French Revolution. The Masonic and Templar Grade, which arises from this tradition, has no links with the Masonic Order of the Temple that is worked in Great Britain and

America today. Its final transformation occurred at the Convention of Wilhelmsbad when it became the Knights Beneficent of the Holy City of Jerusalem. The past history of the Masonic Military and Religious Order remains obscure. The body that descends from the Larmenius Charter via the Strict Observance, Waite claims, is a wilful invention. He finds the positions of the two Masonic Grades are curious in this connection. The Knights Beneficent have abandoned the Templar claim, making their rituals illogical Templar memorials. But the Military and Religious Order suppresses all accounts of its origin.

Waite says that Orders often cease by acts of nature, by falling into desuetude, or by acts of violence against them, but that when they are forcibly suppressed it is reasonable to assume they are not annihilated. Although their suppression means they disappear from public view, this does not always mean extinction. He says that if the Templars preserved some secret knowledge then their ideas did not perish, and if that knowledge is not now with us, then it is because we aren't looking for it in the right place. There are many mysteries of chivalry, and no real theory as to what lies behind it. But Waite says we can see that there is a hidden project. He does not know if it is anything more than a strange growth of the secret life that characterized the Middle Ages, but he detects a Secret Doctrine which the Church did not accept, but which he thinks was a project devised to further the cause of civilization.

If there was a point of junction between Templary and this Secret Tradition, Waite says he could ignore the transmission hypothesis as a subterfuge, and yet he thinks that the connection between Masonry and the Templars must share a common root. It is clear to him that the Military and Religious Order of the Temple has a Masonic symbolic significance that sets it apart from any question of how it arose. He says the ritual of Masonic Templarism is sacramental in nature. It conveys more than appears on the surface as it teaches the soul to search for hidden treasures. Its ritual is a way of bringing an abstract and mystical experience into concrete form. Why then, he asks, is the true meaning so deeply embedded that it can be missed altogether by simple minds? He concludes, firstly, that the great things of the soul are always clouded by any process that tries to render them visible, and the deeper the mystery, the thicker the veil. Secondly, the science of the soul can never be fully expressed in language. The rites of official religion show this. The Sacrifice of the Mass is the greatest ritual in the world, but its true meaning lies so deep beneath the literal surface that few worshippers realize what is involved.

Waite says that Masonic initiations, passings, raisings, exaltings, installations and enthronements are steps by which the mind of the recipient is progressively illuminated. From the first desire to be made a Mason, a Candidate is assumed to seek the light, and the rituals claim that it is revealed in stages. The Craft Grades and the Holy Royal Arch offer material to help understand the reign of law. But the Order of the Temple and other Masonic grades of Chivalry offer a means of realizing the higher side of the eternal law of Grace. The Temple represents a passage from one dispensation to another, and a Masonic preparation of the Postulant is not an arbitrary rule. Those who were responsible for the ordination in old days may not have known what they were doing, but Waite believes they were guided by the traditions of the Instituted Mysteries. Candidates for Temple reception are prepared for a new dispensation of deeper spiritual knowledge. He believes that if this is not communicated, then the rite is folly, but he does not know how these ideas came into the ritual.

He says that the Postulant in the Craft Grades enters a realm of double meaning, designed to show that there was a mystery of wisdom and sanctity that was lost by a revolt from within the camp of initiation itself. The Master Builder perished, and the original plans for the world were lost. But he insists this did not happen as fact. The Craft Legend is not history under a suggestive veil. It is a symbolic way to reveal the existence of a Secret Tradition in the records of Jewry. The path of spiritual experience is explained by a path of symbolism. It is as if man has been remade after the pattern of a lesser angel; this is the experience Waite believes is hidden in the Secret Tradition. He believes that Masonry's quest is to recover this Secret Tradition, and that Masonic ritual is the most sublime indication of the inner meaning of this doctrine that has ever been put into words. He says the Craft Legend and its ritual proclaim that behind the external myth of Jewry a hidden meaning gives life to the doctrine, and this is symbolized by the story of a lost word. The mystery is of death and sorrow; but it ends with a hope of restoration. This is symbolized by the personal experience of the candidate, whose part in the ritual shows that the secret does not die. Waite is certain that those who composed the Craft Grades, and its legend, knew that there was a Secret Doctrine in Israel.

In the Royal Arch the candidate meets a more involved symbolism, and Waite says he has heard thoughtful students who say this Masonic Order is a spurious pretence, because they do not understood what its ritual is saying. They know it claims to repair the loss of the Craft Legend, but they misinterpret the message. The intention of the ritual is to show that the inmost secret of the symbolical Temple is neither diagram nor formula. It is an instruction to look behind the literal sense of the old Scriptures to find a mystery of interior religion. Those who search for this mystery, pass through experiences in the soul, and receive a living truth.

Waite thinks that the Royal Arch has been tinkered out of all true knowledge by excessive editing, but it still serves a purpose. For Masons in England it assumes greater importance when the Candidate proceeds from it to the experience of a Masonic Knight Templar. The ritual of the Knights Templar contains a mystical formula. The candidate passes from the yoke of Israel to the light and easy burden of Christ. The law has become transmuted, but this change does not affect the root-matter of the symbolism. The formula in the Order of Chivalry is like that in the Craft Grade: it offers insight to a secret, more spiritual, meaning behind the surface of religious doctrine. The Postulant for this spiritual Knighthood is given sacred gifts of spiritual knowledge in the symbolic way Masons are familiar with.

Waite explains that the modern Masonic grade of Templar brings from the degrees of Craft Masonry an assurance that the legends of Israel set forth the mysteries of the Old Covenant. But the Old Laws are attacked, as the great artificer was murdered in a rebellion. After this great catastrophe an elect of the official mysteries, symbolized as a chosen Order of knights, are taught in a substituted House of Doctrine, which is Freemasonry.

Waite also says that a Zoharic form of this teaching propounds that when Moses went up the Sacred Mountain, the burden of the Fall was removed from his people, who were to be reinstated in the law of Paradise. But in his absence they turned to rebellion and so reassumed the burden. Then they were put to school under, what Waite calls a substituted law, represented by the Second Tables or the external Temple in Masonic legend. He says that the deeper truths were preserved in the heart of the few, as if within the Sanctum Sanctorum itself. This is the inner and higher law. Masonry describes the succession of those few as the Grand Masters of the several symbolical Lodges. On his entrance into the Preceptory the candidate repeats a formula that he received in another Masonic Grade, and he carries a dismembered symbol. This damaged offering is accepted in the Temple. But he is offered symbolic bread, which is a true Eucharist.

This is his natural Graal as he enters into new knowledge, which is communicated only in symbols. He is put at once upon a quest of search and preparation. He comes forth alive and so proves himself. But in the centre of the Temple there is a place of undeclared mystery that is guarded against his approach.

The postulant is told that he is on a spiritual Graal quest. He is given earthly arms, in the form of a sword, but is told he is not preparing for an earthly knighthood. He is embarking on a pilgrimage of the spiritual life, a striving towards perfection. He is told that he is a part of the things that are above, but he may come into his inheritance by his efforts in this world. He is told that two shall be as one, and that which is without shall become that which is within. The covenant shows that he is entering into its deeper meaning. Next the postulant is shown the symbols of mystical death, which are also the symbols of life. So he completes his term as a Novice of the High Order. But the full mystery is still not revealed. His movements about the floor of the lodge symbolize the spiritual meaning of three counsels of perfection: poverty and denudation in quest; restraint and self-denial in battle with the enemies who are without; and humility and obedience in the ascetic life. He is being prepared for a chivalry that is not of this world.

At a later stage he is told to think of the knighthood that is conferred upon him as a grade of holy priesthood. Then he is given more ceremonial nourishment to complete the symbol of the Eucharist in the Order of the Temple, indicating a deeper doctrine. He partakes of successive reminders of the continuing nature of the Secret Tradition and of the channels through which it has been transmitted.

Waite says this is a ritual of a Saintly Order, presented under the veil of higher understanding using of the deeper side of symbolism. The postulant is being encouraged to understand in the heart. In the stillness of his mind, Waite says, there sounds a tocsin call to become part of holy priesthood, so that he can take his place in the seats of the installed masters who have truly passed the chair.

Chapter 22

The Legacy of Jacques de Molay

The Charter of Larmenius

Waite moves on to discuss an Order of the Temple that is based on a document known as the Charter of Larmenius. The earliest known Grand Master of this Order, in 1805, Dr Bernard Raymond Fabre-Palaprat, was an active Mason, deputy to the Grand Orient of France and a founder of the Lodge Chevaliers de la Croix. From his background, Waite concludes that the grades he offered seem reasonable. These were:

1. Apprentice
2. Companion
3. Master

4. Master of the East
5. Master of the Black Eagle of St John
6. Perfect Master of the Pelican

On 30 April 1808 Fabre-Palaprat is supposed to have issued a decree, changing the names and number of degrees to conceal their Masonic origin. The new degrees were:

1. Initiate
2. Initiate of the Interior
3. Adept

4. Adept of the East
5. Grand Adept of the Black Eagle of St John

The Order was split into three Houses. The first, consisting of the first five degrees, was a House of Initiation, and the last two corresponding to the Elect of Fifteen and the Elect of Nine, but in the reverse of the normal Masonic order. Then came a House of Postulance, which conferred the Grade of Postulant or Perfect Adept of the Pelican – similar to the Masonic degree of Rose-Croix. The third House was called a Convent, and it awarded two further grades:

1. Novice   2. Knight or Levite of the Inner Guard

Waite says this was really a single degree split into in two divisions and was similar to the philosophical grade of Knight of Kadosh.

In 1825, Chevalier Guyot, acting on the authority of the Order, issued a Manuel des Chevaliers de l'Ordre du Temple, in which its Statutes were published. The list of degrees was:

1. Simple Initiates   4. Oriental Adepts
2. Intimate Initiates   5. Adepts-Brethren of the Grand
3. Simple Adepts   Black Eagle of St John the Apostle

The statutes mention Postulants, Squire Novices and Knights, but whether these are additional degrees or alternative titles for listed degrees is not clear. Waite is not sure if these were Masonic degrees, for he knows that during this period ladies were admitted into the Order as Canonesses or Sisters.

Waite explains that the Charter of Larmenius gives a different legend of the Temple. It says that before his execution the last Grand Master, Molay, nominated Larmenius, a Mason, as his successor. Larmenius wrote the original Charter and signed it. From then on every Grand Master added his signature.

Larmenius also excommunicated the Scottish Templars, describing them as deserters and apostates and accused the Knights of St John of being despoilers to be placed outside the pale of the Temple. Waite thinks these are veiled attacks on the claims of the other Masonic Orders of the Strict Observance and the Order of Malta.

He says the association was militantly Latin at the beginning, though a Mason stood at its head, and if it were not for its later history, Waite supposes that it could never have escaped the charge of originating from the Society of Jesuits. He says that both knights and the Grand Master were required to be of the Catholic Apostolic and Roman Faith, and as the Charter testified to the alleged fact of Templar perpetuation, it was logical to hold as far as possible to the original rule of chivalry. The Postulant's pledge of obedience, poverty and chastity was in addition to the ordinary knightly oaths of fraternity, hospitality and military service. But the law of obedience was only applied to the Order and its concerns. It did not lay claim to the material possessions of members, despite the poverty clause, and chastity was interpreted as the purity and high sanctity of sacramental marriage. Following their reception, the Knights were encouraged to visit the Holy Land and the site of Molay's death; it appears, though, there was no insistence on this, and it was probably not performed.

Waite says he could find little about the Order's early history. Some writers said that the Temple was created within the Lodge of Chevaliers de la Croix, but he is not convinced. He thinks that the Lodge was founded in 1805. Five years later the Order became active, and the three continents of the old world were placed under the charge of Lieutenants General, resident in Paris; by 1812 Houses of the Order had been established in Paris, Hamburg, Troyes, Nantes, Basle, Rome, Naples, Lisbon and even New York. At this time the movement was known as the United Orders of the East and the Temple. The name was a reference to its legend of origin, which was supposed to be located in Ancient Egypt. One of the florid ritual discourses delivered by the Grand Master speaks of sages of the East and pontiffs of religion. This growth heralded a crisis in the history of the fraternity.

Waite says that Dr Fabre-Palaprat had married Masonry to Catholicism and, by transmission, revival or invention, had brought about a similar marriage between Masonry and the Temple. However a manuscript of the *Levitikon*, a heretical version of the Fourth Gospel, came into his hands. It included a commentary, attributed to a thirteenth-century Greek monk, Nicephoros who was said to have Sufic connections. The Grand Master decided to transform his Order again, this time into a kind of Johannite sectarian church. He took his lead from a legend of the High Grades and produced a new legend, which may be summarized as follows. The Son of God, meaning Jesus of Nazareth, was brought up at a school in Alexandria. He conferred initiation on his apostles and disciples, dividing them into several orders and placing them under the general authority of St John the Divine, who thus became the Sovereign Pontiff of Christendom. St John never left the East, his doctrine preserved its purity, and his successors maintained the mystic and hierarchic initiation of Egypt, as taught by Christ, until the year 1118. At this time they communicated their knowledge to Hugo de Payens, the first Master of the Temple. Payens was invested with apostolic and patriarchal power and became the lawful successor of St John. In this way the Temple was united with Johannite Christianity.

Waite says this was the historical claim of the Order, and on its basis certain doctrines were authorized. Among these were:

1. A special kind of Divine Trinity was acknowledged.
2. God is the soul of Nature, and its elements are co-eternal with Him.
3. God created only the modes of existence of bodies.
4. The animating principle of all beings returns at death to God.
5. The soul, being immortal and the continuation of personal consciousness, is rewarded or punished in the next life according to its deserts in this one.
6. The spirit of Jesus Christ is ritually communicated via a ceremony of eating bread and wine, and this confers a form of apostolic succession which is the root of a Secret Doctrine within the Order of the Temple.
7. Christ communicated only three sacraments. Baptism, Confirmation and the Eucharist. Any others are of apostolic institution.
8. The resurrection is a matter of tradition.

This was the Order's thesis of primitive Christianity, which it said was the old Templar religion, and it contained a claim of priesthood. On the strength of this idea the Grand Master Fabre-Palaprat soon found that an entitlement to hold the office of Supreme Pontiff was part of his office. When his Statutes of the Fellow-Soldiers of the Order of the Temple were published in 1825, they included a Ritual of Enthronement of a Grand Master, who is endowed with the apostolic power to forgive sins.

Waite describes how the publication of these claims caused internecine struggle, and one dissenting faction appointed a Grand Master to replace Fabre-Palaprat. He, however, refused to resign, and was eventually restored to power. In 1825 he added the *Levitikon* to the Temple archives as a historical monument from the First Temple. In 1839 the Convent General issued a decree that preached tolerance of religious opinions, though it insisted that the Grand Master should be of the Catholic and Roman faith. The year after Dr Fabre Palaprat died, the Order claimed independence of all other associations – which, Waite notes, must have also included Freemasonry. At that time an English Admiral, Sir Sydney Smith, was Regent of the Order and Grand Master Designate, the Duke of Sussex was a member, and its Roll contained some three hundred names from various countries. The Order had signs, passwords and batteries [a system of rhythmic knocks used during rituals] like all the Rites of Masonry. Waite thinks it grew out of Masonry and recruited members of the Brotherhood. Its distinction seems to have been that it did not require the qualification of the Craft Grades from its postulants. By 1850 it was moribund, if not already dead. The Johannite church that Fabre-Palaprat opened in Paris also perished through the lack of money.

The sources of information Waite outlined are scattered throughout fields of Masonic research, but he says that certain rituals from the Order of the Temple came into his hands. From those he discovered that the links between the Temple and Masonry were deliberately concealed by a decree issued on 30 April 1808 by Grand Master Fabre-Palaprat. It was a development that owed nothing to the Craft. The information Waite then reveals he says is new to Masonic literature, and it shows that the Masonic authorities in the past have spoken in error and with unwarranted certitude on points of fact. The degrees he next discusses lie behind the chivalrous section of the Order.

Dr Fabre-Palaprat's conversion to the *Levitikon*, Waite explains, led to the creation of eight grades of Levitical ordination. These ranged from sub-diaconate, diaconate and priestly ordination through to Episcopal ranks. The Grades were called Orders, and the first group was made up of Levite of the Threshold, Levite of the Door within, Levite of the Sanctuary, Ceremonial Levite or Master of the Ceremonies, and Theological Levite. The grades were preceded by question and answer leading to a profession of faith in the religion of Christ, as interpreted by the *Levitikon*.

Once the profession and instruction were complete, the presiding Pontiff constituted the lay Chevalier a Levite of the Threshold, by placing a pick in his hands. Next he made him a Levite of the Door within, by presenting him with a key. Then he was made a Levite of the Sanctuary, and was given two keys. A staff of office made him a Levite of Ceremonies, giving him the staff of his office; finally he became a Levite Theological, when he was handed the Book of the Law and invested with a canonical gown and the insignia of his Orders.

A Candidate for the grade of Levite-Deacon, took no obligation, but was questioned about the Church of Christ and its doctrine. That doctrine was a confused pantheism which said that the Christ of Nazareth was distinct from God, but, despite this, he was God and the

Son of God, in the sense meant by King prophet David when he said that the Elect were gods and sons of the Most High. The Soul of Christ was a perfect divine emanation, unlike that of an ordinary man, but He was not the Son of God in the sense that He was conceived in the body of a virgin. He was the Divine Word, the manifestation of the Eternal, and God in the form of a revelation to man. The Spirit of Divinity was within Him, and He was directed by this Spirit, but It did not take flesh in Him. When the Candidate had thus testified concerning the imputed teaching of St John, the bishop bade the Candidate kneel while he took vows of obedience to the laws of the Temple Church and to his superiors. The Episcopal hands were then imposed on his head and he was told to make himself worthy to receive the gift of the Holy Spirit. He was presented with a thurible [a censer or incense burner] and was told to act as a servant-in-chief among the Levites of the religion of Christ. He was also vested, he kissed the pontifical ring and was proclaimed a deacon of the Church.

The eighth grade was Levite and Priest. The Candidate was brought to the Temple by two armed Knights and two theological students of the Johannite church. He made a ritual demand for the grace of the priesthood and another profession of faith, which furthered the developed doctrine of Jesus of Nazareth. He recognized the Christian Saviour as a guardian of the Secret Tradition, whose local centre was said to be in Alexandria. These Alexandrian guardians consecrated Jesus, and proclaimed Him prophet-in-chief of the world and theocrat of the nations. The ritual involved the laying on of hands, anointing with a mixture of oil of olives and balsam and the invocation of the Holy Spirit. At this point the officiating Pontiff proclaimed the Candidate a Deacon, a Levite Priest of the Church of Christ and a Doctor of the Law. He was now authorized to consecrate bread and wine.

The last grade involved being made a Levite Pontiff or Bishop. The candidate was brought to the chapel by two Knights, two Masters of the Ceremonies, two Deacons and two priests. He wore sacerdotal vestments and carried written proof of his election. Next he made a statement recognizing the *Levitikon* and its Apostolic succession as the doctrine of the true and Catholic religion. He was sworn to obedience and fidelity to fulfil his duties. Then he was made to kneel down and the heretical gospel was placed on his head. He was blessed and told to carry forward the sacred yoke of God's gospel. Then he was anointed, and ordained by the laying on of hands. Once his various insignia had been given to him, a kind of mass was celebrated.

Waite says that these degrees were superposed on the single grade of Chivalry, by which candidates were initiated into the Order. He says that other documents speak of two preliminary ceremonies, or a single ritual divided into two parts, known as Squire (or Novice) and Knight. There were other rites, such as a festival in commemoration of the martyr Jacques de Molay. Others were available for the marriage of a knight or the birth of his child, and finally there was a service for his funeral. There was also a formal Eucharistic ritual after each meeting of the Chapter. The vestments and ecclesiastical body of Levites had nine divisions he listed as follows:

1. Prince of the Apostles
2. Apostolical Princes
3. Apostolical Councillors
4. Primates
5. General Coadjutors
6. Special Coadjutors
7. Priests or Doctors of the Law
8. Deacons
9. Levites from the 6th to the 2nd Order.

Waite says this Order took itself with the utmost seriousness, but he thinks it was cloud piled upon cloud, and it dissolved quickly after Dr Fabre-Palaprat's death.

Chapter 23

The Royal Order of Scotland

An Order of Doggerel Verse

Waite says that the Royal Order of Scotland has two rituals, Heredom of Kilwinning and the Rosy Cross. They are partly in archaic doggerel verse. The ritual called Heredom of Kilwinning is older than any other High Grades that exist.

When Ramsay died in 1743, Waite says, no Continental High Grade was yet available. He says that whatsoever is alleged to have pre-dated 1750 is chronological fantasy. But by the time of Ramsay's death the Royal Order was an established foundation in London. This means it was in existence before the date of the celebrated Oration. It follows that the Grade of Heredom is the first High Grade on record, and it is of British origin. This Waite believes, shows that the High Grades are indigenous to Britain, like the Craft itself. Although the degree of the Rosy Cross has some shadowy analogies with the French Grade of Rose-Croix, it is not the same ritual; there are substantial differences. But he does not suggest that one was copied from the other, or even that the one originated the other. He thinks both sprang from some common root.

He agrees that the grade of Rosy Cross, although later than that of Heredom, was being worked in London between 1743 and 1748. Then he puts forward the possibility that the timing suggested some connection with the French Rose-Croix, without the latter being actually developed from it. His hypothesis gives an insight into the genesis of the Eighteenth Degree, which is one of the three Christian High Grades of Chivalry. But the only evidence is that in 1750 a few members of the Royal Order based in The Hague applied for a constitution to London. It was granted, but no Chapter was incorporated. In this way, he says, the idea of the Rosy Cross may have reached Paris from The Hague. This legend he offers as an alternative to the concept of the Rite of Ramsay.

The other possibility he discusses is that the Rosy Cross was imported from France. But Waite feels this hypothesis just follows the line of least resistance. He prefers to stick to his thought that they sprang from a common but unknown root.

He goes on to warn that one should not be misled by the idea that the existence of the Ecossais system in France can account for the grade of Heredom. He thinks it was earlier than any degree on the Continent, and he thinks, too, that the existence of a Scots Lodge in Berlin in 1741, and of others in Hamburg and Leipzig a little later, does not imply that they worked Ecossais grades.

Part of the ritual of the Royal Order is in ordinary prose and part in very bad verse. But Waite says there is nothing to suggest that the verse was made in Scotland. The ritual is mainly framed as a series of questions and answers. Waite says its lack of a dramatic element is common to most of the lesser High Grades.

The candidate takes his obligation with a sword in one hand and a trowel in the other. He is reminded that this is how the Jews worked at the building of the Sacred Temple in the days of Nehemiah. The lesson of the ritual is patriotic: that in defending our country we should arm either hand for work or war. The candidate is then made a Knight of the Rose Cross and is invested. The Banner of the Order is flown above his head, and this completes the ceremonial.

Waite reveals that the Christian elements of this grade can be found in the lecture that comes next. It covers three points. A Lodge of Knighthood is made up of three persons, symbolizing the Holy Trinity. The chivalry of the Rosy Cross was established in memory of the tree that crucified the Rose of Sharon and the Lily of the Valley – that is to say, Jesus of Nazareth. The Order places implicit belief and entire trust in the articles of faith concerning Jesus. These are that He died upon a cross, between two thieves, for the sins of humanity, that He descended into hell, and now sits enthroned on high till the day of judgment and that the remission of sins depends only on faith. The last statement disposes of the suggestion that the Rosy Cross came from a Catholic source, because, Waite says, this doctrine is the Protestantism of the period.

The second Grade of the Royal Order, Heredom of Kilwinning, is a quest. The Lost Word of the Craft is casually revealed as the password of the Grade, but there is no indication that the Candidate should have previously lost it. As a Brother of Heredom and Kilwinning the Candidate knows all the Royal Order can reveal to him.

Now the Knights combine in a quest, and the candidate joins that quest as part of his ritual reception. He travels symbolically to the four quarters to recover the Lost Word, which is found near the Perpend Ashlar. That is revealed to be the stone that the builders rejected. He is told this Stone is Christ, who perfectly illustrates the three Masonic grand principles of Brotherly Love, Relief, and Truth.

Waite says that this grade has a spectacular element. There are two sections called the Passing of the Bridge and Admission to the Cabinet. He says it is not easy to summarize the instruction, because it is scattered through an unusual array of sections, but nevertheless he attempts it.

The quest of the Word takes the Candidate over the wide world, symbolized by the four quarters of the compass. It is a quest for the Holy Rock or Mount of Adamant. This is symbolized as the Rock of Salvation, and it has a fountain streaming from it. The Rock and the Word are Christ, and the voice of the Word says of the fountain, 'Come and drink'. On the rock is a great cruciform church in the middle of a great city, and it is surrounded by angels carrying flaming swords. This symbolizes the Church universal, its length from East to West, its breadth from North to South, its height immeasurable and its depth unfathomable. But it is a Church of the spirit, not of this world. The work of a Brother of Heredom and Kilwinning is to share in building it.

The vision of this Church and the hope that it inspires to build the City of the living God and the heavenly Jerusalem occur during a visit to a certain Tower, the Tower of Refreshment, which is a symbol of Masonry. The ritual implies that the Masonic art is the path of heaven, and Waite shows how it is worked out. The three great lights of Masonry are the Masonic and Christian laws. The sun shows us the light of revelation, and the moon reflects the sun of Nature, while the Master of the Lodge in the East represents the light of sacred knowledge. The Master of the Lodge is a vice-regent who leads under either light to the finding of Christ, as the end of all Masonic research. The five-pointed star with the letter G in the centre is called the Shekinah – whether on Sinai, in Salem, or the place where eastern Magi saw the

Blessed Face. The mystic pillars show that God alone is our support. The Masonic pavement represents the Law delivered on Sinai. The Blazing Star signifies Divine Glory manifest. The tessellated border shows the adornment of a virtuous life in conformity with the Law. [All these symbols are explained in the ritual and illuminated by tracing boards.] There is only one thing with which the Temple of Solomon suffers in comparison, and that is the body of Christ, which is the mystical Temple. The place of Masons is in the middle chamber, which is the place of the heart on which the head of St John lay. This is the Secret Church, called in this grade the Church of the First-born. The First-born are the first-fruits of the spiritual resurrection after passing through emblematic death. The middle chamber is entered by applying the Masonic virtues of Faith, Hope and Charity. The Trestle-Board is the plane of salvation. The Broached Thurnal is Divine Grace, which penetrates the heart. And the Perpend Ashlar is the Grand Architect of the Church.

So the symbolism of Masonry is put to the service of a new life. Waite thinks that the Grade of Heredom of Kilwinning is the true Masonic knighthood.

The Motive of Chivalry

Waite says that the Masonic urge to create degrees of chivalry carries an implication that is vital, whatever its origin may be. It is that the Crusaders met with something in the East that they brought back to western Europe. It is not a mystery of material building, and can only be a form of secret knowledge. The nature of this knowledge varies according to the legends of its several supporters, but they all share common ground. The secret knowledge is represented by the Masonic Templar rituals, and relates to the charges preferred against the Knights at the time of their destruction.

To support a theory of transmission via the Royal Order of Scotland, Waite says it is necessary to show that some knowledge persisted in Palestine from the far past. It would have to be a kind of Kabbalistic tradition that had become Christian, and it could not be Latin Christianity of the type practised in the kingdoms of the West. It has been called Johannite, though this idea may have arrived late in the legend, through the influences of Fabre-Palaprat and his adoption of the *Levitikon*. Waite notes that other writers have suggested that the

Knights of the Morning were another name for the Essene sect, and says this is also implied by Werner in his *Sons of the Valley*. Werner offered an imaginative creation with a suggestion of strange occult powers and sanctity of design behind it. Waite says he was seeking to celebrate a marriage between emblematic Freemasonry and the instituted mysteries that are part and parcel of the Secret Tradition.

Waite thinks the hypothesis of chivalry is a myth. Its basis was a conventional device to link the root-matter of Masonry with the ancient Mysteries. This gives it its strange charm. He says that behind the primitive forms of expression on the surface of the Rose-Croix there is a deep mystical sense, and it belongs to the House of Secret Knowledge. There is no historical legend attached to it. And it is not especially of the Temple, the Hospital, Palestine, Rhodes or Malta, because its chivalry is not of this world. Waite says it is designed to intimate and conceal the relation of symbolic Masonry to the Mysteries by some Secret Wardens who knew of the relation directly.

Waite believes that the Secret Wardens wrote seriously and claimed special knowledge. He says they were the kind of people who would have passed within the secret circles, or have known about them. He does not believe that Chevalier Ramsay was connected with any secret school, although his thesis was useful as a peg when the Secret Wardens wanted to make use of Freemasonry. He says that Baron von Hund's story is so tangled that it is difficult to reach any decision about it. The Ecossais Grades of St Andrew are curious but they dissolve into the Templar legend of the Rite of the Strict Observance before turning into the strange vision which Werner expresses in the suggestive mystery of *The Sons of the Valley*.

If the secret schools put some ideas into von Hund's hands and left him to sort them out as best he could, then Waite says that he can understand von Hund's apparent personal sincerity. Perhaps he did come across something that he did not fully understand but from which he drew inspiration and expected guidance. This explains why he was utterly at a loss when that direction did not come, and the ease with which he was duped by every impostor who sought to exploit his Rite. Waite thinks it also explains the greatness of some of his materials. He adds that if Werner was also in touch with Wardens of the Secret Tradition, he chose the wiser way of the poet, rather than becoming a maker of rituals.

When he approaches the whole legend of Masonic birth in chivalry in this manner, Waite believes it becomes allegory and symbol. He thinks that to debate its value historically has as little purpose as criticising the mystic death of the Master Builder or the quest of Christian Rosy Cross (also known as Christian Rosenkreuz), the legendary founder of the Order of the Rosicrucians, for the wisdom of Arabia. He says the genesis of the Charter of Larmenius and the four mythical Lodges founded by Jacques de Molay is utterly lost in dark clouds. But up to a certain point the pseudo-historical fact is unquestionably part of the parable.

He ends by saying that the great Grades of Mystic Freemasonry are:

The Rose-Croix
The Order of the Temple
The Knights Beneficent and Heredom of Kilwinning

Each has moving lessons of its own. They are stories of quest, stories of attainment, stories of aspiration after the Lost Word of all-redeeming sanctity, of the Living Gospel, the Mystic Rose of Sharon and the Lily of the Valley. The message they carry is profound, but to understand them properly we must set aside their historical claims and move through their beautiful world of images. Those images represent the hunger of the heart for things undemonstrable. They are a quest for the realities of the Secret Tradition, which is a deep well of experience for the brethren of the Craft to drink at.

Conclusions to Part Four

Waite, who studied mysticism and magic before he came to Freemasonry, is convinced he can see the outline of an ancient mystical tradition in the rituals of the higher degrees of Freemasonry. He thinks it is linked to attempts to address the Christian mystery of death and what comes after, and that there has been a deliberate attempt by the establishment of the United Grand Lodge of England to try and suppress these ideas. We need to remember that Waite made no secret of the fact he was interested in the mystical and symbolic aspects of the Secret Tradition in Christian ideas, so he may simply have been seeing what he set out to find. But he has come to conclusions broadly similar to those reached by Gould and Ward. And he does not differ greatly from the views of William Preston. All four writers think that Freemasonry has grown out of old British traditions, it has been influenced by the Knights Templar and that the true history of the Order is ignored, or even vilified by the official camp-followers of the United Grand Lodge of England.

There is one last Masonic writer I want to look at who also made interesting observations about the origins of Freemasonry, and that is W.L. Wilmshurst. He was impressed with Waite's *Secret Tradition* and wrote a favourable review of it. In doing so he drew the fire of a Quatuor-Coronati-based guardian of the London-origin tradition:

> In the review he produced for The Occult Review, Wilmshurst achieved the almost impossible feat of writing in a style at once more verbose and more incomprehensible than Waite at his worst.

Wilmshurst's main interest was in the spiritual meaning of Masonic ritual but towards the end of his life he produced a paper for the Masonic Study Society in which he set down his reflections on where he thought Freemasonry began. That is what I want to look at next.

Part Five

W. L. Wilmshurst
on
The Origins of Freemasonry

Chapter 24

The Meaning of Masonic Origins

Walter Leslie Wilmshurst

Walter Leslie Wilmshurst was born in Sussex in 1867. He was a cautious and private man, who took as his motto 'Govern the lips. They are the palace doors, and the king is within'. In this way he was a Freemason of his time; he didn't speak of his Freemasonry outside the lodge. Yet he thought deeply about it and sometimes shared his thoughts. He published books, wrote lectures to deliver to his Lodge, created private teaching materials to help his junior brothers, held discussions in lodges of instruction and he kept detailed notebooks of his thoughts.

He spent his whole working life as a solicitor in Huddersfield. He was initiated into Huddersfield Lodge No. 290 in 1889 and soon showed himself to be a keen writer by producing a history of the lodge. In 1899 he moved to another Huddersfield lodge, Harmony No. 275. During this time he wrote many Masonic pamphlets and histories of various lodges and chapters. He was made Provincial Grand Registrar of the Masonic Province of Yorkshire West Riding in 1913. In 1922 he published his first book, *The Meaning of Masonry*, and followed it up with a second, *The Masonic Initiation*, in 1924. Their popularity encouraged him to found a new lodge to study the spiritual meaning of Masonic ritual, which he called The Lodge of Living Stones, No. 4957. In 1929 he was made an Assistant Grand Director of Ceremonies in the United Grand Lodge of England.

Since his death in 1939 Wilmshurst's views on the spiritual purpose of Freemasonry have not been popular with UGLE. In recent years a one-time librarian of UGLE has accused him of 'having his feet planted firmly in the clouds'. This elevated position does, though, give his writing a great breadth of vision, which should not be lost to the present generation of readers.

Most of Wilmshurst's work is concerned with the meaning and practice of Masonic ritual. However, he wrote one short talk, which he delivered to the Masonic Study Society just before his death. In that speech he shared his thoughts on where Freemasonry came from, but he never developed the ideas into a book. I have drawn from the thoughts he expressed in this talk for the final part of this book.

The Home of Freemasonry

In 1938 Wilmshurst attended a meeting of the Masonic Study Society and listened to a paper given by Bro. F.B. Brook, entitled 'Why England became the Home of Freemasonry'. The question Brook raised was interesting, but Wilmshurst was not satisfied with the answer he gave. So he asked himself the same question and came up with his own suggestions as to why Freemasonry originated with the English people.

Brook's detailed study of the historical events and sociological conditions leading up to the formation of the modern craft and of the first Grand Lodge in 1717 convinced him that the beginnings of the Craft was not just a simple accidental impulse by a few London masons. He thought the concept of Freemasonry had to be a principle, which emerged from a number of converging causes, each of which in some way contributed to the strength of the modern Order. And he was curious how this happened.

He reasoned that before the Craft could begin, the people of the British Isles had to become established. Then, once they were welded together and consolidated, they expanded and built a great overseas world-wide empire, becoming a world power. This empire diffused the English language and methods of commerce, but it was also infused with Masonic ideals of universal freedom, brotherhood and goodwill towards all men. Wilmshurst says that the evolution of the British nation into a world power started in the reign of Elizabeth I, with her wars with Spain; thereafter England maintained and expanded its world status. Wilmshurst realized that the formation of the Craft followed soon after England had become an established and powerful kingdom, and from this base Freemasonry spread throughout the world. He did not think this was a chance happening as he explained.

Between 1588, the date of the Armada, and 1717, the formation of our Craft, the English language was shaped and perfected by Shakespeare; learning and scientific method were formulated by Bacon and Newton; and the British ability to open up and govern vast portions of the world was demonstrated by the great explorers and the captains of that time. The decision to re-admit Jews into England brought a great infusion of Hebraic, Kabbalistic and esoteric doctrine, some of which was incorporated into Craft ritual. The symbolism of Freemasonry is markedly Jewish in its construction, and the power of this esoteric symbolism helped the formulation of the ideas within our system.

When the Scottish King, James VI, came to the English Throne in 1603, England and Scotland became intimately united. In 1662 the Royal Society was founded to promote scientific research and encourage the adaptation of scientific knowledge for public welfare. Its early members included men well versed in esoteric knowledge, like Sir Isaac Newton. Now the stage was set to launch our Craft, and to spread Masonic principles world-wide.

When Freemason's Hall was erected in London in 1775, the inscription on its foundation stone stated that our beneficent science was of divine origin and had spread throughout the civilized world. *Descendit e caelo*, it read. The evidence is clear and abundant that England was the focus and starting point of a science that became universal; and the history of England prepared and contributed to the formation of the Craft. Wilmshurst says the choice of motto shows that Freemasonry was raised up by Providence to be endowed and entrusted with a universal purpose.

To understand and appreciate these historic facts he decided to probe back more deeply into the growth of Britain and see what made them possible. He found that the role of Great Britain as a forward-looking, expanding and civilizing power had its roots in a very distant past and in the East. Not without reason, he said, does our ritual include the questions and answers,

Whence come you?

From the East.

Whither directing your course?

Towards the West.

For what purpose?

In search of that which is lost.

To appreciate these ritual words, he said, one must open one's imagination and treat them as being true of our history and development. The origins of Great Britain can be found in the East, and a gradual, persistent westward flow can be traced of the people who ultimately became the present British.

Wilmshurst says that the British originated in the mountains of Northern India in that high Himalayan region called the roof of the world. Variously called Aryans, Caucasians or Indo-Europeans, these people spread gradually westwards. After subdividing into numerous nations on the way across Europe, they ultimately arrived in the British Isles. When they reached the Atlantic these ancient people were temporarily held up. But the halt was only temporary, for in the sixteenth century the occupants of those islands consolidated themselves and became the foremost world power. The westward flow resumed, when the energies of our people, who had conquered and traversed so much earth, conquered the water also, and Britain became Mistress of the Seas. The Atlantic was crossed. The Americas were opened up, and on the western continent streams of European immigrants carried forward the old ideals, impulses and traditions of a wandering race. The people from the East, he says, were still directing their course towards the west.

In speaking of these ancient people, Wilmshurst says he is not referring to the creation of man. In the backward abyss of time many other races of people existed before the Indo-Europeans. He says he is considering how a specific culture arose. The name Aryan comes from an ancient tradition of India. Aryarvarta was traditionally the land of the Aryas. He thinks their speech was probably some early form of Sanskrit. Before their dispersion and westward wanderings began, they had already built up a vast, well-knit and well-governed empire. The epic Indian poems, the *Mahabarata* and *Ramayana* give us glimpses of this lost glory.

But this early empire split into inharmonious tribes, sections and factions. A great drift westward began, and is still in progress. From what is now Afghanistan and north India, wave after wave of emigrants pushed out across Asia and Europe. Some of the emigrants halted, settled and became localized on the way, gradually acquiring separate nationalities and languages. Their offspring built up successive civilizations, like those of Greece and Rome. Others moved on to the British Isles. Wilmshurst says that the biblical legend of the Tower of Babel demonstrates what occurred. From unity of family and uniformity of religion and speech there was dispersion and the growth of a babble of languages.

He says that one valuable piece of evidence shows what happened. Amid all the movement and change, the primitive language of the race persisted. Just as flotsam on water shows the current and its direction, so that westward movement is marked out by tribal place-names that still survive to indicate the course of the flow. He gives some examples.

1. 'Bharata' is the name of a great religious epic of the Indo-European race from India. It records the Aryans' rise and fall. The eventual disruption of the Indo-Europeans is known as the *Mahabharata*, meaning 'the Great Brotherhood', an allusion to the time when universal fraternity prevailed among that race. (He says that '*maha*', becomes *magnus*, 'great' in Latin; '*bharata*' is equivalent to *fratres* or *fraternitas*, 'brotherhood').

To Masons the idea of universal brotherhood is inspiring and illuminating. And it helps understand how deep the roots of our Order run when we realize that we still continue the ideal of universal fraternity that our Ancient Brethren pursued so many thousands of years ago. Even the name this brotherhood coined for itself, 'Maha-Bharata', means the same as the name of our own country, Great Britain. Both imply the same thing, that Indians and Englishmen are brothers.

2. It may be coincidence, but it is amazing that the Latin text on the Foundation Stone of Freemason's Hall – *Descendit e caelo*, which translates as 'descended from Heaven' – should be historically and geographically true of a people who also came down from heaven, in the sense that they originated in the Himalayas, whose great heights are a symbol of heaven. The famous peak Mount Kailas, which is the source of the Indus, has long been a place of pilgrimage and a symbol of Paradise. From its name comes the Greek word for heaven, *koilon*; the Latin *caelum*; and the English 'ceiling' or 'roof'. When a German exclaims '*Himmel!*', or an Englishman says 'Great heavens!', Wilmshurst says they are using phrases that subconsciously perpetuate a memory of the East, whence their ancestors came.

3. The names of the ancient Indian tribes are to be found throughout Europe, especially in Greece and the south-east corner of the European continent through which the great western flow passed. The Caspian and Baltic seas get their names from this source. The Saxons were once '*Saacas*'; other Cymric tribes occupied the Crimea and pushed on to Wales (Cambria), and Cumberland; whilst Dons came up the Danube valley into Denmark and, as Danes, into England. Rome, a kingdom founded by Initiates, owes its name to Rama, the one-time universal King of the Indo-Europeans, whilst that of its first King, Romulus, is an echo and diminutive of Rama; and the Egyptian Rameses is another instance of Rama.

The ancient name of the Indo-European Deity was Brahma, and this appears in Abraham and in the word 'Hebrew'. When the universal religion split into Brahmanism and Buddhism, as Christianity later split into Roman Catholic and Protestant sections, the name of Buddha was carried westwards and appeared as Wotan, Woden or Odin. The 'Kabiri' of the Ancient Mysteries owe their name to tribes who once occupied the Khyber Pass, whilst another form of the word is 'Gabriel' the great Hebrew angel.

The basis of our modern English is Sanskrit. Wilmshurst says that the philologist Max Müller (1823–1900) tells us every word we use today is traceable to one of about seventy primitive Sanskrit roots, and that Sanskrit was a sacred language, as were Greek and Hebrew before they became debased and passed into common colloquial speech. The word Sanskrit might be translated in modern terms by the phrase Holy Writ, or sanctum scriptum. It dates back to a golden age of great wisdom and illumination, and we can learn many useful lessons from studying it.

One of the important Sanskrit roots is 'Br'. 'Br' is a sound you make by a blowing against the lips and releasing your breath. Wilmshurst says that the word 'breath' is built on this root, and you will find any word containing 'Br' as its foundation is associated with the idea of either impelling a breathing forth or of what is breathed forth. He gives as an example the primitive name of the Deity is Brahm, the Holy Spirit or Holy Breath, which created the Universe. When the Deity breathes forth or speaks the Word, something is born, or brought to birth. The creatures born or out-breathed are necessarily His 'brats' (children), to use a good old word, and are related to one another as brothers. The words *Bharata* or *fratres* are based on the 'Br' root, and they transmit that progressive idea of an originating creative Breather-forth, resulting in the creation of Brethren. By this, Wilmshurst says, he is seeking to stress the *raison d'être* and preparation of the Craft to be a Universal Brotherhood under a common Father.

He makes a further point about the root 'Br'. The members of the Indo-European race were not only Brethren, but Brethren charged with a message of Brotherhood to the world. They were not meant to be static and stationary, but to travel from East to West, and they were to be bearers of a message. The strong Hebrew element in the Masonic system, he says, can be explained when you realize that the word Hebrew means a 'bearer', one who is breathed forth to propagate principles of truth. He says that by 'Hebrew' we are wont to limit our ideas to Jews, but the word encompasses more than this restricted connotation. It is true that Abraham the father of the faithful Hebrews founded Hebraism, and that certain Semitic people derive from him. But the Scriptures say 'All are not Israel who are of Israel', and there are 'Jews who call themselves Jews but are not', and Wilmshurst thinks the term 'Hebrew' should be construed in a wider sense as applicable to all bearers and propagators of truths. In the old name of Spain (Iberia) and its river (the Ebro), he says, you can discern the word 'Hebrew', for Spain was one of the Western lands to which the Indo-Europeans spread, and it is to these early colonizers that the country owes the name Iberia. Other Hebrew colonists came to England, Wilmshurst says, and left their mark on the ancient city of York, the Latin name of which was Eboracum, and which has always a famous Masonic centre.

Again, he asks, is it coincidence, or due to something deeper and more purposeful, that 'Br' are the first two letters in our Bible? Look at the original Hebrew version, and you will find its first word to be *B(e)resheth*, meaning 'In the beginning'. This signifies phonetically that God initially created the heavens and the earth by breathing them forth. Surely it is more than chance that we Masons use that same root-sound when we call ourselves Brethren? We seek to promote universal brotherhood, and the birthplace of the modern Masonic movement is Britain, the land of the Brythones or Brothers.

The great migration, he tells us, swarmed from east to west in successive waves over many centuries. As it reached Europe the flow, although a single stream, divided into three groups, just as in a river the water near each bank tends to run slower than the water in the middle. The side currents run off into little bays, creeks and irregularities in the banks, and the flow there is held up, slows down or even stagnates, whilst in mid-river the current rushes on. So, it was the lifestream of westward-flowing people. One part travelled along the

Mediterranean seaboard, through Greece and Italy to Spain and France; this eventually became the Latin peoples, who developed their own distinctive qualities. The second part travelled over northern Europe and became the Nordic or Scandinavian peoples, who also developed their own quite different qualities. A third part travelled midway between the other two, through Central Europe, and also developed special qualities, which partly overlapped with those of the peoples living to the south or north of them.

These three divided portions of the one current all met in Great Britain. The British Isles were peopled by all the types, and they blended into the inhabitants of what we call the United Kingdom. This is a special place: it is isolated from the main continent, and its geographical position, its geological formation, its adaptability to a special purpose, its entire future destiny were arranged long in advance of any facts of ordinary British political or economic history.

Wilmshurst says that if we look upon this idea with Masonic eyes and employ Masonic language, we will recognize that the 'Great Architect first laid out the ground for the intended structure in this dear land of ours, and then in due time used its peoples as His three-fold working tools to execute His further designs. He applied His Square in bringing rude and undressed human material into due form, His Level to teach intellectual equality and brotherhood, and His Plumb-Rule to proclaim universal rectitude and justice.'

He goes on to say that, as we have seen, the great life-flow of people passing through Europe separated into north, south and central divisions, each manifesting a distinctive spiritual characteristic, and these meet and blend in the British people. These characteristics are the three divine qualities that Masonry attributes to Deity: Wisdom (which includes Intelligence), Strength (which implies Power and Executive Ability), and Beauty (which comprises not only moral beauty but any form of aesthetic excellence). In saying this Wilmshurst adds that he does not suggest that the British Isles displayed these qualities in their divine fullness; he prefers to use the rainbow as an analogy. Colourless, white solar light, on passing through raindrops, becomes prismatically broken up into three primary colours. Similarly, the invisible life-stream, colourless but containing all colours, when it passes through myriads of human individuals becomes prismatically divided into a variety of virtues that we may call the primaries: Wisdom, Strength, and Beauty. Every human being manifests a minute glint a greater or lesser measure of these three Divine Qualities that God Himself has out-breathed. He says they are latent in us all and shine out from every single person in such measure as his degree of spiritual development permits but only in the British are they perfectly balanced.

He recommends us to consider these examples.

1. The southern nations excel in reflections of Beauty. The genial climate, which makes life easy and pleasant, contributes to this. They evolved under no great physical stress and were free to indulge their sensuous and artistic nature. Look at Greece. The grandeur that was Greece came from artistic excellence in poetry, language, architecture and sculpture. Wisdom was there too. The Greeks were the first philosophical thinkers, and their thoughts influence us still. But they are not famous for Strength, unlike their successors the Romans who were distinguished for might and power. When one (or even two) of these primary strains is dominant, the other(s) are usually suppressed. The Romans were a forceful rather than an aesthetic people, and only when their Empire had declined, and its power was spent, did the Beauty strain come to the fore, as it did in the rise of Latin Christianity and during the Italian Renaissance.

2. The Nordic peoples, on the other hand, manifest Strength before Wisdom or Beauty. This again is due to climate and the rigours of their struggle to exist in wintry latitudes. The life of the Vikings, Danes and other Scandinavians was rough and violent, a life of exploration and exploitation. Their religion was not gentle, and its symbol was the Hammer of Thor. It took a long struggle to reconcile Odin-worship with Christianity, and even after harmony was achieved the struggle later re-emerged at the Reformation in the conflict between Protestantism and Catholicism.

3. Between these extremes of North and South ran a middle current of influence overlapping its neighbours and to some measure uniting them. Whilst the northern Nordics and the southern Greco-Latin peoples became relatively stationary in their settlements, this centre group was more mobile. They pushed in successive waves, through middle Europe, settling eventually in France, Belgium and the Netherlands, where they were checked by the sea. The British Isles formed the ultimate limit of their reach. From this history the highly composite nature of the British people arises. They are a mixture of many bloods, characteristics, and qualities, some good and some not so good. They inherit, and are suffused with, many race-traditions. They owe their national individuality to this mixture of bloods and combination of qualities. Nature's way of securing good results seems to be by blending racial strains, not by isolating them; the USA is an even more pronounced example of this than our own country.

The marked characteristic of this middle flow of people, Wilmshurst thinks, has been not Beauty or Strength, but Wisdom. He explains that by this he means practical intelligence and *savoir-faire*, which is a reflection and elementary form of it. He says it is a quality that generally makes for prudent and beneficent administration.

Wilmshurst thinks that the British like, admire and have played a part in the Arts, but have never been Beauty specialists. They never had a Periclean age, nor an Italian Renaissance. They have displayed great power in military ways. They make no claim to superior wisdom, and often proceed by way of blunder and stupidity, but he believes that the British have found ways of developing civilization as no one else has. They have often been the shock-absorber for the financial and economic troubles of Europe. No wonder, he says, that it was Britain that gave the Masonic Craft to the world.

All the foregoing has been a briefly sketched survey of matters necessary as a preparation for something deeper. If his survey of human qualities is true, says Wilmshurst, it is a subject that goes to the root of our whole Craft system. But it is a subject that has never yet been explored by any Masonic historian or commentator.

Our Craft doctrine and system, he thinks, rests upon a curious, obscure but remarkably impressive legend or Traditional History. [The legend of the slaying of the Master Builder.] It is a legend that must be either true or untrue. But 'true', he says, does not mean historically true. It can be true in spirit and intention, and in a way that is purposely hidden from the surface-reading eye. He says he has many reasons to reject it as a historically true statement. The system of the Craft, he tells us, explicitly says that its doctrines are to be preached in allegory and illustrated by symbols. He therefore regards it as a myth and sets out to seek the truth covered by that myth.

The myth and its concealed truth are of extreme importance, he believes. This is clear from the fact that it is the final and supreme secret imparted to a Masonic Candidate. To come within even earshot of it he must not only have taken his first two degrees, he must also have taken his third degree obligation to be secret about it. Not till he has done so, is this wonderful story related to him. Clearly it embodies something deeply concealed and of high importance.

Where did we get this legend? Wilmshurst asks. No one seems to know. Our Grand Lodge only says that it turns up for the first time soon after 1717, when the Constitutions and Rituals were being prepared. But of who introduced it, or from what source, nothing is known. It is not Biblical, for it is at direct variance with the Biblical account of the building of Solomon's Temple. The Bible makes no reference to the murder of Hiram Abif; it says that the Temple was finished and dedicated, while the legend tells us that that, owing to Hiram's death, it could not be completed and remains unfinished to this day. It cannot have come from the Operative Guilds of masons, for the legend has no relation to material edifices, and, insofar as their charters and writings contain religious or biblical references, they follow the Bible and orthodox religious teaching. The whole third-degree Ritual is non-operative and derives from another source.

It is often suggested, Wilmshurst tells us, that the legend reached us from the Continent through Doctor Desaguliers, who became Grand Master in 1719. Whilst he does not exclude the possibility, this suggestion seems to him to be without force, because Desaguliers, who was of French Protestant birth, was brought to England by his father at the age of two to escape religious persecution after the revocation of the Edict of Nantes in 1685. Desaguliers grew up to acquire great scientific attainment and became a fellow of the Royal Society. He was a friend of Sir Isaac Newton and other notables concerned with the inauguration of the Craft, and he became its Grand Master in 1717. These facts do not justify the surmise that, because of his foreign birth he kept in touch with the Continent and acquired Masonic material from the there.

Nevertheless, it seems highly probable that Desaguliers had something to do with the inclusion of the legend in our Ritual. In the absence of new documentary evidence, we are unlikely to discover the truth of the matter, but Wilmshurst thinks it quite likely that Desaguliers composed the legend, in substantially the present form, from knowledge he acquired as an advanced Initiate, and that his original draft or copy of it was destroyed as soon as the legend was adopted as part of our Ritual. He says we must not fail to remember that Desaguliers, Newton, and some other great illuminated minds of that time, were members of the Invisible Society, who collaborated in great privacy to launch the Masonic movement. Whilst they inspired and influenced others to get it going, they themselves remained in concealment.

Wilmshurst thinks the legend of the slaying of the Master Builder is pure allegory. He says we have to interpret it without relating it to ordinary history. It tells of the building of a temple, and its imagery is not that of a material edifice, but of a temple of the human body in its collective sense. It speaks of the perfecting of humanity in the Divine Image, for humanity is the ultimate Temple of Deity. It speaks of humanity, immortal, whole and as a unity, not as a scattered multitude of transient mortals. Throughout time, all life – all lives – has been moving towards the perfecting of a humanity that will be the synthesis of us all, who will be at one, even as God is One, and His Name One. That, Wilmshurst believes, is the supreme monotheistic truth behind the Hebrew religion.

He says that our faith, supported by tradition and the scriptural authority of all great religions, is that the making of Humanity in the Divine Image is a gradual and creative process entrusted to, and undertaken by, myriads of spiritual intelligence, called *Elohim*, or Gods. The Masonic work is a process of building: it is analogous to a house being built gradually, stone by stone, brick by brick, and incorporating wood- and metalwork to create the necessary structure. As the Apostle puts it, 'Ye are God's building'. Such work involves the co-operation of hosts of workmen with different grades of skill and ability. It involves intelligence, design and control by superiors. It also involves freedom of choice, methods of trial and error and disharmony among the workmen. For these builders are not mechanical and automatic; they are intelligences given liberty of choice and conduct.

All these facts are envisaged in the legend. It tells us that the creative work was approaching completion when something happened to check it. It tells us this check was due to a disagreement between some of the higher workmen. Human development had reached a certain stage at which an important decision was necessary as to the best method for further advance. The supreme officers – who appear in the legend in the guise of Solomon and the two Hirams – knew, and counselled, a certain method. But some subordinates, themselves also high officers, took a different view and maintained it to the point of a split. There was war in heaven, in the sense of dissension and divided effort.

Wilmshurst sums up by pointing out that the ritual says there were fifteen malcontents, but that twelve recanted and returned to their allegiance, leaving only three most determined to persist in the rebellion. These are spoken of as ruffians, and they eventually slay their Grand Master and are sentenced to death. But again, says Wilmshurst, we must look behind the allegory. We cannot regard these three as vulgar villains and murderers. In the myth they are *Elohim*, or minor gods. One god does not slay another in the fashion of common homicide, nor do gods die. The myth tells of a tragedy, but not a squalid murder. The killing was not committed from base motives or for selfish gain. It was that greater form of tragedy caused by a conflict of two ideas, both noble and honourable, with each side fighting for what it thought to be right.

Conclusions to Part Five

Wilmshurst was widely read in many areas of history, and he bases his argument for the origins of the Craft on an idea which had been first suggested in 1786 when Sir William Jones announced to the Asiatick Society of Calcutta that Sanskrit had to be related to Greek and Latin, starting what we now know as the science of historical linguistics.

In his talk to the Masonic Study Society Wilmshurst shows great interest in the question of the original homeland of the Indo-Europeans, but he could only use linguistic evidence to deduce where it might have been. Some fifty years after his death the archaeologist Professor Marija Gimbutas of UCLA developed a better picture of the movements of the nomadic early Indo-Europeans, using the language of symbols to trace their movements. Then, towards the end of the twentieth century, another archaeologist, Colin Renfrew, put forward a theory that the Indo-Europeans were farmers in Asia Minor who migrated into south-east Europe from around 7000 BC and brought their language and culture with them. Current work in genetics is beginning to confirm many of Gimbutas' and Renfrew's ideas. It also shows that many of Wilmshurst's ideas about the migration of ancient traditions were sound, though no doubt he would have been surprised and interested to learn that his race of Indo-Europeans began in the highlands of Turkey, not the Himalayas.

Conclusions

Wilmshurst is the only one of my Masonic dissenters who does not write of any influence of the Knights Templar on Freemasonry. Instead he looks back over a much broader span of history searching for the genesis of the spiritual ideas he finds in Craft ritual.

But in all the five writers whose ideas I have reviewed and summarized there is a common thread. It is that Freemasonry did not start in London in 1717. All these famous Masonic writers think it is far older. This is an idea that the United Grand Lodge of England considers to be subversive in any form. Let me explain why and review the pattern of response that all five writers experienced.

Over the nearly three hundred years of its existence the Grand Lodge of London and its successor the United Grand Lodge of England have come to believe their own founding propaganda. Since they began to aspire to respectability and set out to lure Hanoverian princes to become their Grand Masters, they have had a problem with the origins of Masonry. Both Preston and Gould make strong claims for the involvement of the Stuart kings in the Craft, and say that it was already well-established by the time the Stuarts got involved in it. Both claim that Freemasonry has evolved from ancient sources within the British Isles. Whilst they do not agree in detail, the thrust of their separate messages is clear. There is no chance at all that Freemasonry was invented in eighteenth-century London. But it is this that forms the basis of the United Grand Lodge of England's claim to be the 'Premier' Grand Lodge of the Craft.

When Preston was writing the various editions of his *Illustrations of Masonry* a power struggle was taking place over two alternative claims to be the 'Premier' Grand Lodge. The contestants were the

Antient Grand Lodge of Free and Accepted Masons, based in London, and the Grand Lodge of All England, which was based in the City of York and sometimes known as the Grand Lodge of York. (At that time the majority of Freemasons knew the Grand Lodge of London as the 'Moderns'.) The battle to decide which was to be the 'Premier' Grand Lodge was won by the Moderns, who persuaded the Prince of Wales to become their Grand Master and then, in 1799, used a coercive Act of Parliament to force through the creation of the United Grand Lodge of England. This came to fruition in 1813 under the Grand Mastership of the Duke of Sussex. Sussex put into place a corrupt system of patronage and favouritism to make sure there was no more dissent. He established layer after layer of petty ranks, each carrying its own pompous title and ornate apron, and made sure that only Brethren who were prepared to take an oath of allegiance to obey 'each and every edict of the United Grand Lodge of England' were appointed to them. This strange method of appointing senior officers of the Order in England still exists, although it is increasingly being called into question by younger recruits, because of its lack of transparency and ease of manipulation by those already in office.

Gould was the first Masonic writer to break ranks with Sussex's New Order. He was an army officer turned solicitor, with a sharp inquiring mind and a passion for detail. The questions he asked about the origins of Freemasonry had answers that the United Grand Lodge of England did not like. However, as he had already been promoted to Senior Grand Deacon in UGLE, Sussex's method of control by patronage was of no use to curb him. So a new technique was used: Gould was invited to become a founder member of a new 'Premier' lodge of Research, to be named Quatuor Coronati, after the Roman legend of the Four Crowned Martyrs killed by the Emperor Diocletian for refusing to work on pagan buildings. Gould was fond of this legend and devoted an entire twenty-page chapter to it in the first book of his three-volume *History of Freemasonry*. He became a founder member of this lodge and went on to be Master of it. And in due course he gave permission for another member of Quatuor Coronati, Dudley Wright, to create a new five-volume edition of *Gould's History of Freemasonry*, which played down the role of other British sources and stayed much closer to the UGLE line of 'it all began in London in 1717'. From then on Quatuor Coronati became a breeding ground for pseudo-academic Masonic historians, who would attack any views that did not fit UGLE's chosen view of history – i.e.

the one that established it as the world's 'Premier' Grand Lodge.

Ward graduated from Cambridge with a degree in History and membership of the University Lodge. The more he read about Freemasonry and the more he looked at ancient customs and rituals, the more he was convinced that many of the features of Freemasonry were very old. When he dared to suggest that Freemasonry might *not* have started in London in 1717, the wrath of Quatuor Coronati was unleashed on him. Not only was his work described as worthless, he was personally vilified as not being worthy to hold his Cambridge degree. The following quotation from a book review written by a Past master of Quatuor Coronati illustrates the method:

> There are very strong arguments to be made in favour of an Aryan origin for certain Masonic conceptions, but such arguments gain no help from the puerile phantasies of Brother Ward. As a BA of Cambridge, he should know better.

And Ward's crime? To put forward the idea that Freemasonry might predate 1717.

Waite suffered even more at the hands of Quatuor Coronati members. He was in his forties, an established writer in the field of the esoteric and magic and the designer of a famous Tarot pack, when he decided to join Freemasonry. He saw many interesting similarities between Masonic ritual and other traditions, and became convinced that there was a much older tradition hidden in the Masonic myth. I have already mentioned some of the criticism which he received from Quatuor Coronati but the name of one of Waite's most outspoken critics caught my eye as I was reading a paper by Professor Andrew Prescott, who holds the chair of Freemasonry at Sheffield University. The paper, *Druidic Myths and Freemasonry,* can be found on Sheffield University's website and refers to links between Freemasonry and the Eisteddfod. It also points out the poor scholarship of JES Tuckett, who was at the forefront of the attack on Waite . . . for poor scholarship!

Waite asks if there is a long-standing secret tradition behind Freemasonry and then tries to answer his own question. You may not agree with his conclusions, but he does make a coherent argument that is worth thinking about. Perhaps it is even worth taking a new look at his question in the light of new historical knowledge.

Wilmshurst is still one of the most popular writers on the spiritual meaning of Freemasonry, even so long after his death. He is convinced that Freemasonry is an ancient science of understanding the human soul, and he traces its ideas back for thousands of years, linking it to the westward spread of civilization from Asia Minor. He founded a new type of research lodge. In his address during the consecration of the lodge in 1927 he said:

This Lodge has been formed to meet a demand for a fuller understanding of the latent teachings of our Order. The lodge is being formed at a time when the bulk of members are content with the routine formalities and social amenities of their Lodges, but there is a constantly increasing minority who feel that the Craft was intended to mean more and are eager to learn what that more is.

This new lodge is a first step to a new form of lodge, one which devotes itself to advanced work which cannot be conveniently pursued in the usual form of lodge. The purpose of the new lodge falls within the three great foundation principles of the Masonic Order, Brotherhood, Relief, Truth. Hitherto the energies of the Craft have been directed to the two former, to the neglect of the third.

We have reached a time in the historical development of the Masonic Order when the pressure of existence and the conditions of social, intellectual and religious life are forcing thoughtful minds to a more intensive search for Truth than ever before. By Truth, I do not mean the personal virtue of truthfulness, nor even the sectional truths of sciences, philosophies, churches, but rather that larger Truth which lies behind everything. It has always been the maxim of the Initiate to penetrate to the truth of oneself and to solve the riddle of existence. Our lodge will seek to discover what Truth meant to the Initiates of earlier times, who left their hints concealed beneath heavy veils of allegory and symbolism for their successors in the modern Craft to unravel and profit by for themselves.

Wilmshurst's words are as true today as they were when he spoke them over eighty years ago. He founded his new lodge to investigate Truth at a time when the Craft was thriving. Now, three generations later, Freemasonry is dying because it is failing to question its own purpose. It is failing to offer any reason for young people to join it, and, so long as it hides from its own spiritual truths, it will deserve to die.

The common thread linking all the writers I have chosen to revisit is that they dared to ask the question that UGLE has forbidden any Mason wanting promotion even to think about: When and where did Freemasonry start? And asking this question is a necessary preliminary to any attempt to understand the purpose and truth of the Craft. Not one of these great writers came to the conclusion that Freemasonry started in London in 1717. No wonder, then, UGLE attacked each of them in turn. But so long as the United Grand Lodge of England insists on playing its self-appointed role of 'Premier' Grand Lodge of the World, and continues to assert that Freemasonry was set up as a simple form of amusement for bored London gentlemen to play at being Bob the Builder, why should anybody else take the Craft seriously?

The writers whose ideas I have explored afresh in this book are the big names in Masonic writing over the last 250 years, and they all think Freemasonry started long ago, that it has civilizing purpose and that it has evolved over a long time. They disagree over exactly where and when it all began, but they have all sensed a deep spiritual undercurrent to the ritual, which they variously ascribe to the Druids, the Scots, the Knights Templar or the mysterious Wardens of the Temple of Sion, who are the guardians of the secret knowledge of the human soul.

Are they right in their claims? That is not a question I have set myself in this book; all I have attempted to do here is to modernize their prose, lay out their claims and repeat their chains of reasoning, so readers can make up their own minds. Whatever the outcome of that exercise, the one thing I am certain of is that they were right to ask the question. Where *did* Freemasonry come from, and what is it for?

Bibliography

Preston, W., *Illustrations of Masonry*, Preston, London, 1795

Gould, R. F., *A History of Freemasonry*, Caxton, London, 1883

Ward, J. S. M., Freemasonry and the Ancient Gods, Simpkin, London, 1921

Waite, A. E., *The Secret Tradition of Freemasonry*, Rebman, London, 1911

Other works mentioned

Gimbutas, M., *The Language of the Goddess*, Thames & Hudson, London, 1989

Levi, E. *The History of Magic*, trans. A. E. Waite, William Rider, London, 1913

Renfrew, A. C., *Archaeology and Language: The Puzzle of Indo-European Origins*, Cambridge University Press, Cambridge 1987

Wilmshurst, W. L., *The Meaning of Masonry*, William Rider, London, 1922

—— *The Masonic Initiation*, William Rider, London, 1924

Relevant websites

http://www.brad.ac.uk/webofhiram/

http://www.freemasonry.dept.shef.ac.uk/

http://www.robertlomas.com/preston/

Appendix 1

The St Clair Charters in the Original Scots

First St Clair Charter

Be it kend till all men be thir present letters ws Deacons Maistres and freemen of the Masons within the realme of Scotland with express consent and assent of Wm Schaw Maister of Wark to our Souane Lord ffor sa meikle as from aige to aige it has been observit amangis that the Lairds of Rosling has ever been Patrons and Protectors of us and our priviledges likeas our predecessors has obey'd and acknowledged them as Patrones and tectoris while that within thir few years throwch negligence and sleuthfulness the samyn has past furth of use whereby not only has the Laird of Rosling lyne out of his just rycht but also our hail craft has been destitute of ane patron and protector and overseer qlk has genderit manyfauld corruptions and imperfections, baith amangis ourselves and in our craft and has given occasion to mony persones to conseve evill opinioun of ws and our craft and to leive off great enterprises of policie be reason of our great misbehaviour wtout correction whereby not only the committers of the faults but also the honest men are disapoyntit of their craft and ffeit. As lyikwayes when divers and sundrie contraversies falls out amangis ourselfs thair follows great and manyfald inconvenientis through want of ane (Patron and Protector) we not being able to await upon the ordinar judges and judgement of this realme through the occasioun of our powertie and langsthe freeumness of process for remeid qrof and for keeping of guid ordour amangis us in all tymes cumyng, and for advancement of our craft and vocatioun within this realme and furthering of policie within the samyn We for ourselves

and in name of our haill bretherene and craftismen with consent
foresaid agrees and consents that Wm Sinclar now of Rosling for
himself & his airis purchase and obtene at ye hands of our Souane
Lord libertie fredome and jurisdictioun vpone us and our successors
in all tymes cummyng as patrons and judges to us and the haill
fessoris of our craft wtin this realme quhom off we have power and
commission sua that hereafter we may acknawlege him and his airis
as our patrone and judge under our Souerane Lord without ony kind
of appellation or declynyng from his judgement with power to the
said Williame and his airis to depute judges ane or mae under him and
to use sick ampill and large jurisdictione upon us and our successors
als weill as burghe as land as it shall pleise our Souerane Lord to grant
to him & his airis.

William Schaw, Maistir of Wark

Second St Clair Charter

Beit kend till all men be thir present letters ws the Deacones Masteris
friemen of the Maissones and Hammermen within the kingdome of
Scotland. That forsameikill as from aidge to aidge it has been
observet amangis us and our predecessors that the Lairdis of Rosling
has ever been patrons and protectors of us and our priviledgis. Likeas
our predecessors has obeyit reverencet and acknowledget them as
patrons and protectors qrof they had letters of protection and vtheris
richtis grantit be his Maties most noble progenitors of worthy
memorie qIkis with sindrie vtheris of the Lairdis of Rosling his writtis
being consumet and brunt in ane flame of fire within the Castle of
Rosling. The consumation and burning hr of being clearly knawin to
us and our predecessors deacons maisteris and freemen of the saidis
vocations, and our protection of the samyn and priviledgis thereof of
negligence and slouthfulness being likely to pass furth of us where
throw not only wald the Lairdis of Rosling lyne out of their just richt
but also our hail craftis wald haif bene destitute of ane patrone
protector and oversear quhilk wald engenner monyfald imperfectionis
and corruptionis baith amangis ourselves and in our craft and give
occasione to mony persones to conceive evill opinioun of us and our
craft and to leave af many and grit enterpryces of policie whilk wald
be undertaken if our grit misbehaviour were suffered to goe on
without correctioun For remeid qrof and for keeping of good ordour

amangis us in all time coming and for advancement of our craft and vocation within his Hienes kingdom of Scotland and furdering of policie yaireintill the maist pairt of our predecessors for themselves and in name and behalfe of our bretherene and craftsmen with express advice and consent of William Schaw Maister of Wark to his Hienes umqle darrest father of worthy memorie all in ane voce agreit consentit and subseryvet that William Sinclar of Rosling father to Sir William Sinclar now of Rosling for himself and his airis should purches and obtain at the hands of his Majestie libertie freedome and jurisdictioun upon us and our predecessors deacons maisteris and freemen of the saidis vocation, as patrones and judges to us and the haill professors thereof within the said kingdom qrof they had power and commission sua that they and we micht yairafter acknowledge him and his airis as patrone and judge under our Soverane Lord without any kind of appellation or declinatour from thair judgement forever, as the said agreement subscryvet be the said Mr of Wark and our predecessors at mare length proportis In the whilk office priviledge and jurisdictioun over us and our said (voca)tioun the said William Sinclar of Rosling ever continuit to his going to Ireland qr he presently reamanes sen the quhilk of his departure furth of this realme there are very many corruptiounes and imperfectiounes risen and ingennerit baith amangis ourselfis and in our saidis vocatiounes in defect of ane patrone and oversear over us and the samyn Sua that our saidis vocatiounes are altogether likely to decay And now for safety thereof we having full experience of the efauld good skill and judgement whilk the said Sr William Sinclar now of Rosling has in our said craft and vocatioun and for reparation of the ruines and manifold corruptiounes and enormities done be unskilfull persones thereintill we all in ane voce have ratified and approven and be thir presentis ratifies and approves the foresaid former letter of jurisdictioun and libertie made and subr be our brethrene and his Hienes umqle Mr of Wark for the time to the said Williame Sinclar of Rosling father to the said Sr William whereby he and his airis are acknowledget as our patrone and judge under our Soverane Lord over us and the haill professors of our said vocatioun within this his Hienes kingdom of Scotlande without any appelation or declinator from their judgements in ony time hereafter. And further we all in ane voce as said is of new have made constitute and ordainit and be thir presentis makis constitutes and ordanes the said Sir William Sinclar now of Rosling and his airis maill our only patrones protectors and overseers under our

Soverane Lord to us and our successors deacons maisteris and freemen of our saidis vocatiounes of Masons hammermen within the haile kingdome of Scotland and of our haille priviledges and jurisdictiounes belonging thereto wherein he his father and their predecessors Lairdis of Rosling have been in use of possessioun thir many aidges bygain with full power to him and them be themselves thair wardens and deputis to be constitute be them to affix and appoint places of meeting for keeping of good ordour in the said craft als oft and sua oft as need shall require all and sundry persones that may be knawin to be subject to the said vocatioun to be called absentis to amerciat transgressuris to punish unlawes casualities and vtheris duties whatsomever pertaining and belonging or that may fall to be pait be whatsomever persone or persones subject to the said craft to aske crave receive intromet with and uplift and the samyn to their own proper use to apply deputtis under them in the said office with clerkis seruandis assisteris and all other officers and memberis of court needfull to make create substitute and ordain for whom they shall be holden to answer all and sundry plentis actions and causes pertaining to the said craft and vocation and against whatsomever person or persones professors thereof to hear discuss decerne and decyde acts duties and sentences thereupon to pronunce And the samyn to due execution to cause be put and generallie all and sundrie other priviledges liberties and immunities whatsomever concerning the said craft to doe use and exerce and cause to be done and exercet and keipit siklyke and als freely in all respects as any vyeris thair predecessors has done or might have done themselves in anytime bygane freely quietly well and in peace but any revocatioun obstacle impediment or again calling quhtsomevir.

Index